COMPETENCE, EDUCATION AND NVQs

s book on or befr   ᴜst date
stamped bel

Also available from Cassell:

L. B. Curzon, *Teaching in Further Education* (4th edition)
P. Mizen, *The State, Young People and Training*

Competence, Education and NVQs

Dissenting Perspectives

Terry Hyland

CASSELL

Cassell
Villiers House
41/47 Strand
London WC2N 5JE

387 Park Avenue South
New York
NY 10016–8810

First published 1994

British Library Cataloguing-in-Publication Data
A catalogue record for this book is available from the British Library.

ISBN 0–304–32934–7 (hardback)
     0–304–32932–0 (paperback)

Typeset by York House Typographic Ltd, London
Printed and bound in Great Britain by Redwood Books, Trowbridge, Wiltshire

Contents

For John Hyland, 1919–92

Abbreviations

APA	accreditation of prior achievement
APL	accreditation of prior learning
BTEC	Business and Technology Education Council
CATS	credit accumulation and transfer systems
CBET	competence-based education and training
CBI	Confederation of British Industry
CGLI	City & Guilds of London Institute
CPVE	Certificate of Pre-Vocational Education
DES	Department of Education and Science
DFE	Department for Education
DOE	Department of Employment
ED	Employment Department
EDAP	Employee Development and Assistance Programme
ERA	Education Reform Act
FE	further education
FEFC	Further Education Funding Council
FEU	Further Education Unit
GCSE	General Certificate of Secondary Education
GED	General Education Diploma
GNVQ	General National Vocational Qualification
HE	higher education
HEC	Higher Education for Capability
HEFC	Higher Education Funding Council
HMI	Her Majesty's Inspectorate
MSC	Manpower Services Commission
NATFHE	National Association of Teachers in Further and Higher Education
NCC	National Curriculum Council
NCE	National Commission on Education
NCVQ	National Council for Vocational Qualifications

NETTs	National Education and Training Targets
NIACE	National Institute of Adult Continuing Education
NPS	National Preferred Scheme
NROVA	National Record of Vocational Achievement
NVQ	National Vocational Qualification
OFSTED	Office for Standards in Education
OU	The Open University
PICs	Private Industry Councils
RSA	Royal Society of Arts
Scotvec	Scottish Vocational Education Council
SCUE	Standing Conference on University Entrance
SVQ	Scottish Vocational Qualification
TA	Training Agency
TDLB	Training and Development Lead Body
TEC	Training and Enterprise Council(s)
TEED	Training, Enterprise and Education Directorate
TVEI	Technical and Vocational Education Initiative
UDACE	Unit for the Development of Adult Continuing Education
VET	vocational education and training
YTS	Youth Training Scheme

Introduction

Since the establishment of the National Council for Vocational Qualifications (NCVQ) and the introduction of National Vocational Qualifications (NVQs) in 1986, the NCVQ and the system of competence-based education and training (CBET) which underpins its strategy has extended its influence throughout all levels of the system, from school to university. What Burke (1989b) called a 'quiet revolution' (p. 1) has gathered both momentum and considerable sound and fury in the last few years.

The chief thesis of this critical and dissenting examination of NVQs* and CBET is that this approach to education and training is fundamentally flawed, disastrously misguided and entirely inappropriate to our current and future education and training needs. The introduction of general NVQs (GNVQs) in 1992 can be regarded as an attempt by the NCVQ to remedy some of the worst failings and shortcomings of CBET, and, though these experimental courses still have to be fully evaluated, there is considerable doubt about whether, without other radical changes, GNVQs will be enough to meet our education and training requirements in future years (Smithers, 1993).

From its base and original home in work-based vocational education and training (VET), the NCVQ model of CBET has extended its influence downwards into schools (Hyland, 1991a, 1992f) and upwards into teacher education, higher education and professional studies in general (Hyland, 1992c, 1993a). The idea of CBET has insinuated itself into just about every sphere of contemporary educational discourse, with the upshot that the slogans of 'competence' and 'competence talk' are now difficult to resist. One of the most worrying aspects of all this is the fact that the

---

* Scottish Vocational Qualifications (SVQs) are the counterparts of NVQs north of the border. There are, in fact, a number of significant differences between the two systems. Unlike the NCVQ, the Scottish Vocational Education Council (Scotvec) is both an awarding and an accrediting body, and SVQs are seen as 'education-led' as opposed to the 'industry-led NVQs' (Wojtas, 1993, p. 8). However, though my concern is primarily with NVQs, the criticisms are also meant to apply to SVQs in so far as these are influenced and informed by the CBET strategy employed by the NCVQ.

relatively few critical studies of NVQs are almost totally overshadowed by the massive public relations exercise mounted by the NCVQ and its supporters (NCVQ, 1993a; Targett, 1993) in order to sell NVQs to colleges and other providers. More worrying still (and also more puzzling) is the apparently uncritical endorsement of the NCVQ enterprise by the Department for Education (DFE, 1993a), often in the face of all the contrary research evidence (Nash, 1993d).

NVQs and the CBET system which underpins and informs them are logically and conceptually confused, epistemologically ambiguous and based on largely discredited behavourist learning principles. In the chapters which follow, this thesis is explained, elaborated and justified. The key shortcomings and weaknesses of the system are revealed in an examination of the influence of NVQs and CBET on assessment, learning, teaching and knowledge, before looking at the impact of the CBET onslaught on VET, adult and further education, higher education and professional studies. I conclude by suggesting that NVQs are simply not up to the task of enhancing VET, upgrading the skills of the workforce or bringing about the 'learning society' of the kind recommended by the CBI (1989) and in the National Commission on Education report (NCE, 1993).

The examination of competence and NVQs will be partly 'philosophical' – if philosophy is taken to be a concern with logical analysis of discourse, criticism of arguments, and engagement in an activity which 'pursues the ideas of common sense and clarity far enough' (Wilson, 1977, p. 3) – and also 'empirical' in the sense that I will draw on evidence from a range of research studies on NVQs and CBET (including our own recent and ongoing research at Warwick University, Hyland, 1993d; Hyland and Weller, 1994). Critical analysis and 'dissenting perspectives' provide a theme which runs throughout the book, though an initial critical summary and overview of the NCVQ enterprise is included as a postscript to Chapter 1.

All educational discourse and argument is based on value positions which stand in need of justification. In order to counterbalance and frame the 'negative' criticism of NVQs, my own 'positive' positions about education and training – commitments to active and experiential learning, to Dewey's theory of vocationalism, to a broad general 14 to 19 curriculum for all students which includes a rationally defensible 'education for work' core, and to a democratic community-oriented model of educational provision – are stated throughout the following chapters and summarized in Chapters 9 and 10. The central argument is that, not only is CBET not nearly enough to remedy our current education and training ills, but that the NCVQ model actually fosters an approach which is part of the very problems which we are currently trying to solve.

Chapter 1

Origins of Competence-based Education and Training: NVQs and the Rise of the NCVQ

COMPETENCE-BASED EDUCATION AND TRAINING

Although the competence-based education and training (CBET) strategies currently growing in influence and popularity at all levels of the education system have their more recent origins in this country in the establishment of the National Council for Vocational Qualifications (NCVQ) in 1986, the roots of this general approach to education and training go back much further than this.

There is general agreement that the more immediate origins of CBET are to be found in the performance-based teacher education movement which gained prominence in American educational circles in the 1960s (Tuxworth, 1989; Elam, 1971; Houston, 1980). The apparent precision of programmes based on closely defined and pre-specified outcomes had a powerful attraction for American administrators whose overriding concern was public accountability and control of certification in professional teacher education (factors not dissimilar to the ones which appealed to proponents of input/output efficiency in the British climate of economic realism in the 1980s).

In spite of strong academic criticism of CBET in America (Broudy, 1981; Smith, 1975) and, as Tuxworth notes, the fact that there 'was little or no research evidence to show superiority over other forms of teacher preparation' (1989, p. 12), programmes informed by the general competence approach continued to influence professional and higher education there throughout the 1970s (Hertzberg, 1976). Although the approach began to lose favour and decline in influence in America in the 1980s – ironically, just as those concerned with vocational education and training (VET) in Britain were turning their attention to CBET approaches – the philosophy underpinning this general approach to education and training had a clear populist appeal, with its roots in the 'social efficiency' theory which was influential in American educational circles earlier this century. It is worth looking at these earlier origins in more detail, for they not only contain all the essential ingredients of mainstream CBET strategies currently informing much policy and practice in British education, but also serve to explain the political, economic and philosophical attractions of CBET as well as indicating the educational shortcomings of this approach.

COMPETENCE AND SOCIAL EFFICIENCY

As Norris (1991) noted in his wry comment on the origins of competence strategies in education and training, 'we have been here before and others have been here before us' (p. 338). Among those 'others' must be included leading pioneers in the behavioural objectives field such as Tyler, Thorndike, Bloom and Popham. Tyler, in particular, has observed that his research in the 1920s on statistical techniques for evaluating teacher-training curricula was inspired by the prevailing climate of opinion concerned with 'finding the competencies of teachers and trying to focus on them' (Norris, 1991, p. 338). Reference will be made in Chapter 7 to the recent rediscovery of CBET approaches to teacher education in Britain by those who wish to achieve greater control and accountability of the teaching profession in the current climate of market forces, consumer choice and policies of de-professionalization (Chitty and Simon, 1993).

The climate of opinion in education referred to by Tyler was established in the main by the theories of educators such as Snedden and Prosser who criticized the educational practices of the early twentieth-century American public system and recommended instead a system of 'utilitarian training which looks to individual efficiency in the world of work'. The ultimate aim of such training was 'the greatest degree of efficiency' (Wirth, 1991, p. 57), and this was to be achieved by making schooling completely responsive to the contemporary and developing needs and demands of industry.

This philosophy of social efficiency represented the attempt to provide a theoretical rationale for the technocratic ideas being propagated by the National Association of Manufacturers, which, following the 1893 depression in America, became a 'powerful force advocating the addition of a vocational component to the school system' (p. 55). The writings of Snedden and Prosser were

> marked by a conservative social philosophy, a methodology of specific training operations based on principles of S-R psychology, and a curriculum designed according to a job analysis of the needs of industry, and by a preference for a separately-administered set of vocational schools. (p. 56)

The parallels between social-efficiency philosophy and the more recent vocationalizing elements surrounding the establishment of the NCVQ in the 1980s are quite striking. All the essential ingredients of NVQs are present in the early American model – a conservative ideology, a foundation in behaviourist psychology and a determination to serve the specific needs of industry.

These ideas were brought to full prominence in the America of the early 1900s by educators who, influenced by Manual Training and Trade schools pioneered by Woodward in the nineteenth century (Lewis, 1991), sought to establish a no-nonsense vocationalism which tied the principles of schooling directly to the needs of industry. Taking the view that in the interests of 'social efficiency . . . it was the business of society to fit each individual to a station in life' (p. 99), Snedden and Prosser (Snedden as Commissioner of Education in Massachusetts and Prosser as Secretary of the National Society for Industrial Education, Wirth, 1991, pp. 57–8) campaigned nationally for the reform of schooling along utilitarian lines.

As with the more recent vocationalizing tendencies of the last two decades, this early movement was dismissive of the claims of traditional liberal education and the so-called 'culturists' who were said to be cut off from the world of work (see Weinstock's 1976 assertion mentioned later). Vocational education, Prosser argued, 'only functions in proportion as it will enable an individual actually to do a job . . . Vocational education must establish habits: habits of correct thinking and of correct doing. Hence, its fundamental theory must be that of habit psychology' (Prosser and Quigley, 1950, pp. 215 20, the 'habit psychology' referred to was that of Thorndike, a pioneer of behaviourism). All these notions resulted in prescriptions for a utilitarian vocational curriculum (including such things as 'manipulative skills', 'shop chemistry', 'shop physics', and the like, Prosser and Allen, 1925) in which non-vocational general education played a marginal role.

Although such views held sway for a while with the National Education Association in America during the inter-war years, their educational limitations and vocational short-sightedness were eventually acknowledged, thanks largely to the work and writings of John Dewey. Pointing to the folly of narrowly defined vocational programmes, Dewey (1966) argued that when 'educators conceive vocational guidance as something which leads to definitive, irretrievable and complete choice both education and the chosen vocation are likely to be rigid, hampering further growth' (p. 311). Moreover, he pointed out that the needs of a constantly evolving industrial society can never be met by a narrow skills training which neglects aspects of general education. He was convinced that any scheme for vocational education which 'takes its point of departure from the industrial regime that now exists' was likely to 'assume and to perpetuate its divisions and weaknesses' (p. 318).

Dewey's powerful message is as relevant today as it was when it was first issued in 1916, and, as I will be suggesting in later chapters, Dewey's theory of vocationalism has much to offer those currently concerned with the reform of VET and the attempts to upgrade vocational studies and bridge the academic/vocational divide in the post-16 curriculum. Certainly, the utilitarian principles which Dewey was attacking have striking parallels in the development of policy and practice in Britain since the 1970s, and, amidst the pendulum swings and recyclings of educational theory, contemporary liberal educators have felt it important to attack the 'economic utility model' (Bailey, 1984) on the grounds that it is divisive, counter-productive and totally inadequate to contemporary educational requirements. It is worth examining this recent period of the 'vocationalization' of the curriculum (Hyland, 1991b) in more detail, since the more immediate origins of CBET and NCVQ philosophy are clearly discernible in the generation of policy and practice during this period.

THE TRAINING CULTURE AND THE VOCATIONALIZATION OF EDUCATION

The end of the liberal consensus and the reassertion of the economic and vocational function of education in recent times is typically dated from the time of the Great Debate following Callaghan's Ruskin College speech in 1976 (Whitty, 1985, ch. 5). Throughout the years that followed, the role of education in helping to improve industrial performance was taken up by public figures and politicians and was subsequently reflected in various Department of Education and Science (DES) publications.

Arnold Weinstock, then head of GEC, could be confident of a warm reception for his charges of 'anti-industry bias' and a preference for 'the life of the mind over the practical life' (Weinstock, 1976, p. 2) levelled at the teaching profession during this period of re-evaluation of educational priorities. In the struggle for the curriculum during the late 1970s and early 1980s the vocational lobby gained a noticeable edge. By 1984 Sir Keith Joseph, in his North of England Conference speech, was urging the adoption of a curriculum with a 'practical element' which was 'relevant to the real world'; the 'technical and vocational aspect of school learning should have its proper place' and 'all pupils should be introduced to the economic and other foundations of society' (Joseph, 1984, p. 4).

The Green Paper *Education in Schools: A Consultative Document* (DES, 1977) had stressed the vital role of education in aiding Britain's economic recovery through the improvement of manufacturing industry, and the change of ethos is clearly reflected in the DES publication *Better Schools* which recommended a 5 to 16 curriculum which would encourage

> the qualities, attitudes, knowledge, understanding and *competences* which are necessary to equip pupils for working life. With this aim in view the Government has established the Technical and Vocational Education Initiative (TVEI) which explores how best to fit work-related skills within full-time education. (DES, 1985, p. 6, my italics)

From the outset, TVEI schemes were guided by the Manpower Services Commission (MSC) definition of vocational education as that 'in which students are concerned to acquire generic or specific skills with a view to employment' and TVEI was intended ultimately to influence 'the whole curriculum including such areas as mathematics and English' (Pickard, 1985, p. 23).

The influence of the 'new vocationalism' (Esland, 1990) has been widespread and pervasive, perhaps most noticeably in the post-compulsory sector in which the MSC, at a stroke, took control of 25 per cent of work-related non-advanced further education in 1985/86 (Statham *et al.*, 1989, p. 177). In subsequent years the Training Agency and later the Training, Enterprise and Education Directorate (TEED), a branch of the Employment Department (ED),* and the regional Training and Enterprise Councils (TECs) have effectively continued the restructuring of VET policy and practice and, in latter years, the NCVQ framework has played an important role in the process (Evans, 1992; Smithers, 1993).

The CBET strategy which informed the development of NVQs grew out of these policy changes in VET and the emergence of a new training culture in the 1980s. Mansfield (1989) shows clearly how the notions of 'outcomes' and 'job competence' – now key elements in NCVQ philosophy – were developed through MSC experience with Youth Training Schemes (YTS) in the early 1980s (pp. 27–8). The Training Agency was subsequently charged with the responsibility of developing standards of

---

* The Employment Department (ED) tends to be cited/referred to as the Department of Employment (DOE) prior to the 1990s.

training based on occupational competence (Debling, 1989), and since the White Paper *Employment for the 1990s* (DES, 1990) this function has been regionalized through the work of the network of TECs around the country. Government policy on training in the last few years has been dominated by the achievement of the National Education and Training Targets (NETTs, see Table 1.1) which arose out of the original CBI recommendations, and in so far as TEC funding is now closely tied to their success in meeting these NVQ targets (Evans, 1992, pp. 179–80), there is a perfect symmetry between contemporary VET policy and practice and the principles and objectives of the NCVQ.

THE ESTABLISHMENT OF THE NCVQ

The foundations for a major overhaul of VET programmes and qualifications were laid with the publication of *A New Training Initiative* by the Department of Employment (DOE) in 1981. If Britain was to meet its training needs in a rapidly changing and increasingly competitive economic climate, urgent reforms were needed in both the design and delivery of VET programmes. Even at this early stage the concern with 'outputs' – the 'standards that need to be achieved at the end of a learning programme' (Jessup, 1990, p. 18) – was given prominence; as the report stated, 'at the heart of the initiative lie standards of a new kind' (DOE, 1981, p. 6). The implementation of these new output standards was to provide the impetus for the development of NVQs and the CBET strategy which underpins them, particularly during a period when VET policy and practice was almost exclusively influenced by the powerful MSC and later the Training Agency (see Finn, 1990).

This theme was taken up and reinforced in subsequent White Papers – *Training for Jobs* (DOE, DES, 1984) and *Education and Training for Young People* (DOE, DES, 1985) – and was ultimately brought to fruition and operationalized in the 1986 White Paper *Working Together: Education and Training* (DOE, DES, 1986). Following this publication the NCVQ was set up with a remit which included the design and implementation of a new national framework of vocational qualifications with the aim of securing national standards of vocational competence throughout all occupational sectors.

Table 1.1 *National education and training targets*

Foundation Learning
1. By 1997, 80% of young people to reach NVQ 2 or equivalent (4 GCSEs, Grades A–C).
2. Training and education to NVQ 3 (or equivalent) available to all young people who can benefit.
3. By 2000, 50% of young people to reach NVQ 3 or equivalent (2 A-levels).
4. Education and training provision to develop self-reliance, flexibility and breadth.

Lifetime Learning
1. By 1996, all employees to take part in training and development as the norm.
2. By 1996, 50% of the employed workforce to be aiming for NVQs or credit towards them.
3. By 2000, 50% of the employed workforce qualified to at least NVQ 3 or equivalent.
4. By 1996, 50% of the medium to larger organisations (200 or more employees) to qualify as Investors in People.

(*Source*: Smithers and Robinson, 1993, p. 4)

From the start, the key aims of the NCVQ were to 'improve vocational qualifications by basing them on the standards of competence required in employment' and to 'establish a National Vocational Qualification (NVQ) framework which is comprehensible and comprehensive and facilitates access, progression and continued learning' (NCVQ, 1989, p. 2). The NCVQ is not an awarding body, but will undertake to accredit or 'hallmark' qualifications awarded by other vocational bodies such as City & Guilds, the Business and Technology Education Council (BTEC) or the Royal Society of Arts (RSA), but insists that it will 'only accredit qualifications which meet employment needs' (NCVQ, 1989, p. 3). It will be well worth remembering this primary focus on *qualifications* and *employment* when we come to consider the massive expansion of NVQs in later chapters.

THE NATURE AND STRUCTURE OF NVQs

All NVQs must consist of 'an agreed statement of competence, which should be determined or endorsed by a lead body with responsibility for defining, maintaining and improving national standards of performance in the sectors of employment where the competence is practised' (NCVQ, 1991, p. 1). For NCVQ purposes there are 11 key occupational sectors (Jessup, 1991, pp. 186–90), plus lots of subsidiary sectors, and, at the last count, there were around 160 or so separate industry lead bodies (St John-Brooks, 1992; including industry training organizations as well as lead bodies, Smithers puts the total at 186, Smithers, 1993, p. 20) which had been responsible for awarding some 354,005 NVQ certificates up to the end of March 1993 (NCVQ, 1993a).

The agreed statement of competence in each occupational sphere 'should be derived from an analysis of functions within the area of competence to which it relates' (NCVQ, 1991a, p. 2), and should be accompanied by 'performance criteria' which 'identify only the essential aspects of performance necessary for competence' and 'range statements' which 'express the various circumstances in which the competence must be applied, and may detail, for example, differences in physical location, employment contexts or equipment used' (p. 3).

This process of 'functional analysis' used by lead bodies to determine competence involves examining 'the expectations in employment as a whole . . . breaking the work role for a particular area into purposes and functions' (Mitchell, 1989, p. 58). The end result is the identification of 'key purposes' in the various occupational sectors (an example from the Building Society Sector is 'promote the sale of associated products and services to customers', p. 59) and, on this basis, key 'units' and constituent 'elements' of competence are constructed, each accompanied by the appropriate performance criteria, range statements and assessment guidance (see Table 1.2 for a practical illustration).

In addition to all this, there is a hierarchy of five levels of competence – from 'competence in the performance of a range of varied work activities, most of which would be routine and predictable' at Level 1 to 'competence which involves the application of a significant range of fundamental principles and complex techniques' at level 5 (NCVQ, 1991a, p. 4; for a full description of each level see Table 1.3). These levels are intended to provide uniformity and harmony in terms of the national

Table 1.2 *Business Administration (Administrative) NVQ Level 2*

UNIT: RECEPTION
ELEMENTS:
01 receive and direct visitors
Notes:
Underpinning skills and knowledge: structure, location and responsibilities of people in organisation; policy and procedures of organisation on greeting visitors, security, safety and emergency; messaging procedure; telephone system and operation; effective use of information sources; dealing with difficult/aggressive visitors (e.g. recognise and react appropriately to physical communication signals); car parking arrangements available to visitors; effective communication (oral and written)
Range:
Routine and non-routine visitors must be dealt with. Contingencies must be dealt with: callers without appointment (with both urgent and non-urgent requirements), callers who are late/early for appointments, callers who require baggage or other effects to be cared for during visit, receipt of deliveries, emergency situations
Performance Criteria:
1. All visitors are greeted promptly and courteously.
2. Visitors' names and needs are identified.
3. Visitors are only given disclosable information.
4. Visitors are directed and/or escorted in accordance with organisation policy.
5. Reasons for any delay/non-availability are explained politely.
6. All records are up to date, legible and accurate.
7. Messages are accurately recorded and passed on promptly to correct location.
8. Security and safety procedures are followed at all times.

(*Source*: COVTEC, 1992, p. 1)

Table 1.3 *The NVQ framework*

The following definitions of the NVQ levels provide a general guide and are not intended to be prescriptive.
Level 1: competence in the performance of a range of varied work activities, most of which may be routine and predictable.
Level 2: competence in a significant range of varied work activities, performed in a variety of contexts. Some of the activities are complex and non-routine, and there is some individual responsibility or autonomy. Collaboration with others, perhaps through membership of a work group or team, may often be a requirement.
Level 3: competence in a broad range of varied work activities performed in a wide variety of contexts and most of which are complex and non-routine. There is considerable responsibility and autonomy, and control or guidance of others is often required.
Level 4: competence in a broad range of complex, technical or professional work activities performed in a wide variety of contexts and with a substantial degree of personal responsibility and autonomy. Responsibility for the work of others and the allocation of resources is often present.
Level 5: competence which involves the application of a significant range of fundamental principles and complex techniques across a wide and often unpredictable variety of contexts. Very substantial personal autonomy and often significant responsibility for the work of others and for the allocation of substantial resources feature strongly, as do personal accountabilities for analysis and diagnosis, design, planning, execution and evaluation.

(*Source*: NCVQ, 1992c, p. 12)

standards of competence, and also to offer broad foundations for future progression for NCVQ candidates.

Since the NCVQ framework was given official government endorsement as a model for future VET reform in the 1991 White Paper *Education and Training for the 21st Century* (DES, 1991), there has been an increasing tendency to use the five NCVQ levels of competence to indicate some kind of equivalence between NVQs and other vocational and academic qualifications. This exercise has become even more popular since the introduction of general NVQs (GNVQs) in 1992, and a typical table of equivalence would be as follows:

NVQ Level	GNVQ Level	General Education
5 (Professional, Managerial)		Higher Education
4 (Higher Technician, Junior Management)		
3 (Technician Supervisor)	Advanced	2 GCE A-Levels
2 (Craft)	Intermediate	4 GCSEs, A-C
1 (Foundation)	Foundation	Other GCSEs

(Smithers and Robinson, 1993, p. 43)

It should be noted, however, that any equivalence here between NVQs, GNVQs and academic qualifications can only be regarded as a *claim* or an assertion which has yet to be substantiated. NVQs are not normally regarded as being equivalent to GCSE or A level by colleges and universities, and GNVQs have still to be empirically tested and evaluated. The announcement that GNVQs at level 3 were to be known as 'vocational A levels' (Nash, 1993a), made in July 1993, some time before the evaluation of the first limited pilot runs of the new qualifications, was entirely typical of the recent policy implementations and publicity exercises surrounding NVQ developments.

Referring to developments in education more generally, Gipps (1993) has described this recent mode of policy-making as a 'misuse of evidence' – and a shift away from 'discussion and evidence'. A standard policy-making process is now one in which 'think tanks promote policy through strong value assertions and then proceed directly to detailed prescriptions. Argumentation is intuitive; there is appeal at most to anecdotal evidence but not to research' (p. 36). Although directed primarily at National Curriculum policy decisions, this comment might easily apply to some of the developments surrounding the implementation of NVQs.

RECENT DEVELOPMENTS

Over the last few years there has been an exponential growth of NVQs, accompanied by a massive increase in the power and influence of the NCVQ. The 'quiet revolution' referred to by Burke in 1989 has become rather noisier in subsequent years! Without doubt, the most significant feature of these later NVQ developments has been the official government endorsement of the NCVQ framework through the Department of Employment (DOE) and, latterly, the Department for Education (DFE – formerly the Department of Education and Science, DES).

Although the NCVQ was always unofficially sponsored jointly by the Employment Department and the DES, according to Maclure (1991), it was generally 'seen as a creature of the ED' (p. 27), arising as it did out of the training culture of the Manpower Services Commission and the Training Agency. Maclure describes the NCVQ system as the 'government's chosen instrument for giving structured recognition to the acquisition of the skills which industry and commerce value' (p. 27). An overt DES interest in this sphere, however, was revealed in the 1991 White Papers concerned with the future of education and training.

The White Papers were intended to provide solutions to a number of perceived problems in the post-school sector generally and VET in particular, including Britain's comparatively low post-school participation rates, the unsatisfactory state of VET and what Maclure describes as the 'historic failure of English education to integrate the academic and the practical, the general and the vocational' (Maclure, 1991, p. 28). A key element in the government's strategy for the solution of these problems was the utilization of the 'clear framework of qualifications' provided by the NCVQ. The government thus 'instructed the National Council to have a comprehensive framework of NVQs in place by the end of 1992' which would 'cover 80% of the working population at Levels 1 to 4 in the NVQ framework, and all the major sectors of employment' (DES, 1991, vol. 1, pp. 16–17). More significantly, the implementation of all NVQs was to be accelerated, and the Secretary of State for Education would use reserve powers under the Education Reform Act 1988 as a 'means of requiring colleges and schools to offer only NVQs to students pursuing vocational options' (p. 19). More recently, the Employment Secretary launched a massive publicity campaign designed to 'put NVQs on the map' and, in addition to the achievement of the NETTs, to establish one thousand 'NVQ advocates' by the end of 1995 (NCVQ, 1993a, p. 6).

In addition to other measures such as the introduction of training credits for 16- and 17-year-olds and the establishment of advanced and ordinary diplomas which would record achievement in both academic and vocational areas, it was announced in the White Paper that the government saw 'the development of more general NVQs as an important priority' (p. 18). It seems that, like NVQs, the new qualifications may be *doomed* to succeed, and educators, lecturers and trainers will simply have to make the best of the new system, just as teachers coped with the National Curriculum and its assessment procedures.

What few commentators seem to have noticed in the midst of all this hectic and impromptu innovation, however, is the crucial difference between GNVQs and their more occupationally specific counterparts, especially in so far as these indicate a discernible retreat from cherished foundational NCVQ principles and practice (GNVQs are discussed in more detail in Chapter 8).

The development of GNVQs was representative of a marked tendency over recent years for the NCVQ remit to stray far beyond its original and natural home in work-based VET. Jessup's speculation in 1989 about whether CBET would 'impact upon the mainstream of school and academic education' (1989, p. x) has proved uncannily accurate. NVQs and the philosophy which underpins them have moved downwards into schools and upwards into higher education, with what can only be far-reaching and (as I will argue in later chapters) potentially disastrous results for learning, teaching, and education and training in general in these spheres.

A model of assessment developed to facilitate and enhance workplace qualifications is a most unlikely candidate for the reform of either the post-school sector in general or VET in particular. More significantly, as Professor Woolhouse observed in the 1993 John Baillie Memorial Lecture, a 'system in which the predominant mode of provision is employer-based training is unlikely to satisfy the criteria for a national system of studentship', and 'undue reliance on a voluntary employer-led system . . . will lead only to mistakes of the last 40 years' (Woolhouse, 1993, p. 7).

POSTSCRIPT: AN INITIAL CRITICAL OVERVIEW OF THE NCVQ ENTERPRISE

The NCVQ is fond of issuing glossy brochures and videos outlining the benefits of NVQs for employers, for students, and for colleges. By way of an initial summary of the criticisms and dissenting perspectives which are a primary focus on this book, it would be useful to offer an early critical review of the alleged NVQ benefits in each of these areas.

Employers

Among the many practical benefits which employers can expect from the NVQ framework is 'improved profitability and economic performance through education and training provision which is more relevant to employment and better structured to meet the needs of industry and commerce' (NCVQ, 1990a, p. 4). The promotion of NVQs has now been inextricably bound up with the general demands for the upgrading of VET and the development of a flexible and highly trained workforce initially outlined by the CBI task force in 1989 and repeated in countless documents and general prescriptions since. As Debling (1992) correctly notes, 'NVQs are now fully recognised as an integral part of the national education and training effort' (p. 5), are given prominence in the NETTs mentioned earlier and are currently receiving massive publicity and promotion by all relevant agencies.

The easy assumption of a direct link between VET and economic performance is almost certainly mistaken (Esland, 1990), as is the connection between qualifications and employers' requirements (Moore, 1989; these issues will be taken up in more depth in later chapters). However, for the sake of argument we can accept that there may be some sort of relationship between changes in VET and industrial and economic developments, and go on to ask whether any of the main claims can be justified and, after eight years of NCVQ development work, whether we are any nearer to the achievement of the aims of improving vocational qualifications and establishing a national framework which facilitates access, progression and continued learning.

NCVQ apologists would naturally answer all such questions in the affirmative, and indeed do so in a constant stream of publicity material. However, independent research and evidence – for example, the Smithers report which claimed that the NCVQ system was leading us into a 'disaster of epic proportions' (1993, preface) – tends to paint a rather different picture of these matters.

In the first place, employers – who are supposed to be the key players in this area – are largely indifferent to or ignorant of the nature of NVQs. A report by Her Majesty's Inspectorate (HMI) on NVQ implementation in 1991 involving consultations with colleges and employers revealed that the 'level of NVQ awareness among some employers and in the community is low'. Lecturers in many colleges were expressing concern that many employers 'do not know what NVQs are and, correspondingly, show little interest in them' (Dean, 1991, p. 4). This state of affairs has now been belatedly acknowledged by the DOE and the NCVQ, and in 1992/93 a new publicity campaign – coinciding with the introduction of GNVQs and benefiting from Mr Major's personal endorsement (NCVQ, 1992b) – was launched and later taken up with enthusiasm by the Employment Department.

It becomes increasingly difficult in these times of 'hard sell', however, to separate fact from fiction, and it is less obvious that employers (outside the members of industry lead bodies, that is) are either involved in or are gaining anything of value from all this activity. In 1991 Field's study recorded low employer participation in NVQ implementation at shop-floor level and lukewarm or indifferent trade union attitudes (1991), and in 1993 Field was still expressing disappointment and regret that 'far too few employers see NVQs as anything more than a new acronym on the certificates that young people bring' (1993a, p. 6) when applying for jobs (see also Nash, 1993d).

Moreover, there is no evidence of any links between NVQs and the promotion of high-level technological change and the upgrading of skills currently being called for by the CBI and other relevant bodies. The research by McHugh *et al.* (1993) reported 'limited opportunities for progression beyond level 2' (p. 45) for both employed and unemployed candidates. Of the hundreds of thousands of NVQ certificates thus far awarded, the overwhelming majority were at the lower levels 1 and 2 (with 37% at level 1), and, more significantly, a 'quite extraordinary proportion of the NVQs awarded are in areas where labour supply has been perfectly adequate for some years' (Field, 1993a, p. 6). Typically, the awards are in areas such as fast food, hairdressing and basic business administration, not the sort of sectors likely to lead to the 'World Class Britain' called for by Mr Major (NCVQ, 1992b, p. 1) or take us into an economic lead over European competitors! Indeed, as Smithers (1993) reports, many senior executives are convinced that, because NVQs are 'so narrowly defined, they are likely to fail industry in the longer term'; Smithers also cites recent research by Steedman and Hawkins which suggests that 'NVQs represent a retrograde step in the development of vocational education and training for young people in Britain' (p. 21).

What of the harmonization of vocational qualifications and the improvement of access which were initially key elements in the NCVQ remit? There is some evidence that the NVQ framework has provided an opportunity for more people to gain vocational qualifications, particularly in areas not previously covered by a recognized qualifications system (Shackleton, 1990). In a similar way, it could be said that NVQs are potentially a 'powerful tool for the extension of equal opportunities to access to vocational qualifications' (McKelvey and Peters, 1991, p. 65). The large number of awards at lower levels is logically connected with such considerations of access (though, as I argue below, the long-term value and benefits of such new qualifications are less obvious).

In terms of the establishment of a national system of vocational qualifications, however, there is little evidence that – over and above the 'national' printed in the NVQ kitemark – there has been all that much standardization, uniformity and coherence achieved over the last seven or eight years. Certainly, there was something of a 'complex and untidy array of vocational qualifications' (Jessup, 1991, p. 9) in existence prior to the establishment of the NCVQ. However, the 'jungle' of qualifications and awarding bodies has been replaced by the equally dense and impenetrable jungle of lead bodies and rival interpretations of occupational competence and assessment procedures (not to mention fierce territorial disputes, see Smithers, 1993, p. 18).

The awarding bodies (BTEC, City & Guilds, RSA) are, of course, still there, since NCVQ is meant to accredit awards made by other bodies. Indeed, a review of NVQ developments published in 1993 by the Employment Department's Methods Strategy Unit saw the 'rapid increase in the number of awarding bodies and of qualifications' (ED, 1993a, p. 35) as a potentially serious problem. What we now have is another administrative layer of over 180 industry lead bodies (with all the various sub-committees), each one jealously guarding its new-found power and control over a particular section of occupational standards and VET. Callender (1992) recorded the 'confusing duplication and proliferation of NVQs within industries and especially in occupational areas that cut across different industrial sectors, contrary to one NVQ aim to streamline the qualification jungle' (p. 26).

There is every sign that these lead bodies will continue to multiply and breed new levels of administrative bureaucracy far in excess of anything which existed in pre-NCVQ days. The Employment Department at least seems to have identified the dangers here, and, at a conference for the lead bodies in Autumn 1992, the head of the ED's qualifications and standards tentatively floated the idea of some future rationalization involving the replacement of lead bodies with around fifteen or so 'occupational standards councils' (St John-Brooks, 1992). The fact that this announcement was met with cool resistance and some trepidation from lead body representatives is an indication of the new-found power and status of these bodies and the problems in store for those who, having given such responsibility to employers, may now want to place curbs and restrictions on this power and responsibility.

Students

In the new discourse of education, it is more correct to speak of NVQ 'candidates' or 'customers' rather than 'students'. In any case, whatever we call them, it is clear that the impact of the new qualifications on people in education and training wishing to achieve vocational qualifications is of prime importance.

This point is worth stressing, for, in spite of contemporary publicity about NVQs, access and flexible learning, students are, in fact, something of an afterthought, since the NCVQ framework was, as noted above, designed in the main to serve the interests of employers, not those of people seeking vocational qualifications. Moreover, in conjunction with the tendency towards lower-level accreditation referred to above, there may in fact be a de-skilling element of NVQs which is certainly not in the interests of those pursuing vocational studies (see Raggatt, 1991, 1994; Jarvis and Prais, 1989; Callender, 1992).

In later chapters I will be referring to studies which have shown how NVQs have led to a narrowing of skills, knowledge and occupational focus, and suggesting that this state of affairs is in nobody's interests. For the present it is worth noting in particular the way in which NVQs severely restrict and circumscribe learning and, at another level, provide employers with substantial power and control over the functions and work activities of employees. Field (1991), for instance, has suggested that a potentially sinister feature of NVQs is the high degree of control over job specification and function which the system offers to employers. In this respect, the 'routinization' and 'mechanistic behaviourism' of the NCVQ approach is ideally suited to the 'reinforcement of the divisions between different aspects of the work process', thus offering employers the means to 'narrow the scope of initiative and field of responsibility of each individual in her work' (pp. 49–50).

All this is a long way from the open and flexible system described in the NCVQ literature as providing the client with 'more control over the process and assessment of learning' (Jessup, 1991, p. 115). The reality is that 'employees find it hard to demonstrate all required competences at a particular level because NVQs cannot hope to precisely reflect/describe the content of real jobs' (McHugh *et al.*, 1993, p. 46). Moreover, the key characteristics of NVQs 'also penalise candidates with learning difficulties who can only complete selected units' (p. 46). The 'autonomous learner' depicted in CBET writings is largely mythical, a popular slogan which, along with notions of open access, the accreditation of prior learning (APL), individualized learning contracts, action plans, records of achievement and student-centredness, has been appropriated by the industrial-training lobby from the progressive and experiential tradition and utilized to achieve particular training objectives (Edwards, 1991).

A number of points need to be made about the appropriation of progressive terminology and methodology by the industrial trainers in general and NVQ supporters in particular. In the first place, it is dishonest to suggest that procedures such as APL, action planning, credit transfer, and the like were either developed by or necessarily connected with the development of NVQs. As Ecclestone (1993a) points out, none of these popular and fashionable learning concepts now linked with NVQs is 'exclusive to competence-based education' (p. 270), but all are presented as such. In a similar vein, Chown and Last (1993), in discussing the benefits of open and distance learning, flexible patterns of attendance, modularization and credit accumulation and transfer systems (CATS), go on to stress that

> First, not one of them is exclusive to competence-based curricula. Second, a great many institutions have already incorporated these features into their existing provision, in some cases – like the Open University, for example – for many years, without necessarily adopting competence-based curricula. (p. 17)

Furthermore, not all of these fashionable trappings of contemporary practice (often associated in adult-education contexts with Knowles' theories of andragogy; see Knowles, 1970) should be regarded as unmixed blessings. Critics of these trends such as Collins (1991) speak of the emergence of a 'technicist obsession' which has reduced adult learning to 'situations managed by mechanical formulations such as standardized pre-packaged curricula and preconceived needs assessment instruments put together by experts'. All of this has resulted in learning being 'reduced, with technocratic abandon, to a series of critical thinking skills or competences' (pp. 4–6).

This alternative perspective on current learning trends helps us to explain how what appear to be superficially the oddest of bedfellows – open/autonomous learning and CBET approaches – can at one level manage to coexist (though not without resultant tensions and paradoxes). Edwards (1991) has described how many of the REPLAN schemes for unemployed adults had managed to adopt the 'discourse of learner-centredness', but pointed out that such putatively flexible and open learning schemes frequently functioned as a 'mask for coercion and poor training' (p. 115). On this account, flexible and open learning may be adopted, not for educational or even good VET reasons, but because it is necessary to cope with structural under-employment and the rapid rate of technological change in post-Fordist economies.

The NVQ system is an ideal instrument in this respect, for it combines apparent openness of procedures and methods with the necessary control over outcomes through employer-defined competences. There is admittedly a sense in which it is true (though neither unequivocally nor absolutely, as I will suggest later) that NVQs are 'independent of any course or programme of learning' and 'can be gained through any mode of learning' (Jessup, 1990a, p. 24). But this statement is both incomplete and disingenuous. NVQs are not primarily concerned with learning, but with the *collection of evidence* to satisfy competence criteria. If evidence is successfully collected, then an NVQ is awarded. It may be that some useful learning does take place during the gathering of evidence (though this will be unsystematic and not an integral part of the whole enterprise), but this pales into insignificance beside the need to satisfy all the pre-specified units and elements of competence, performance and supplementary criteria required for certification. Now it has already been established that all these assessment procedures are established by employers through the industry lead bodies. Consequently, since learners play little or no role in determining the ends of the exercise, the claims about 'autonomous' learning become less easy to sustain.

This is brought out well by Edwards (1993) in a later paper in which he argues that the changes in education and training brought about by the introduction of NVQs have served to support the 'development of post-Fordism in the economy'. Against this background, 'open learning can be articulated as another aspect of post-Fordism, strategically arranged to normalize a view of the future of work . . . persons will be disciplined into certain forms of behaviour and more readily managed within a social formation of structural inequality' (pp. 180, 185).

When examined against these alternative perspectives, the benefits of NVQs to learners become rather less obvious and a good deal less appealing than the official NCVQ version would have us believe!

Colleges

In this context, 'colleges' is really a shorthand way of referring to all the providers of VET and qualifications, including schools, higher education (HE) institutions, private training companies, TECs, and the like. And since the so-called NVQ revolution is said to be in large part a movement away from a provider-led to a client-led system, the implications for colleges cannot but be far-reaching and significant. In the brave new world of NVQs the 'key process on which to concentrate is not the teaching or training by the providers, but that of learning by the students or trainees, the clients in the system' (Jessup, 1991, p. 99). This client-led system is itself part of the process fuelled by the opening up of the whole system to market forces and input/output accountability through policies now enshrined in legislation such as the Education Reform Act and the Further & Higher Education Act 1992 which removed institutions from local authority control (Hyland, 1992a; Simon, 1992).

This official client-led ideology has, like the fashionable learning practices discussed above, been around for some time in the post-compulsory sector and publicized extensively through the work of the Further Education Unit (FEU). As a recent FEU publication noted:

> Colleges of further education have long been concerned to provide flexible learning opportunities to meet the needs of individuals, and this evolution can be traced through the early development of evening classes and the more recent provision of open learning, distance learning, learning workshops, resource-based learning and participation in the Open College. (FEU, 1992a, p. 1)

The more recent changes – motivated partly by government policy and the new economic realism and accountability of the 1980s (DES, 1987) and partly by changing needs of industry, and the development of more 'responsive' institutions (Thompson, 1987) – have led to the new concept of the post-school institution as a provider of 'learner services'. This inevitably entails a movement away from a traditional 'course-based' system of education and training (with fixed exit and entry points) towards a 'flexible' system through which colleges may support access to guidance, counselling, tutorial support, and 'flexible access to assessment and accreditation' (FEU, 1992a, p. 9).

According to the NCVQ, the new framework of NVQs has a number of benefits to offer colleges as they strive to realize their potential in the new era of flexibility. The role of colleges in delivering NVQs can lead to:

1. more people seeking opportunities to learn . . .
2. opportunities to tailor arrangements to individual needs, with the possibility of qualifications being obtained through credit accumulation
3. a higher profile for the Further and Higher Education sector . . .
4. the improved development and use of the skills of college staff, and of college services generally
5. more influence over the training and quality process . . .

(NCVQ, 1990b, p. 4)

Even allowing for the fact that these claims are taken from a glossy marketing brochure, it is really quite remarkable how all of them manage to be either half truths or just plain wrong. It would be worth looking briefly at each one in turn.

1. No matter what is now being said, NVQs were meant to promote work-based training outside formal institutions, and it is only in the last four or five years, once it was realized that this original plan was short-sighted, that NVQs have been linked with programmes offered in FE colleges. Moreover, the market for FE services has been growing steadily over the last twenty or thirty years, quite independently of the development of either NVQs or flexible services. There was a 'phenomenal post-war growth in the further education sector in England and Wales by which the number of students more than doubled', between 1946 and 1975 (Cantor and Roberts, 1983, p. 3). The much canvassed 'Cinderella' status of the sector has always been semi-mythical, and what was left of the myth has been finally dispelled by the incorporation of colleges in the wake of the Further & Higher Education Act 1992. Participation rates in post-school education (influenced considerably, it has to be said, by the recession and deepening youth unemployment) have increased massively since 1987, and are projected to rise by another 30 per cent or so by 1995/96 (Nicholson, 1993). The FE sector

now educates as many 17- and 18-year-olds as do the schools, and 'caters for two million students a year at a cost of about £2.5 billion' (Smithers and Robinson, 1993, p. 1). NVQs are, of course, linked to all these developments in the NCVQ literature and the NETTs, but there is no shortage of independent factors to account for the expansion of this sector of education (and also, as the 1993 National Commission report concluded, 'much that needs to be improved', NCE, 1993, p. 12).

2. Recent developments in post-school learning programmes have served to emphasize the activity of learning and the importance of continuous and flexible assessment (Gibbs, 1988). GCSE courses for mature students and BTEC courses, for example, allow for individualized learning development assessed by a range and variety of techniques. These trends were themselves developed in opposition and as a reaction to the 'traditional' examinations system which NVQ supporters are fond of attacking. As I argue in more detail in Chapter 4, the NCVQ rhetoric about learning is a very long way from the reality, since CBET is quite seriously at odds with the preferred methods of experiential learning employed in the post-school sector. Moreover, as mentioned earlier, CATS schemes were fully operational before the establishment of the NCVQ, and the Open College Network, perhaps the most common and flexible system for mature students in FE, is operated quite independently of the NVQ framework and does not employ CBET strategies (Mager, 1993).

3. Further and higher education, as suggested above, already has a high profile which, reinforced by the provisions of the 1992 Act, is likely to provide for expansion of numbers and increased access for years to come. NVQs and the NETTs may be a part of this, but they are not the *cause* of it. Arguably, it is the access movement in general, starting in the 1970s and gaining momentum in the 1980s, which has had the greatest impact in this sphere (Parry and Wake, 1990).

4. Post-school institutions have undergone massive changes over the last decade or so, and the process has accelerated in the era of incorporation since April 1993. In spite of 'innovation fatigue' and low morale caused by deteriorating conditions of service and poor industrial relations in recent times, college staff have responded well to the new demands and are now being given due credit for enhancing the quality of service in the sector (Melia, 1993). It is worth remembering, after all, that the separation of VET and FE in many vocational sectors occurred not with the introduction of NVQs but in the period following the Industrial Training Act of 1964. After that, 'training was the responsibility of industry and was not to be provided by colleges except as a contract service at full cost' (Millington, 1990, p. 117). This process of colleges competing for training contracts was reinforced during the MSC/TA period in the 1970s and 1980s, and continues under the TECs.

Most post-school institutions have proved themselves more than a match for the changing conditions, and staff have responded flexibly and intelligently in the new era of incorporation. Naturally, there are areas of tension and anxiety, but, as with the introduction of the National Curriculum into schools, these could have been avoided by the adoption of a more rational approach to innovation and reform. All the research evidence on curriculum innovation suggests that reforms which are 'top-down' or 'centre-periphery' are either short-lived or outright failures (Macdonald and Walker, 1976), and the introduction of National Curriculum assessment procedures into schools has provided a recent and particularly graphic illustration of this (Lawton, 1993).

The implementation of NVQs bears all the hallmarks of these failed 'top-down' models. As with the recent introduction of competence-based Training and Development Lead Body (TDLB) standards into further education teacher training (Chown and Last, 1993), there was a minimum consultation with FE staff about the introduction of NVQs into colleges. Shackleton (1990) paints a rosy and idealistic picture which, without wishing to deny the qualities and strengths of one particular college, is self-evidently not confirmed by the more general experiences of institutions in this sphere. Burke (1989b), for instance, noticed a sharp division in attitudes between proactive managers and departmental heads in colleges and staff at lecturer level who 'are far less in control . . . Policy decisions may be made above their heads and they have to live with the consequences . . . ' (p. 129). Similar unease and frustration is reported throughout the survey by Smithers (1993).

The crucial message about full staff participation and the need for development programmes to cope with the change process was also a conclusion reached in the study by Haffenden and Brown (1989) which revealed 'widely differing perspectives about the nature of competence' among FE staff, in addition to widespread misgivings about workplace assessment and fears that 'possession of knowledge might be undervalued' (pp. 139, 149). All the good will and staff development in the world cannot alter the fact that in many occupational areas NVQs were simply imposed on college staff without very much consultation or preparation, and lecturers simply had to make the best of it. As one of the catering lecturers whom we interviewed as part of our research at Warwick commented about the department's involvement in NVQs: 'To a certain extent we were forced into it because a lot of the part-time students were on YT programmes and the managing agents had to have NVQ qualifications to qualify for their financing' (Hyland and Weller, 1994, p. 23). This theme can be discerned in the initial implementation of NVQs in all the key occupational sectors.

What made this external imposition of new standards even more difficult to accept for many lecturers was their perspective that, in certain areas, the new system was quite sloppily introduced and resulted in rather lower standards than had previously existed. Again, this was of particular concern to the hairdressing lecturers we interviewed, and seemed to confirm Raggatt's findings about the narrowness of focus of many NVQs, which compared unfavourably with the BTEC 'process' model (1991, pp. 73–4). In a more recent study, Raggatt (1994) noted that the 'narrowness of NVQs put pressure on employers who often wanted students on work placement to undertake a wider range of activities' (p. 66). Throughout many of the studies there is a concern that CBET undervalues knowledge and theory, and studies in the areas of catering (MSC, 1988), engineering (Millington, 1990), plumbing and electrical engineering (Smithers, 1993) and construction (Callender, 1992) made specific references to the erosion of standards in this respect. This last study in particular painted a dismal and depressing picture of restrictive and mechanistic training, de-skilling and a lack of co-ordination between courses. More recently, a technical report on NVQ progress commissioned by the Employment Department noted in its list of 'problem areas' the 'poor quality of some of the standards on which qualifications are based' and the 'restriction of some lower level qualifications to very narrow skills' (ED, 1993a, p. 35). When all this is taken together, there is more than enough evidence to justify Smithers' (1993) damning critique of NVQs.

5. Given what has just been said above, the notion of NVQs offering more influence over the training and qualifying process is a little difficult to swallow. How can a system imposed externally and incorporating criteria devised by employers and accredited by a national quango possibly provide institutions with greater influence and freedom? The NCVQ document might well note the opportunities for colleges to become involved in a 'strengthened partnership with employers, training organisations and awarding bodies' (1990b, p. 4). This is not a matter of choice – colleges either do this or they go to the wall!

The erosion of colleges' autonomy in this respect has continued since the intervention of the MSC into the sector in the 1970s, and there is no evidence to suggest that the introduction of NVQs has offered institutions (and certainly not lecturers) any more power. Indeed, once the honeymoon period of independence is over the newly incorporated colleges may find that their activities are even more circumscribed by the demands of outside paymasters than they were under the aegis of the local education authority. Particularly worrying is the possibility that, in the new system of 'outcome-related funding', colleges 'now have a financial incentive to pass their students whatever standards they reach' (Smithers, 1993, p. 21). Nash (1993c) has reported that 'as the euphoria following incorporation disperses, some colleges appear to be experiencing management difficulties, and there have already been casualties at senior executive level' (p. 10). As far as college staff are concerned, the new era of incorporation has already indicated that there will be a deterioration of conditions of service (Utley, 1993a) to match the de-skilling and de-professionalization of roles likely to be brought about by the introduction of TDLB standards into the sector (Hyland, 1992b; Chown, 1992).

The long-term future of the further education sector in general and the roles of lecturers and trainers in particular is likely to be determined, not by considerations about NVQs, VET the 16 to 19 curriculum, or anything else 'educational', but by a struggle between the opposing 'market forces' model of provision in line with current ideology and the 'community college' model favoured by professional bodies such as NATFHE (NATFHE, 1992; I examine this in greater depth in Chapter 10). Perhaps it is just as well that the Further Education Funding Council is pledged to funding expansion in the sector over the coming years (FEFC, 1992), and that the economic climate is such as to encourage youngsters to stay on after 16, most of them likely to be pursuing vocational studies in the form of GNVQs!

After offering an initial critical response to the key NCVQ claims, it is now time to inspect more closely the alleged flaws, weaknesses and inconsistencies in CBET and NVQs in the areas of learning, assessment and knowledge, before looking at the impact on VET, adult, further and higher education, and professional courses. However, in order to establish a foundation for this closer analysis, it is necessary to examine the central concept of competence in greater detail.

Chapter 2

The Nature of Competence

COMPETENCE: THE AMBIGUITIES OF THE CONCEPT

> Everybody is talking about competence. It is an El Dorado of a word with a wealth of meanings and the appropriate connotations for utilitarian times. (Norris, 1991, p. 331)

Although Norris is correct about both the meanings and the connotations of the concept of competence, I will reserve judgement about its alleged 'El Dorado' qualities! Just as there is nothing particularly new about CBET strategies, so the term 'competence' itself has a long-established history both in ordinary language and in the discourse of VET. The notion of the competent craftsman or artisan goes back a long way; in the British coal-mining industry, for instance, 'certificates of competency' for various job functions were being issued as long ago as the middle of the nineteenth century (Berkovitch, 1977; Osborn, 1993).

Although the positive overtones of the concept are obvious, they are not necessarily always dominant, and there is in fact a strange ambiguity about the notion of competence. Although competence is a term of approbation, it also carries with it 'lowest common denominator' characteristics. Indeed, dictionary definitions of competence which include such synonyms as 'sufficient', 'adequate' and 'suitable' serve to reinforce this sense of the term. If a plumber, bricklayer or doctor is deemed to be competent, then he or she is normally considered to be able to work within and satisfy certain basic requirements of the trade or profession. What is more, this 'lowest common denominator' feature seems to apply even in what might be considered to be higher level theoretical pursuits. In the sphere of literary theory, for instance, Eagleton (1983) has described the idea of the 'competent reader' as a 'static conception'. The idea of a competent reader as 'one who can apply to the text certain rules' is a 'limited one' which

> tends to suppress the truth that all judgements of 'competence' are culturally and ideologically relative, and that all reading involves the mobilization of extra-literary assumptions for the measuring of which 'competence' is an absurdly inadequate model. (p. 125)

Jessup (1991) is clearly fully aware of these 'basic minimum' overtones of competence, and early on his book tries (unsuccessfully in my view) to pre-empt further discussion by asserting that competence 'does not refer to a lowish or minimum level of performance' but to 'the standard required successfully to perform an activity or function' (p. 25). But, in the face of both ordinary language and usage in the area of technical and vocational education, this claim is less than convincing. The particular model of functional analysis employed by the NCVQ – the analysis of tasks and functions (Mansfield, 1989) rather than the identification of the characteristics of superior performers (Tuxworth, 1989) – seems to lead inevitably to this lower order kind of concept. Moreover, there is now considerable research evidence to suggest that, even at this relatively low level, occupational standards are still not being achieved (Callender, 1992; Smithers, 1993).

Ordinary language is, of course, never the last word in discussions about the ultimate meanings of terms, but, as the linguistic philosopher J. L. Austin (1970) once remarked, it *is* the 'first word' (p. 185). Consider the following everyday conversation between two work colleagues, one of whom is seeking to determine the work capability, industry, conscientiousness, quality of performance of a third colleague:

A: What do you make of her?
B: Well, she's quite competent.
A: But . . . ?
B: No buts . . . she's highly competent!
A: Yes, but is she any good?

In this context and many others linked to work roles, competence cannot but be a term of praise, but it is neither undiluted nor unequivocal praise. We may be justified in thinking that if someone is described as being competent then this is not the highest recommendation which might be made of that person's ability!

The basic minimum aspect of the concept – which is partly responsible for the confusion and ambiguity which surrounds much of the debate in this area – seems to place the term in the category of 'trouser words' (Austin, 1970, pp. 70ff.), that is, words such as 'real' and 'proper' whose negative usage, so to speak, wears the trousers. There is, for instance, a definite sense to the claim that something is real or proper only in the light of specific ways in which that thing is *not* real or proper (e.g., it is a fake or an illusion). In a similar way, competence seems to gain much of its meaning from a consideration of ways in which people or actions might be 'incompetent'. This point is significant in terms of the use of competence as a slogan or persuasive device (we are all against incompetence, after all!), and also in terms of the technical NCVQ interpretation. It is worth remembering that this latter usage, in spite of recent attempts to extend the scope of competence beyond its original home in work-based occupational VET, has an overriding concern with protecting employers and the public against incompetence in the performance of occupational roles and tasks.

THE VARIETIES OF COMPETENCE

It is worth prefacing this closer analysis of the concept with an examination of a troubling, and largely unnoticed though highly significant, tendency to confuse and conflate the terms 'competence' (plural: 'competences') and 'competency' (plural: 'competencies'). As a matter of preference, I am using the former term throughout this book, but there is some evidence to suggest that there are relevant differences between the pairs of concepts, and that the failure to make the necessary distinctions has fuelled the appalling confusion and opacity which has characterized much of the discourse in this sphere.

We can usefully begin the analysis here with the important distinction noted by Carr (1993) between competence as a *capacity* and competence as a *disposition*. In the capacity sense (what I have called the 'holistic' versions of competence; Hyland, 1993c), the term is employed broadly when we 'evaluate individuals as more or less successful in realising their aspirations to the standards of whichever professional activity they are engaged in' (Carr, 1993, p. 256). This is the sense in which we might speak of a competent electrician, plumber, lawyer or doctor. There is, however, the narrower or more atomistic dispositional sense of competence in which the term is used 'to label particular abilities or mark episodes of causal effectiveness with respect to these abilities' (p. 257). In this more restricted sense we might speak of a competent piece of driving or writing, or the competent performance or handling of a situation.

Against this background, there are good grounds for arguing that the capacity sense of the term normally applies to the evaluation of *persons*, whereas the dispositional sense refers to *activities*, and that it is the former which is more properly connected with 'competence' and the latter with 'competency'. On this account, 'competences' would presumably be used to pick out broad groups of general capacities, and 'competencies' would be a label for specific performances or aspects of activities.

However, it must be admitted that no such awareness of distinctions and gradations of meaning is revealed in the mainstream literature on NVQs and CBET, and the terms are used interchangeably and randomly as if 'competence' and 'competency' were all of a piece. Ashworth (1992) is broadly right in suggesting that the NCVQ 'adopts an individualistic orientation by emphasising *personal* competences' (p. 8, author's italics), but then goes on to talk about 'competencies' or 'elements of competence' (p. 9) as if there were no relevant distinctions to be made here. Since NVQs are based on occupational roles or functions, it might be thought that the broader capacity sense of the term was the more appropriate, and indeed 'competent' is the favoured term in the overwhelming majority of writings on the topic. However, since the NCVQ model tends to fragment whole work functions into units and elements, there seem to be grounds for arguing that it is 'competencies' that are really being picked out in much of the NCVQ and mainstream literature.

These questions of meaning and definition are neither trivial nor purely academic. After all, how can a system which claims to be based on precise standards and explicit outcomes (Jessup, 1990b; Fletcher, 1991) be allowed to get away with such confusion about the basic terms which are at the heart and foundation of the whole process? In addition, the nature of the particular concepts and categories that are used picks out concrete items and properties in the real world which educators and trainers wish to emphasize in relation to particular programmes. In other words, questions of status and *value* are inextricably bound up with questions of meaning and application.

Some such value considerations, for instance, influence Jessup's distinction between 'job competence', when a person's competence is 'limited to a particular role in a particular company', and 'occupational/professional competence', which involves a person acquiring a 'repertoire of skills, knowledge and understanding which he or she can apply in a range of contexts and organisations' (1991, p. 26; incidentally, Jessup uses the term 'competence' throughout almost the whole of the book, but unaccountably changes his preference to 'competency' when discussing assessment in ch. 7, pp. 54–9). There is a clear wish to provide the NCVQ model with the gloss of this broader, more prestigious notion of professional competence, but in terms of the *actual* NVQ assessment procedures based on the functional analysis of occupational roles in terms of key purposes this is mere wishful thinking and not justified by the evidence. Some sort of distinction between job and professional competence may serve to characterize the difference between lower (say 1, 2 and 3) and higher (4 and 5) levels of the NVQ framework, but even here I would want to say that procedures which are perfectly adequate for the assessment of competence at the lower level are hopelessly unsuited to the assessment of professional competence. As I will be arguing later in Chapter 7, at these higher levels the notion of competence, and indeed the whole NCVQ system, should be abandoned and replaced (or at least radically modified) by alternative models of education, training and assessment.

The imprecision and confusion about definitions of the key terms characterizes almost all the literature on CBET but does not seem to worry or dismay NVQ proponents overmuch. In recommending CBET strategies for teachers in further and adult education, for instance, McAleavey and McAleer (1991) apparently found no embarrassment in admitting that there 'is no agreed definition of the term competence' (p. 20). Indeed, this is a howling understatement, since definitions of competence 'abound in the literature' (UDACE, 1989a, p. 15), the term 'competence has different meanings to different people' (Debling and Hallmark, 1990, p. 90), and 'both employers and educationalists have found competence strangely difficult to define' (Greenacre, 1990, p. 95).

All this was confirmed by the empirical research of Haffenden and Brown (1989) on the implementation of NVQs in further education (FE) colleges. They discovered a wide range of different conceptions in operation, and a 'plethora of opinions about competence and its definition' and 'widely differing perceptions about the nature of competence' (p. 139). In a similar vein, Ashworth and Saxton's (1990) examination of the concept of competence picked out some of the inconsistencies and ambiguities outlined above. They concluded that competences were of 'unclear logical status' and that the meaning of the term had 'not yet been clearly defined'; in particular, 'it is not clear whether a competence is a personal attribute, an act, or an outcome of behaviour' (pp. 3, 9).

This relates to the capacity/disposition conflation identified above, a confusion which is partly responsible for the vast and varied range of definitions of competence – from the simplistic and specific to the complex and all-embracing – evident in the literature. What follows is a typically representative sample taken from mainstream accounts:

1. ' . . . competence is essentially concerned with performance in employment' (NCVQ, 1988, p. v.)
2. Competence is a 'performance capability needed by workers in a specified occupational area' (FEU/PICKUP, 1987, p. 1)
3. Competence 'entails the ability to perform activities within an occupation' (Fletcher, 1991, p. 32)

4. 'Competence is concerned with what people can do rather than with what they know' (UDACE, 1989a, p. 6)
5. Competence embraces 'the possession and development of sufficient skills, knowledge, appropriate attitudes and experience for successful performance in life roles' (FEU, 1984, p. 3)
6. Competence should be described in general terms as 'being able to perform "whole" work roles . . . to the standards expected in employment . . . in real working environments' (Mansfield, 1989, p. 28)
7. Competence 'can be defined in terms of four interrelated components: the ability to perform a set of specific tasks – the ability to use task skills in an appropriate way to achieve the overall job function – the ability to respond to breakdowns in routine, emergencies, etc. – the ability to adapt one's work performance to natural constraints imposed by particular working environments' (Bartram, 1990, pp. 55–6)
8. ' . . . aspects of competence which go beyond the technical have been classified under the headings of "task management", "contingency management" and "role/environment skills" . . . All are considered necessary to be fully competent in an occupation or profession' (Jessup, 1991, p. 27)

This spectrum of definitions illustrates not just the differences in interpretation of competence in terms of breadth, specificity and the capacity/disposition distinction outlined above, but also serves to mark different emphases which characterize the evolution of competence talk from the 1980s to the present.

Definitions 1 to 4 cited above represent the earlier conception of competence which attempted to remain true to the behaviourist origins of CBET (discussed in more detail in Chapter 4) by specifying precisely what was to be achieved in terms of performance 'in the workplace' (NCVQ, 1988, p. v). This represents a determined effort to maintain the alleged precision, functional objectivity and workplace relevance of CBET by insisting that only measurable and observable job performance is to be taken into account. Competence is 'concerned with what people can do rather than what they know' (UDACE, 1989a, p. 6).

In more recent writings on NVQs and competence (particularly those published since 1990, see Fletcher, 1991, pp. 55ff.) there is a marked attempt to move away from the narrower conceptions and towards a more holistic model which identifies the role played by knowledge, understanding and context in the assessment of competence. It was considered that the use of performance alone to measure competence was (except the very basic, routine tasks) far too simplistic and context-specific; it did not provide an 'indication that a person will continue to be competent or will become more competent' (UDACE, 1989a; in fact, this notion of a person becoming 'more competent' is highly problematic, as I will explain later). There was a growing recognition of the 'need to assess knowledge in NVQs to cope with variation in practice which cannot be assessed through performance demonstrations' (Jessup, 1991, p. 123).

To deal with these newly perceived difficulties, the notion of 'range statements' – which attempt to 'describe the limits which performance to the identified standards is expected if the individual is to be deemed competent' (Fletcher, 1991, p. 52) – is now emphasized in the assessment procedures. This newer, more comprehensive process has been described in terms of a 'recontextualizing' of competence and has produced a new language of assessment in which 'first order measures' (which look at performance alone) are distinguished from 'second order measures' (which examine performance) and 'underpinning knowledge and understanding' (Wolf, 1990, pp. 33–4).

There has been, it must be said, some reluctance on the part of the more 'fundamentalist' (Black and Wolf, 1990, p. 14) NVQ proponents to make any such radical concessions to knowledge and understanding. Moran (1991), for instance claims that 'even in most professional occupations the proportion of knowledge-heavy competences is quite few' and that 'in many cases it is the recognition of how little we know which makes us more competent' (p. 8; I will be challenging and attempting to show the naivety of such populist attacks on knowledge in Chapter 5). In a similar vein, Debling and Hallmark (1990) assert that although 'standards are ashamedly about ability to perform effectively', this does 'not deny that sustained effective performance, in different contexts, may well depend on the individual owning *relevant* knowledge and understanding and applying it to good effect' (authors' italics). Relevant knowledge and understanding is that which is 'directly related to expected performance' (p. 10).

If we add to this the recently introduced notion of 'generic' competences (Jessup, 1991, p. 30; Fletcher, 1991, p. 52), which are meant to ensure the transferability of occupational skills, then the rich and ever-expanding metaphysical universe of competence is almost complete. Just for good measure though, a new star in the heavens has recently been identified – something called 'meta-competence', which draws attention to the fact that there are 'competences which work on other competences' (Fleming, 1991, p. 10).

Since the idea of 'generic' competence is connected with the new emphasis on core skills and common learning outcomes in the current debates on VET and the 16 to 19 curriculum (examined in Chapter 8), it is worth looking at this conception a little more closely before completing our survey of the logical geography of competence and competence talk.

GENERIC COMPETENCES, CORE SKILLS AND META-COMPETENCE

The extension of notions of competence to incorporate generic skills, knowledge and understanding can be seen both as a tacit acknowledgement of the inadequacies of the early performance-based CBET schemes and also a recognition that such approaches are too narrowly focused to capture all that is required in quality VET provision. The 1989 CBI report had pointed out that a serious shortcoming of our current provision was a failure to provide a solid general foundation on which to build VET. A part of the CBI solution was the inclusion of 'core skills' into VET programmes, and, as Maclure (1991) has noted, there now seems to be a consensus on this issue, with BTEC, HMI and various school curriculum bodies all calling for post-16 programmes which incorporate a 'core of related knowledge, skills, qualities and attitudes' (p. 38; these VET trends are discussed at greater length in Chapters 6 and 8).

The discussion about core skills tends to become entangled in broader debates about 'generic competences, general competences, process skills and common learning outcomes' (Jessup, 1991, p. 30), and a key difficulty in this area lies in determining just what it is that people are wanting to pick out and recommend for practice. There does seem to be some broad educational justification and legitimate use for generic skills such as literacy and numeracy which obviously have a wide applicability. In this respect, areas like 'communication', 'application of number' and 'information technology', which are included as core elements in GNVQs (NCVQ, 1993d), can fairly readily be seen to span vocational domains and subject and skill areas to provide for the desired flexibility and transferability of application.

I am less sure, however, whether notions such as 'knowledge about industry and commerce' and 'practical skills' (HMI, 1989) actually mean very much at all until they are applied to specific contexts. Similarly, 'problem solving' and 'personal social skills' are, in spite of their popularity as educational slogans, highly problematic and 'fraught with difficulty' (Maclure, 1991, p. 40). As for the notion of 'personal autonomy' as a core skill competence (Jessup, 1991, p. 84), however, the idea is breathtakingly naive and illogical, and about as far away from reality as the 'autonomous learners' said to be found on NVQ schemes (pp. 115–17). Autonomy is a highly complex philosophical concept which has been the subject of a long history of debate within philosophy of education (Dearden, 1984; Callan, 1988). As Dearden explains, a person is autonomous to the degree that

> what he [*sic*] thinks and does in important areas of his life cannot be explained without reference to his own activity of mind. That is to say, the explanation of why he thinks and acts as he does in these areas must include a reference to his own choices, deliberations, decisions, reflections, judgments, plannings or reasonings. (1972, p. 453)

Whatever particular philosophical perspective on autonomy is favoured, it is quite certain that autonomy is definitely *not* any sort of competence!

It is not clear how such omnibus and heterogeneous notions such as 'practical skills' and 'problem-solving' could possibly have much of a core status, and the newly fashionable conception of generic competences is as problematic as the older versions (consider the so-called 'skills' of doing history and riding a bicycle, for instance, and the difference between 'problem-solving' in mathematics and literature; see Barrow, 1987). Of course, anything can be *described* as a core skill, just as anything may be *stipulated* as a competence; whether it makes educational or logical sense to do so is quite another matter. As was noted in the analysis by Ashworth and Saxton (1990), competence statements sometimes strive to be so macroscopic and universally applicable that they are 'in grave danger of being empty and uninformative' (p. 19).

In spite of the current popularity of the idea of core or generic skills and abilities, there is a respectable and long-established philosophical tradition which fiercely opposes the notion of general powers of the mind. Ryle's (1973) famous account of 'intelligent performance' (discussed in more detail in Chapter 5), for instance, is context-specific and insistent that there are vast differences between learning how to be 'inventive, prudent, acute, logical, witty, observant, critical, experimental . . . etc.' (pp. 32ff.). On this account, 'competence' would only be one in a long list of discrete mental and physical qualities that educators and trainers may wish to foster and promote.

A common error in this sphere involves making the false move from identifying features common to certain skills and, from this, inferring the existence of a common *skill*. As Dearden (1984) notes in this respect, there may indeed be features common to all skilled performances in virtue of which we call them skilled, but it does not follow that it is the same skill which is present in each case; in the skater, the juggler, the flautist, the chess player and the linguist. (p. 45)

Powell (1968) makes a similar point when he argues that epithets such as 'careful', 'vigilant', 'accurate' and 'thorough' are without meaning until the details of their context and application have been filled in, and 'it follows from this that they will be field-dependent and of low generality'. He goes on to argue that

there is no such animal as 'Careful Man'; there are simply men who do particular things in particular ways and it is always necessary to specify these in some detail before we can understand what is meant by careful surgery or careful driving. (p. 45)

This context-bound character of high-level skills and qualities is also endorsed by Phillips Griffiths (1965), who argues forcefully against the widely held belief (resurrected recently in the attempt to identify the 'outcomes' of higher education; see Otter, 1992) that higher education can be regarded as general preparation for working life. As he notes, although the use of 'imagination, wisdom and intelligence' is required for high-level study, this does not imply or entail any general fostering of such qualities. In 'pursuing history or physics or philosophy . . . one becomes better at history, physics or philosophy', but this does not mean becoming 'a wiser father or trade union leader; or a wiser, more imaginative, more logical and intelligent man' (p. 205).

All these arguments count against the implausible notion of 'meta-competence' which has been identified to allow 'competence to extend beyond the bounds of tested situations' (Fleming, 1991, p. 10). Meta-competence is said to be 'about lining subject-specific knowledge with the particular competences that should be practised by the learner' (p. 11). However, meta-competence is as problematic as the more down-to-earth generic competences and core skills discussed above. As I have argued elsewhere on this subject (Hyland, 1992d), the concept of competence is being asked to bear far more weight than it can possibly carry in the attempt to extend the boundaries ever wider so as to answer criticisms about the NVQ narrowness of occupational focus (alternative concepts and models such as vocational expertise and reflective professionalism are examined in Chapter 7).

The debate surrounding the notion of competence is shrouded in conceptual fuzziness and equivocation, and the introduction of new conceptions such as core and generic competences has not helped matters much in this respect. If there is a sense in which the idea of generic competence may be described as logical nonsense, then meta-competence is a prime candidate for the label (once used by Bentham to criticize the idea of natural rights) of 'nonsense on stilts'!

THE ANATOMY OF A SLOGAN

In spite (and also partly *because*) of the conceptual imprecision and logical and epistemological equivocation surrounding discussions of competence, the term has proved most effective as an educational slogan and has generated a massive influence, following and field of applicability within education and training. As a way of completing the discussion of the concept, it is worth looking at the nature and evolution of this sloganizing status of competence talk in the attempt to explain the influence and power of the concept. The first thing to say is that the conceptual and general theoretical vacillation of competence talk takes nothing away from the potency of competence as an education slogan. As Norris (1991) wryly observes, words like 'competence and standards are good words, modern words; everybody is for standards and everyone is against incompetence' (p. 331). But these words are 'good', not because they have a precise and definite meaning, but because of their very vagueness and ambiguity which is able to suggest something broadly positive and honorific without actually having to say what this is.

Such words are the life-blood of effective educational slogans in which the persuasive and hortative meaning is far more important than any descriptive content. For example, even though we cannot say exactly what 'democracy' or 'family life' mean, it is not easy to gainsay them without encountering considerable resistance. In a similar way, terms such as 'relevance' (Haydon, 1973), 'openness' (Hyland, 1979) and 'skill' (Barrow, 1987) have been used to support and popularize educational programmes of all kinds, and have been largely successful without having to define precisely their key concepts and principles.

In more recent times, terms such as 'quality' and 'standards' have featured most prominently as educational slogans and have been used in debates about policy at all levels of the system. Naturally, everyone endorses high quality and standards, so it is understandable that educators try to get the force of these slogans behind their own particular proposals for practice. Quality is a term which is especially effective in this respect, and, no doubt for just this reason, it has tended to dominate debates about further and higher education. However, although it is now impossible to read a college prospectus or mission statement without coming across at least one reference to quality, there is no general agreement about what precisely is being conveyed by this term in educational discourse (Mortimore and Stone, 1990). In a similar way, the positive connotations of competence and its 'El Dorado' properties make it an ideal candidate for slogan status.

According to Scheffler (1960), slogans claim neither to define terms in educational discourse nor to facilitate such discourse, but act rather as 'rallying symbols' (p. 36) of the key ideas and attitudes of educational movements. This account is certainly an apt one as far as competence is concerned, for it has become a banner under which all manner of educational activity has found a place, from its original base in the industrial-training camp to courses of general education in FE, and even to Masters courses in higher education (Glasgow University, 1992).

Komisar and McClellan (1961) noticed that a feature of most educational slogans was that they appeared to summarize a whole series of assertions which had become associated with the general import of the slogan. Slogans, however, do not embody or logically entail the particulars they summarize in the way that, for example, generalizations do; rather, they become attached to a more or less clearly specified group of proposals, together with various sorts of empirical and anecdotal evidence which purport to justify them. In the case of competence talk this range of associated particulars is now comprehensive and well developed. Typically they would include such claims as:

- 'NVQ statements of competence are derived, not from an analysis of education and training programmes, but from an analysis of employment requirements . . . ' (Jessup, 1990a, p. 22)
- ' . . . an NVQ can be gained through any mode of learning . . . ' (Jessup, 1990a, p. 24)
- 'Assessment is being brought into the real world and de-mystified within the new model of education and training.' (Jessup, 1991, p. 135)
- 'Because of the emphasis placed on outcomes, the logical place to assess competence is at the demonstration of that particular task or skill in the workplace . . . ' (Greenacre, 1990, p. 109)
- 'Assessment processes collect valid and reliable evidence of performance, to be matched against the standard, and learning is designed to achieve competent performance.' (Mansfield, 1990, p. 17)
- 'The new competence-based movement is attempting to go back to fundamentals and look at what is really required for successful performance or the achievement of successful outcomes in any field of learning.' (Jessup, 1991, p. 129)
- 'Within a competence-base [*sic*] model of qualifications there is no justification for assessing knowledge for its own sake but only for its contribution to competent performance.' (Jessup, 1991, p. 123)

By means of such assertions we arrive at a subtle (though not always transparent) linking of the slogan with key ideas concerned with the importance of performance, evidence and outcomes, and, by implication, a favourable recommendation of such notions over other 'traditional' forms of learning and assessment. Furthermore, once these prominent ideas have been connected with other widely endorsed educational principles – modularization, open access, credit accumulation, raising employers' standards and workforce skills, and the like – the upshot is a complete slogan system with potentially wide-ranging influence and applicability.

The examination by Eastwood (1964) of the way 'slogan systems' of this kind typically evolve can help to provide further insights into the current state of competence talk. The evolution of a slogan system embraces three stages (pp. 208ff.):

1. the selection and definition of the key slogan word (e.g. 'quality', 'standards', 'competence');
2. the justification of the system so that it gains currency and recognition;
3. the creation of a wide field of applicability for the slogan term.

It would be useful to examine competence talk within the framework of this analysis.

1. According to Eastwood the choice of a suitable slogan word is guided primarily by the need for a term which channels some pervading contemporary interest and uses it to provide an educational banner for the proposals being advocated. In the case of competence this climate can be located in the rise to prominence of the 'industrial trainers' (see Ball, 1990) and the emergence of a widespread belief in the need to make education more relevant to the world of work. As mentioned in Chapter 1, the NCVQ agenda was to a large extent dictated by these concerns, and it is interesting that, in the drive for a world-class workforce, almost all the key targets are connected with the achievement of NVQs. There is now almost complete equivalence between CBET and the notions of upgrading VET, enhancing workforce skills, providing an industrial and

economically competitive nation and improving generally our systems of education and training at all levels.

2. Once the slogan has been attached to appropriate principles and proposals for practice (such as an emphasis on performance at work or employer-defined criteria), the next step is to offer some sort of justification for the whole enterprise. For many NVQ proponents, of course, no justification for NCVQ principles beyond their role in generally improving vocational qualifications (in ways only vaguely specified) is needed. Perhaps it is for this reason that the mainstream literature on NVQs often seems so uncritical, platitudinous and sometimes downright sycophantic! However, if educational debate is to remain on a rational level, it is perfectly legitimate to ask questions about NVQs of all kinds and at all levels, such as why employer-defined standards are necessarily more preferable to standards defined by other agencies or why the CBET stress on outcomes is an improvement on VET programmes (such as BTEC) which place a corresponding stress on learning and experience.

Eastwood claims that the justification of slogan principles often involves the 'emotive linking' (Eastwood, 1964, p. 214) of the slogan to principles that are already well known and popularly endorsed. This move is what Scheffler (1973) calls a 'relative' (p. 118) kind of justification, that is, the justification of a proposal by showing that it is a member of a sub-class of proposals which are already justified. NVQ supporters are now adept in such matters. By linking key CBET objectives with generally approved aims such as opening up access and creating equal opportunities for people to acquire vocational qualifications, a kind of relative justification of NVQs in terms of 'standard practice' is achieved. And, naturally (as mentioned in the first chapter), the fact that such generally endorsed objectives may be logically and educationally independent of and temporally prior to NCVQ activities is not something that is normally mentioned!

O'Connor (1968) argues that all the questions that may be asked about an education system can be reduced to just two: '(i) what is held to be valuable as an end?; (ii) what means will effectively realize these ends?' (p. 7). A relative justification of the kind discussed above only seeks to answer questions of the second sort, about the most effective means of achieving some desired or approved end. There is, however, a deeper 'general' (Scheffler, 1973, p. 119) level of justification which is concerned with the justification of ultimate ends, and, in educational terms, this demands an engagement with fundamental values and the justification of standard practice itself or the proposed reform of such practice.

Most of the literature on NVQs is concerned with instrumental matters, with taking a means to an end, and there is very little attempt to offer more general justifications of ultimate ends and values. Thus, although the NCVQ 'revolution' has indeed been fundamental in its impact on VET courses, colleges and students, the reforms tend to be justified mainly in terms of trends and developments (e.g., access, employer-defined standards) which were already approved and under way. There is, consequently, no really substantial theoretical or intellectual underpinning of the 'revolutionary' practical proposals for reform. Justificatory arguments at the relative means–end level have apparently proved themselves to be more than adequate.

However, as I will note in later chapters, it would be wrong to imply that there are no discussions of values and fundamental educational issues in the NVQ literature. The debates on knowledge and competence, and on the relative weight to be given to validity and reliability in assessment are both fundamental and intellectually sophistic-ated. Moreover, the attempt to shift the emphasis away from process to outcomes, from learning to assessment, from knowledge to performance, and from education to industry represents, without doubt, a shift in emphasis as radical as the recent changes accompanying the Education Reform Act 1988. In addition, there are clear connec-tions between the NCVQ project and the economic individualism and 'market forces' model of planning and provision which dominates current policy and legislation on education and training. It is just that such change is so rarely justified by a discussion of fundamental values concerning the ultimate ends and purposes of educational activity and that, in spite of the origins, nothing as coherent and systematic as the social efficiency philosophy of Snedden and Prosser is to be found in the NCVQ literature.

3. Once the proposals summarized by a slogan have been justified, the next stage requires supporters to establish a wide field of applicability for their term. The establishment of such comprehensiveness involves the presentation of the slogan in a series of sub-contexts coupled with a demonstration of its applicability to each, or, in some cases, a reformulation of certain ideas in order to achieve this necessary relevance. There can be little doubt that this condition has been fully satisfied in the case of competence talk.

Competence has achieved an unprecedented degree of popularity and has found its way into every conceivable sphere of educational activity, from school to university, from lower-level craft skills to postgraduate professional courses, and from hair-dressing and catering to teacher education and higher management. Moreover, if the context demands something new – such as a broader-based vocationalism or alternatives to standard competence assessments, as was the case with GNVQs – then competence talk is easily versatile enough to deal with the 'reformulation' of principles necessary in these situations. In a similar way, competence can be applied to abstract conceptions such as 'autonomy' (Jessup, 1991) or 'morality' (Wright, 1989), just as much as it can to greeting visitors at a reception desk or operating a photocopying machine.

Like quality and standards, competence is now *de rigueur* for all mission statements, course outlines and textbooks – irrespective of content, level or subject matter – if the programmes are to stand any chance of gaining approval and (more important these days) financial support. A complete competence slogan system is now fully operational in British educational theory and practice.

CONCLUSION

The development of a fully operational and widely influential competence slogan system by the NCVQ in only seven or eight years is without doubt a considerable achievement. However, the main themes and critical perspectives which inform this study suggest that the NVQ 'revolution' cannot be considered to be much of an achievement in any other sense of the term. The analysis of the nature and scope of the concept of competence has served to indicate some of the basic flaws and inconsisten-cies in the NCVQ model.

Although it is possible to distinguish between broadly based holistic versions and narrower specific conceptions of competence in the literature, there is widespread confusion and equivocation over the precise meaning and definition of the very term which, presumably, is intended to play a central and pivotal role in CBET strategy. The systematic ambiguity about competence is caused partly by a failure to take note of the distinction between the capacity/dispositional senses of competence and partly by the need to extend and 'recontextualize' the NVQ assessment procedures so as to accommodate desired changes and answer criticisms of excessive specificity and narrowness of focus.

Disagreement about definitions and differing views about the role of performance as against knowledge in the literature neither inspires confidence nor lends much support to claims about the validity, accuracy and precision of the NCVQ assessment system. Moreover, the 'recontextualizing' of competence by means of range statements and talk of generic competences merely compounds the confusion surrounding the concept and presents further problems of definition and interpretation. Although there may be some legitimacy to the notion of core skills in such areas as literacy and numeracy, there is very little evidence, of either a philosophical or an empirical kind, to support the idea of generic competences, and, on this account, the notion of 'meta-competence' can only be a metaphysical illusion.

Competence and competence talk may have powerful persuasive power at the slogan level, but it is conceptually imprecise, logically equivocal and systematically ambiguous.

Chapter 3

The Assessment of Competence

Broadfoot (1979) has claimed that to arrive at a full understanding of the philosophical, political and theoretical nature of any system of education we need to look closely at its methods of assessment. To be sure, the specifically *political* nature of public systems of education needs to figure prominently in any analysis of education systems. The links between education and state formation, as Green (1990) has demonstrated so comprehensively, are crucially formative influences on the development of particular models of schooling, and the differential development of national systems in England, France, Prussia and America in the nineteenth century provides a graphic illustration of this. Notwithstanding the variation between national systems, Green felt justified in making the general observation that

> The major impetus for the creation of national education systems lay in the need to provide the state with trained administrators, engineers and military personnel; to spread dominant cultures and inculcate popular ideologies; and so to forge the political and cultural unity of burgeoning nation states and cement the ideological hegemony of their dominant classes. (p. 309)

Green's comment serves to highlight the key role played by vocational education, in the broad sense of preparing people for particular roles and functions in society, and, in this respect, the forms and methods of assessment employed have a vital part to play in determining the ends and purposes of the enterprise.

The need to control the certification of professionals in Britain as the nation moved from an essentially static agrarian state to a dynamic and more fluid industrial nation as a result of the Industrial Revolution functioned, as Broadfoot explains, as the prime motive and originator of the first national examinations and assessment systems in this country. In 1815 the first professional qualifying examinations were instituted by the Society of Apothecaries to ensure that doctors were adequately trained, and this was followed by examinations for solicitors in 1835 and for accountants in 1880. In explaining these developments, Broadfoot quotes the Beloe Report, which noted that 'the lazy doctrine that men are much of a muchness gave way to a higher respect for merit and for more effectual standards of competence' (1979, p. 30).

Along with the elements of control and competition, the certification of competence – at least 'demonstrated competence' (p. 42) – is viewed by Broadfoot as a key component in the development of the meritocratic ethos which has played such a central role in the development of schooling and assessment systems both in Britain and in Western culture generally. Certainly the concepts of control and competition help to explain the evolution of examinations in Britain up to the time of the 1944 Education Act in which selection, competition and the notion of achieving social status on the basis of merit came to full maturity and prominence. Over the last few decades the 1944 social settlement has been altered radically as a result of a whole range of shifts in social, economic and political conceptions, though, in terms of the implications of these changes for educational policy and practice, the role of assessment is again crucial and paramount.

Reference was made in the first chapter to swings in political opinion and ideology which influenced the vocational turn in education in the 1970s and 1980s. There are various ways of characterizing recent changes, and Williams' (1961) description of three dominant ideological groups – the liberals (or old humanists), the industrial trainers, and the public educators – still provides a useful tool for understanding contemporary educational change.

In brief, the industrial trainers were concerned with 'education in terms of future adult work' and stressed habits of 'regularity, self-discipline, obedience and trained effort', whereas the old humanists argued that 'man's spiritual health depended on a kind of education that was more than training for some specialised work'. Against both these conceptions of the role of education, the public educators gradually gained the initiative in the middle of this century with a view which held that 'man had a natural right to be educated, and that any good society depended on governments accepting this principle as their duty'. The notion of natural rights, however, did not prescribe any content or rationale for education, and, as Williams notes, the public educators in fact drew heavily 'on the arguments of the defenders of the old liberal education as a way of preventing universal education being narrowed to a system of pre-industrial instruction' (pp. 161–3).

The views of the public educators may have held sway until relatively recent times but, as Ball (1990) convincingly argues, this is no longer the case. In the 1980s 'the public educators are in disarray' and the 'field of education policy making is overshadowed by the influence of the old humanists and industrial trainers' (p. 5). The industrial-training influence can be seen clearly in the activities and aims of the MSC, the Training Agency and their associated lobby described in Chapter 1, and this provided the ideological backdrop for the establishment of the NCVQ. However, politics, and perhaps especially the politics of education, is never quite so simple, and Ball's reference to the continuing influence of the old humanists in New Right politics (represented in Ball's view by shifting alliances in the FEU/DES camp) alongside the newly acquired power of the industrial trainers (with a power base in the Department of Trade and Industry) illustrates the dangers of over-simplification in this area.

The impact of New Right policies on recent educational trends is, in fact, neither coherent nor uniformly systematic. Whitty (1990), for instance, has outlined the tensions and conflicts between the 'neo-conservatives' (those who, like the Hillgate group, as opposed to all aspects of progressivism and stress 'traditional' methods and content) and the 'neo-liberals' who favour opening up the whole education system to the influence of market forces (through open enrolment, opting out, league tables of schools, and so on). To complicate matters even further, both of these groups would claim to support increasing parental power and local democratic control of education, whereas, in *fact*, the thrust of all reforms stemming from the Education Reform Act 1988 (ERA) has been towards a steady reinforcement of centralized control over all aspects of the system (Simon, 1992; Maclure, 1989). Furthermore, there is ample evidence to suggest that this centralized power is increasingly harnessed to a 'management' perspective on education which, according to Hartnett and Naish (1986), accords primacy to the 'requirements of industry and commerce' (p. 185) and regards schooling as essentially a preparation for work and a means of providing a service for industry and commerce (for a broadly similar perspective, see also Halliday, 1990).

Echoing such views, Wadd (1988) interprets the move towards a National Curriculum in 1987/88 as being motivated by a desire to raise standards in order to meet the competitive challenge of rival industrial nations. Although this would be broadly accurate in reflecting the emerging vocationalizing tendencies in the 1980s, the subtle and painstaking analysis of the political underpinnings of ERA by Lawton (1989) reveals a whole host of factors at work during this period. The National Curriculum and its assessment procedures can be interpreted as an attempt by the Secretary of State to handle a state of affairs in which a number of contending ideologies were making rival and contradictory demands from the system. The upshot was a fairly confused, backward-looking and incoherent set of provisions, with the 'privatizers' (those opposed to state intervention in education) or the neo-liberals (using Whitty's terminology) and the 'minimalists' (those favouring concentration on the basics) both finding something to please them in ERA (Lawton, 1989, pp. 48–52). Furthermore, the assessment mechanisms and procedures linked with the National Curriculum can be taken as characteristic of an examination structure which for years has tended to 'exaggerate the vocational function of schooling' (p. 81).

In the years since ERA the influence of the minimalists and privatizers has been consolidated through a range of measures which have led to an emphasis on selection rather than a broad entitlement for all pupils, a narrowing of the curriculum and an instrumentalist assessment framework concerned more with control and accountability than with educational standards (Lawton, 1993). If we add to this the Further & Higher Education Act 1992, which increased centralized control over the system (Bogdanor, 1991; Hyland, 1992a), and recent legislation designed to encourage schools to opt out of local authority control, then the centralizing tendencies noted by Maclure, Simon and other commentators can be seen to reach their fruition (ironically, at a time when most other European nations are moving in opposite directions!; see Corbett, 1993).

Since the review of vocational qualifications which led to the establishment of the NCVQ in 1986 grew out of the vocationalizing and industrial training culture of the period, its subsequent development could not but be influenced by the ideological and political factors outlined above. Of course, since the remit of the new vocational body was precisely to harmonize and enhance *vocational* qualifications in particular, it would appear odd, if not bizarre, not to connect this move with the general vocationalizing of the system. After all, vocationalism is what NVQs are all about! However, the particular model of CBET which developed out of the currents of change in the 1980s was heavily influenced by the dominant trends of the period, and for this reason an 'industrial' rather than an 'educational' (Greenacre, 1990, p. 95) model of VET qualifications eventually emerged (though this itself has been modified over the years and, with the introduction of GNVQs, substantially altered).

THE NATURE AND STRUCTURE OF NVQ ASSESSMENT

The broad outlines of the NVQ framework – concerned with functional analysis, performance criteria, range statements and units and levels of competence – were sketched out in the first chapter. Against this background the NCVQ definition of assessment is couched in terms of

> the process of collecting evidence and making judgements on whether performance criteria have been met. For the award of an NVQ a candidate must have demonstrated that he or she can meet the performance criteria for each element of competence specified. (Jessup, 1991, p. 48)

Moreover, performance has to be 'demonstrated and assessed under conditions as close as possible to those under which it would normally be practised'. This entails 'demonstrations in context' in the workplace, or, at least, 'simulations which replicate the important contextual features' (p. 49). This latter area of simulations has been important in relation to the increase in FE provision of NVQs, where, in the context of work experience placements becoming more difficult to find, assessment increasingly takes place in model offices, college restaurants and college hairdressing salons.

There is, it needs to be said, some equivocation about this notion of 'work-based' learning. Boffy (1990), for instance, talks about work-based learning in FE in terms of 'workshop approaches where students have access to a range of learning resources' and 'integration between the various locations in which learning linked to the work role may occur' (p. 192). The reality is that, except for part-time students in employment, it is becoming increasingly difficult for colleges, often in competition with youth training schemes and schools vocational projects, to find work placements with employers willing to co-operate. In Raggatt's (1994) recent survey of NVQ provision in the FE sector, the problems of finding suitable work places and lack of employer interest were cited by lecturers as two of the most serious long-term difficulties. These will inevitably increase with the expansion of GNVQs, and indeed this much is now tacitly acknowledged in the NCVQ literature. It is work-*related* rather than work-based learning that is given prominence in GNVQ prescriptions, with statements of attainment 'presented in a form which encourages the use of projects, assignments and other forms of simulation' (NCVQ, 1991b, p. 22). This makes such programmes very like existing BTEC ones, and marks a radical departure from original NVQ principles (this will be discussed in greater depth in Chapter 8).

In the context of this work-based, work-related or workshop learning, the role of assessment is of paramount importance since NVQs are, after all, concerned with the *assessment* of competence, not with learning (this basic fact is often overlooked, as I emphasize in the next chapter). Jessup was quite right in admitting that the 'credibility of assessment at work still needs to be established' (1991, p. 53). The evaluation of the NVQ Caterbase scheme noted a wide variation in assessment practices. Although some supervisors were 'extremely conscientious', assessment practices ranged 'from a very regular event between trainee and supervisor to the rather more common "as and when" there was time to do it'. Furthermore, there was 'considerable variation in the degree of involvement from the supervisor', and the 'process of assessment was not without criticism from some users' (MSC, 1988, pp. 8–9).

Similar difficulties were noted in the evaluation of NVQs in the construction industry by Callender (1992), who reported 'considerable resistance' from 'providers, employers and supervisors' to the idea of workplace assessment by charge hands or overseers (p. 23). The lecturers interviewed in our own research in Warwickshire expressed a number of misgivings about the NVQ system of assessment. We asked FE lecturers in twelve Coventry and Warwickshire colleges questions about NVQ implementation in three vocational sectors: business studies, catering and hairdressing (response rates were 58 per cent, 51 per cent and 75 per cent respectively). Comments on the implementation of NVQs in the three spheres were organized in terms of what the lecturers themselves perceived to be the main advantages and disadvantages of NVQs.

Business Studies

Advantages	*Disadvantages*
Full coverage of all relevant outcomes	Evidence logging was far too time consuming
Chance for students to work at their own pace	Marking/assessment load too heavy
Standards relevant to industry	Lack of emphasis on underpinning knowledge and understanding
More practical experience for students	Too narrow – does not develop students' wider perspective of the business world
Helps lower ability students to achieve some competences	Can do/cannot do assessment
	Too undiscriminating

Hairdressing

Greater practical emphasis	Lowering of standards
Less time pressure on students	Too much paperwork
Students able to work at their own pace	Excessive administration for staff
No student failures	Lack of merit/distinction grading scheme
Flexibility of roll on/roll off approach	

Catering

Relevance to industry	Too much paperwork
High degree of validity	Too great a gap between levels 2 and 3
Practical assessments	Narrowness of focus
Greater access and flexibility	Too skill-specific

(Hyland and Weller, 1994, p. 29)

Even acknowledging the positive perceptions of lecturers in terms of the flexibility and practical relevance of NVQs, the criticisms of the assessment system in terms of its undiscriminating nature and narrowness of focus appeared with worrying regularity in all three vocational areas. The excessive skill specificity and lack of theoretical/ knowledge base, in particular, echoed the findings of the MSC evaluation of NVQs in catering (MSC, 1988) and also the studies by Haffenden and Brown (1989), Raggatt (1991, 1994) and Smithers (1993).

The cumbersome and costly nature of NVQ assessment was also a prominent criticism which cropped up in all the studies. In the 1993 Employment Department evaluation of NVQ implementation the assessment system was picked out as a particularly problematic area. In addition to 'uncertainty on how to foster and assess the knowledge and understanding necessary for successful work performance', there were 'assessment difficulties including the cost, the amount of paperwork involved, practical difficulties of assessment in the workplace and concerns about the *reliability* of assessments' (ED, 1993a, p. 35, my italics).

This last observation is particularly worrying, since it is legitimate to ask how an assessment system which is unreliable and dogged by so many practical problems can possibly produce the precision, accuracy and 'new kind of standards' (Jessup, 1991, p. 14) claimed by NVQ proponents. Moreover, it is worth stressing that the critical comments and views of lecturers about NVQ assessment mentioned above are an expression of those who are the *assessors* in the system! Since the whole enterprise depends to a large extent on the activities of supervisors and college lecturers who are asked to make assessments of competence, such criticism must raise further doubts about the reliability of the whole system (especially when funding is linked to the award of NVQs!; see Smithers, 1993, p. 21).

RELIABILITY, VALIDITY AND CRITERIA

The NVQ model of assessment is said to be one in which 'assessment is related directly to the elements of competence and sufficiency of evidence is the key concept' (Jessup, 1990b, p. 32). Evidence is indeed the key NCVQ concept; as Mansfield (1990) observes, the 'assessment process can be described as the generation, collection and *interpretation* of evidence which is then compared to the standard and used to make a judgement which *infers* competent performance with respect to the standard' (p. 17, my italics).

An examination of the notions of interpretation and inference used by Mansfield brings out the fact that, in the last analysis, the 'evidence' in question is neither objectively given and obvious (as in the evidence of our senses), nor is it absolute and incorrigible. Such evidence is nothing more nor less than the *judgements* of assessors working within the system, and this is worth underlining in view of the reliance on this concept of evidence as a kind of gloss which justifies all aspects of the NVQ system

In dealing with judgements of assessors, questions of objectivity, possible bias, reliability, and so on, naturally arise. However, I would not wish to imply that the NVQ framework is especially culpable in this respect, since the potential problems of prejudicial judgements and possible subjectivity have been recognized (Jessup, 1991; ED, 1993a) and remedies are currently being applied in the form of assessor training, external verification and the research and development work of the Employment Department's Methods Strategy Unit (Martin, 1992). Black's admission that 'there is no formula for gathering evidence which will make an assessor absolutely certain about competence' (1992, p. 3) certainly needs to be noted in the light of the excessive claims made about 'evidence' in the CBET literature, but, on the other hand, such a caveat could equally well be applied to *any* system of educational assessment and measurement.

What is particularly worrying about the NCVQ position on assessment, however, is the cavalier way in which issues of reliability are dealt with. Much is made in the literature of the inadequacy and unfairness of 'norm-referencing' in standard examinations and assessments, in which student performances are compared with each other and graded, as against the 'criterion-referencing' of NVQs, in which the performance of students is measured against the 'standards required in employment' (Jessup, 1990b, p. 20). Now, although it seems to be perfectly sensible for VET qualifications to be linked in some way to occupational standards, it is quite another thing for these standards, defined by employers and industry lead bodies, to be the sole determinants of the criteria by which student or trainee performance are to be judged.

I will be arguing in later chapters that commentators tend to make too much of the alleged difference between assessments made in educational and those made in industrial settings. Greenacre (1990), for instance, claims that whereas 'competence in educational terms has meant the ability to perform to a given standard test . . . In industrial terms, competence quite simply means the ability to perform a task, or range of tasks, to the standards demanded by the employer' (p. 95). This dichotomy is rather too tidy and simplistic. Not all measures of industrial competence are defined exclusively by employers. The tests of competency in the coal industry, for example, were traditionally based on the view of a wide range of experts in the field (Berkovitch, 1977), and the very first national tests of competence introduced for apothecaries and accountants at the beginning of the nineteenth century was largely designed by professional bodies assuming the role played by medieval guilds in relation to craft apprenticeship (Broadfoot, 1979). Moreover, in terms of general VET as reflected in the programmes devised by BTEC, City & Guilds and the Royal Society of Arts (RSA), it is fair to say that standards are jointly set by representatives of education and industry (greater democracy in this area with the reconstitution of the NCVQ so as to 'better reflect the views of employers, employees, educators and the general public', was one of the key recommendations of Smithers, 1993, p. 42).

In addition, the recommendation of CBET in terms of its basis in criterion-referencing as opposed to the norm-referencing of traditional assessments is a little disingenuous. In the first place, criterion-referenced assessment covers a vast territory which stretches well beyond the NCVQ framework. Criterion-referencing does, in fact, take place routinely in a wide variety of educational contexts in which formative assessments by teachers or students are considered to be important aspects of the total learning programme. The General Certificate of Secondary Education (GCSE) exams introduced in the 1980s are both criterion-referenced, in the sense that student performances are measured against graded criteria relating to specified standards and measures of subject matter, and also include formative (or diagnostic) assessment, which allows students to consolidate progress over a given period rather than being examined on the 'sudden-death' basis of traditional exams. Indeed, it is for this reason that supporters of GCSE assessment have sought to defend its basic principles in the face of attempts to reduce the course-work elements and return to the old norm-referencing of traditional modes of examination (Scott, 1989; Hyland, 1992f).

Although criterion-referencing, as Rowntree (1977) notes, does fit well with formative assessment, its origins are in fact behaviourist, since it 'became popular along with the programmed learning movement' in which a 'criterion test' was related to sets of prespecified learning objectives (p. 180). This is the sense in which the NCVQ version of criterion-referencing should be understood. It is concerned not with formative development or diagnosis, but with the summative evaluation of predetermined outcomes. Consequently, there is a world of difference between the criterion-referencing of, for instance, GCSE, which takes account of a range of cognitive abilities, skills and values, and the criteria of NVQs, which are largely concerned with *performance* criteria which assess demonstrated competence in employment and occupational contexts.

In addition, as Rowntree suggests, 'norm-referencing and criterion-referencing have more in common than is usually recognized' (p. 185), and in practice the rigid dichotomy tends to break down. This can be illustrated by a consideration of the process by which standards or criteria are initially established. If they are to be operational standards or criteria (whether the area of measurement is intelligence, specific subject matter, skills or competence), then, logically, they must have been *standardized* by testing them out on students or trainees. The criteria thus established are based on the *norms* derived from those initial trials, and the only difference between criterion-referencing and standard norm-referencing comes down to the fact that the former uses comparisons based on norms established by *other* candidates elsewhere, whereas the latter compares students *directly* with their immediate peers and fellow students. On this account, the standards and performance criteria of NVQs are nothing more nor less than the *norms* of occupational standards which are defined, established and maintained by the relevant industrial lead bodies!

These issues surrounding the precise nature of CBET assessment are of crucial importance, since it seems clear that, in the excessive concentration on performance criteria linked to predetermined employer-defined standards, the NCVQ model has sacrificed *reliability* of assessment in the drive for *validity*. Broadly speaking, a test or assessment instrument is valid if it 'measures what it is supposed to measure' and reliable if it 'consistently measures whatever it measures' (Gay, 1987, pp. 128, 135). Validity is, without doubt, the linchpin of NVQ assessment procedures and is pursued with almost religious zeal. Jessup (1991), for example, is adamant that the 'sole objective of assessment within the NVQ model, within cost and resource limits, should be to maximise its validity'. He goes on to propose that 'we should just forget reliability altogether and concentrate on validity, which is ultimately all that matters' (pp. 191–2). This is a quite staggering claim, and warrants closer examination.

There are several different types of validity, and it is important to identify precisely the sort of validity being claimed for NVQs. 'Content' validity refers to the extent to which a test 'measures an intended content area' (e.g., in science, history or biology), and 'construct validity is the degree to which a test measures an intended hypothetical construct' (Gay, 1987, pp. 129, 131) such as intelligence or creativity. In addition, there is 'concurrent' validity, by which performance on a test is related to performance on another test 'or to some other valid criterion administered at the same time', and, of particular significance in the area of VET, 'predictive' validity, which indicates the 'degree to which a test can predict how well an individual will do in a future situation' (p. 132).

Against this account we may ask what particular kind of validity is being claimed for NVQs and how justified the claims are. Tuxworth is quite clear on this matter and states that

> There is a lack of research evidence that CBET is superior to other forms of education/ training in output terms. *Face* validity is acknowledged to be high and it is easy to show *content* validity. What is more problematic is *predictive* validity . . . (1989, p. 17, my italics)

What is referred to by Tuxworth as 'face validity' is, I would argue, hardly of the first importance in this context, since it relates only to the 'degree to which a test appears to measure what it purports to measure' and thus is 'not a psychometrically sound way of estimating validity' (Gay, 1987, p. 130). Claims about the validity of NVQs, I take it, ultimately rest not on what they *appear* to measure, but on what they *do* measure.

Attempts to determine what NVQs do in fact measure are not quite so simple as it might at first glance be assumed, and for this reason Tuxworth's reference to 'content' is a little puzzling. Do NVQs have any content? They certainly contain lots and lots of units and elements of competence along with performance criteria and range statements, but it seems odd to call this their content (indeed, Smithers criticizes NVQs for just this lack of content, 1993, p. 9). Surely content is more accurately applied to courses or learning programmes, and, as the NCVQ literature insists, NVQs are completely independent of these. It seems far more appropriate, particularly in the light of the analysis of the concept in the last chapter, to characterize NVQ assessments in terms of 'construct' validity.

Wolf (1989) helps to throw some light on matters here in her assertion that '*competence is a construct*, and not something that we can observe directly' (p. 40, author's italics). Of course, this 'hypothetical' feature is not specific to competence but would be shared by other general conceptions like capability, imagination, knowledge and understanding. However, in the case of measuring competence in terms of operational definitions and constructs, we should bear in mind the vast range of definitions and quite considerable logical and conceptual confusion described in Chapter 2. What this means is that, when validity of competence assessment is claimed, this claim needs to be qualified by referring it to the particular theoretical construction operating in the relevant occupational sector. Thus, since a wide range of theoretical constructions operating in different occupational sectors seems to be in evidence, any claims to validity can only be domain- or sector-specific, and this would appear to weaken substantially the case for any *general validity* of NVQs. It is just a short step from this to the raising of serious questions and doubts about the legitimacy of the 'national' component of NVQ standards and titles.

Furthermore, the problematic status of CBET in terms of predictive validity must also be a cause for concern in relation to NVQs. It is true that predictive validity can be regarded as a general problem for measures of educational attainment or capability, and even though so-called 'traditional' examinations such as A levels and externally set professional examinations do score quite highly in terms of predictive validity, it needs to be remembered that any such 'predictions' are often logically linked to the examinations as a form of entry into higher and professional levels (Broadfoot, 1984).

Yet in the case of NVQs, which are said to be based on the standards defined by employers, predictive validity might be assumed to be crucial. If candidates deemed to be competent turn out not to be quite so competent once they are in employment, there can be no basis for NVQ claims about validity. In this respect, the studies already referred to which indicate a lowering of standards, narrowing of occupational focus and de-skilling in certain sectors must be a cause of the gravest concern.

Moreover, the official NCVQ line of concentrating on validity rather then reliability is at odds with all that is recommended in terms of good practice in the social and educational research community. Mouly (1970), for instance, argues that a 'measuring instrument must be *reliable*, i.e., it must be consistent in the measurement of whatever it measures' (p. 115, author's italics), and Borg (1981) suggests that 'reliability is an extremely important characteristic of educational measures' (p. 97). Gay takes an even stronger line on this issue with the assertion that 'an unreliable test is essentially useless' (1987, p. 135), and Burroughs (1971) wishes to recommend that 'some index of reliability ought to appear on the label sewn into every data-gathering device ever produced' (p. 68). In the face of this testimony the NCVQ position would seem to be at best short-sighted and at worst dangerously untenable.

The fact is that validity and reliability are both necessary and complementary aspects of any form of assessment. It does not make sense to opt for one as against the other, since both are required if the measurement of knowledge, skill or competence is to mean anything. Prais (1991) expresses the position clearly and succinctly in his observation (with the NCVQ model specifically in mind) that

> any argument that bases itself on the notion that Validity (i.e. lack of bias) is all that matters is essentially wrong. We need to be concerned with the total expected error associated with a qualification-procedure (i.e. Validity plus Reliability); we are likely to be misled if we focus on only one component. (p. 87)

Prais takes his criticism of the NCVQ model even further by suggesting that written tests of vocational capability are not only more reliable than 'practical' ones, but also cheaper and easier to administer and ultimately fairer on candidates and trainees (pp. 87–8). With this in mind, Smithers (1993) suggests that the 'assessment of both NVQs and GNVQs should include both written examinations as well as assessments of practical skills, independently set with marks externally verified' (p. 43). All this serves to undermine substantially the NCVQ model of assessment in the very areas in which its main strengths are purported to lie, and should cause all those concerned with VET provision to look again at the claims made for CBET.

CHANGES AND DEVELOPMENTS IN NCVQ ASSESSMENT

In response to some of the criticisms and identified areas of weakness mentioned above, the NVQ assessment procedures have been altered and modified in a number of respects over the last few years. The earliest developments were concerned with the patent inadequacy of the existing framework to deal with the complexity of skills and knowledge required for work roles beyond the basic levels of competence. In this respect the fact that the vast majority of NVQs thus far awarded are at levels 1 and 2 becomes both understandable and explanatory of the more recent trends.

It should be remembered that NVQs were originally designed to be used only in the context of work-based VET, and perhaps for this reason the initial systems were rather unsophisticated in terms of their appreciation and conception of the precise nature of performance-based assessment and its links with related and cognate variables such as skills, understanding and knowledge. The relative naivety of the early approach is well brought out in Jessup's (1991) comment that arguments for the assessment of competence were initially based on the assumption that 'if a person performs competently we need not be concerned with what he or she knows' (p. 121). It was soon discovered however, that this theoretical position was untenable when the assessment concerned anything beyond the most basic routine tasks.

The shortcomings were noticed first in connection with questions of predictive validity (which, as mentioned earlier, cannot easily be separated from reliability issues). If a person was deemed competent on the basis of a number of observed performances, this could be far too context-specific and may not provide 'an indication that a person will continue to be competent or will become more competent' (UDACE, 1989a, p. 6). To deal with this difficulty the idea of 'range statements' – which 'describe the limits within which performance to the identified standards is expected if the individual is to be deemed competent' (Fletcher, 1991, p. 52) – was introduced, and now constitutes a standard component of the NVQ system.

In addition, it was acknowledged that performance-based assessment could not by itself cope with the range and variety of variables which emerged as the framework was developed at the higher levels of 3, 4 and 5, and that, particularly in relation to professional and management education, some serious modifications and changes would be required. As Debling and Hallmark (1990) explain, although NVQ standards are 'unashamedly about ability to perform effectively', this 'does not deny a recognition that sustained effective performance, in different contexts, may well depend on the individual owning *relevant* knowledge and understanding' (p. 10, authors' italics). Relevant knowledge and understanding is elaborated as that which is 'directly related to expected performance' (p. 10). Similarly, Mansfield (1990) speaks of the 'gap' between the evidence collected in the working environment and 'evidence which is needed to make a safe inference of competence'. The suggestion is that this gap can now be filled by 'knowledge evidence' – generated by the testing of 'knowledge and understanding which increases the inference of competence' (p. 17).

Wolf (1989, 1990) has examined the role of underpinning knowledge and understanding in CBET in some detail, and in response to evolving requirements and developments has constructed a two-tier system for the assessment of competence. Commenting on the development of range statements as a way of 're-contextualising competency statements', Wolf suggests a pragmatic approach to knowledge and understanding on the grounds that the 'more evidence we have which comes from direct measures of competence . . . the less we need other indirect measures, which look only at the knowledge and understanding elements' (1990, p. 35). This leads to recommendations of a recontextualized assessment scheme in which 'first order measures' which look at performance are supplemented by 'second order measures' which examine the knowledge and understanding said to underpin performance (p. 34).

This new recontextualized conception of competence – with its different measures in the form of direct observation, skills and proficiency tests and oral/written evaluation of underpinning knowledge – is rather involved and complex. If we add to this Wolf's speculations about whether to base range statements on ideas drawn from 'heuristics' or 'algorithms' (p. 36), we arrive at a rich and varied picture of the field which might be described as a sort of 'metaphysics' (Hyland, 1992d) of competence assessment. So much for Jessup's claim that 'assessment is demystified in the NVQ model' (1991, p. 59). Nothing could be further from the truth! As the framework of NVQs expands in vertical and horizontal directions, the sense of labyrinthine complexity – units and elements of competence, range statements, performance criteria, underpinning knowledge requirements, APL procedures, and the like – grows exponentially. The discourse on 'standards' illustrated in the various Employment Department Methods Strategy Unit publications – and especially the technical matters discussed in the in-house journal *Competence & Assessment* – is now entirely esoteric, and it is not surprising that employers and lecturers find all this growing NVQ bureaucracy difficult to understand (Smithers, 1993; Nash, 1993d). Certainly, the lecturers interviewed in the Warwick University study were unanimous in their views about the cumbersome assessment procedures of NVQs, and Raggatt (1994) also reported that negative views about assessment seemed to be based on the 'appearance of the NVQ units and lengthy lists of performance criteria' (p. 6; Prais also offers similar criticisms in relation to the complexity of the system, 1991, pp. 88–9).

I would suggest that the development and seemingly unbridled growth and complexity of assessment procedures owes more than a little to the behaviourist origins of the NVQ procedures and its attachment to functional analysis. The check-lists of units and elements of competence bear an uncanny resemblance to those used in programmes based on behavioural objectives, and the hierarchy of NVQ levels is not unlike aspects of Bloom's taxonomy of educational objectives (1956; more will be said about these links in Chapters 4 and 5). Reference was made earlier to two broad models of CBET: 'occupational analysis', which involves 'consultations with role holders and their supervisors to establish provisional lists of competence elements', and a more 'generic' approach concerned with 'identifying the characteristics of superior performers in the occupational role' (Tuxworth, 1989, p. 18). It is clear that the former individualistic strategy is what informs the NCVQ procedures, and it is important to note that this is neither the only nor the most effective model of CBET on offer.

Mansfield (1989) suggests that the 'VET world uses at least six models of competence' (p. 27), and provides a classification of these in terms of whether they are based on 'inputs' or 'outputs'. It would be useful to outline these briefly as a background to the criticisms of NVQ assessment already noted. Mansfield describes the models as follows (p. 38):

Input Models

SED/TA Action plan (National Certificate) 1984, which picks out the key areas of knowledge and its use, skills and behaviours (attitudes)

FEU 1984 based on the 'possession and development of sufficient skills, knowledge and appropriate attitudes and experience for successful performance in the roles'

YTS (MSC) 1985 which emphasises competence in a range of occupational skills, competence in a range of transferable core skills, the ability to transfer skills and knowledge to new situations, and personal effectiveness

NCVQ 1986 which establishes that a statement of competence should incorporate specified standards in the ability to perform a range of work-related activities, and the skills, knowledge and understanding which underpin such performance in employment

Output Models

TSO (MSC) 1983 which highlights competencies which meet or contribute to the key purpose of the occupation and the organization, competencies which contribute to creativity and improvement of systems, and competencies which contribute to the maintenance of the overall efficiency of the organisation

Mansfield & Mathews 1985 which is based on four interrelated components: task skills, contingency management skills, task management skills and role/job environment skills.

It is interesting to note here that, in addition to the existence of alternative, more broadly based versions of CBET than the NCVQ model, Mansfield chooses to characterize the mainstream model as one which is 'input based, even if stated in output terms' (1989, p. 38). Mansfield explains that, although all the CBET models share the view that competence is essentially about performance, the input models stress the content of performance (skills or tasks) whereas the outcome models are concerned with roles or elements of roles. On this account, the different models would generate different formulations of competence performance; for example, applied to the routine activity of photocopying, the input model might result in a statement such as 'operate a photocopier', whereas an outcome approach would describe the same event as 'reproduce copies of documents' (p. 28).

Mansfield's own 'job competence model' is thus quite different from the standard NCVQ approach that is implicitly criticized for its 'narrow task approach' (p. 32), which was originally developed for YTS foundation or entry-level occupations (NCVQ Levels 1 and 2). Due acknowledgement is given by Mansfield to NCVQ developments which herald a movement towards his own preferred model and towards an increased emphasis on underpinning knowledge, though, as some of the critical studies referred to earlier indicate, the narrowness of focus and mechanistic conceptualization is still very much a feature of NVQ implementation.

The case argued throughout this book is that, apart perhaps from the basic routine tasks identified by Mansfield at the first two NVQ levels, *no* CBET system can provide an adequate foundation for VET, since its basic rationale of functional analysis and behaviourist theory is fatally flawed. The differing emphases and nuances of the different models are therefore not enough in themselves to support a general justification of CBET, though they do point towards a strategy for improvement. I will note in later chapters that some of the other so-called alternative models of competence-based education (e.g., Hodkinson, 1992; Winter, 1992) only succeed by simply paying lip-service to competence while avoiding the wholesale adoption of CBET strategies (they are therefore not really CBET strategies at all!).

Particularly when taken in conjunction with the fuzziness surrounding the concept of competence discussed in Chapter 2, Mansfield's description of the differing models of CBET, each with its own priorities for assessment, serves to undermine seriously the NCVQ claims about the transparency, precision and objectivity of its assessment system. Moreover, the input/output distinction also provides scope for asking fundamental questions about whether the NCVQ's rhetoric about the value of outcomes really can be justified.

Jessup (1991) makes much of the idea of NVQs being developed in opposition to the traditional models of education and training that are concerned with such things as 'institutional arrangements, curriculum theory, the practice of teaching' (p. 3), and contrasts all of these unfavourably with the allegedly revolutionary new emphasis on outcomes in NVQs. In the light of what was said above about the NCVQ position in relation to inputs and outputs, this alleged new emphasis on outcomes may turn out to be as distinctive as the links with criterion-referencing discussed earlier. There is a sense, after all, in which many of the so-called traditional courses and qualifications can be said to be concerned with 'outcomes'; it is just that such outcomes tend not to be expressed with the specificity of elements of competence or overly concerned with observable performance criteria.

In this respect, the recent FEU (1992b) publication urging the adoption of a national and uniform system of post-16 qualifications is informative and interesting. As part of a project concerned broadly with the advocacy and development of a uniform and coherent national post-16 CATS systems, the FEU seeks to establish a system within which a credit value may be attached to the outcomes of the diverse range of courses and qualifications available in the post-school sector. However, the notion of outcomes employed here – 'what a learner can be expected to know, understand and do in order to achieve credit' – is far wider than the NCVQ conception and includes, in addition to competences, the assessment objectives of A levels, the learning objectives of BTEC, the learning outcome statements of open college networks, and the statements of attainment of the National Curriculum, GCSE courses and GNVQs (1992b, p. 4). Other possible outcomes cited in a study of this area made by the Unit for the Development of Adult Continuing Education (UDACE) are 'subject-based outcomes' such as knowledge and comprehension, and 'personal outcomes' which might include 'interpersonal skills like teamwork and negotiation, and intra-personal skills like motivation, initiative and critical self reflection' (UDACE, 1989b, p. 3).

These wider perspectives indicate, first, that there is nothing particularly new or distinctive about the NVQ stress on outcomes and, second, that when outcomes are interpreted as simply the benefits or consequences of undertaking a learning programme, then just about *anything* could be described as a learning outcome. Certainly, there seems to be no reason why outcomes should be restricted to vocational education, since the consequences of attending courses in Egyptology or flower-arranging can be described in terms of learning outcomes. Indeed, the arguments put forward in recent years by the National Institute of Adult Continuing Education (NIACE) against the artificial distinction between vocational and 'leisure' courses in the Further & Higher Education Act 1992 draw attention to the value of this broader notion of learning outcomes. Moreover, even if courses lacked specific outcomes and did not carry certification, there is still great potential value in general education and learning of any kind as an essential part of a 'continuum of educational opportunity' and a system which 'encouraged the development of a learning culture' (NIACE, 1992, p. 13).

This last point is of vital importance, since two of the key NCVQ claims are concerned with enhancing access to and openness of learning. However, the general thrust of arguments and evidence surveyed in this chapter is that the NVQ assessment system is far too narrowly focused – and is based on much too behavioural and task-specific a conception of outcomes – to justify these claims. Any putative openness of access and flexibility of certification pales into insignificance beside the mechanistic and essentially closed NVQ framework of assessment.

CONCLUSION

Although recent changes in the NVQ assessment system – including a greater emphasis on underpinning knowledge and understanding and the use of wider notions of competence linked to range statements – are to be welcomed, they do not go far enough to solve the basic problems inherent in CBET procedures. The evidence suggests that, even when allied to experiential learning methodologies, NVQs lead to a reduced curriculum, a narrowing of focus and a neglect of important theoretical considerations. Considerable change and development will have to take place if NVQs are to foster 'both vocational capability *and* educational achievement' (Smithers, 1993, p. 43). Moreover, the predictive validity of NVQs is problematic, and the associated abandonment of reliability flies in the face of all that is recommended in terms of acceptable practice in the field of educational measurement and assessment.

There is nothing particularly new or distinctive about the stress on criterion-referencing or outcomes in the NVQ system, and, indeed, both these concepts are interpreted and utilized in a more coherent and educationally valuable way in the context of GCSE, BTEC and open college courses. Even though the obsession with evidence now seems to have been tempered by the adoption of perspectives which look beyond the level of immediately observable performance, the upshot of introducing NVQs still seems to be a 'minimalist' (Raggatt, 1994, p. 8) approach to VET which leaves out vital components. The NVQ assessment system is mechanistic, cumbersome and costly, and does not even seem to meet the basic minimum of VET requirements by providing what employers want. Such an assessment system is a most improbable vehicle for the enhancement of VET and the promotion of a learning culture.

Chapter 4

Competence, Learning and Teaching

In discussing the notions of learning and teaching within the context of CBET we immediately come face to face with the extreme strangeness and apparently paradoxical business of attempting to describe teaching and learning processes against the background of systems which are allegedly concerned only with *products* and the assessment of *outcomes*. If NVQs are genuinely intended to be 'independent of any specific course, programme or mode of learning' (NCVQ, 1988, p. v) and based on a model which is 'firmly rooted in the functions of employment . . . without imposing an educational model of how people learn and behave' (Jessup, 1991, p. 39), how can such a system, at the same time, achieve the aim of fostering the 'autonomous learner' (p. 115)? Indeed, if NVQ assessment is genuinely independent of learning programmes – and it really is the case that 'NVQs have nothing whatsoever to do with training or learning programmes' (Fletcher, 1991, p. 26) – how can a key feature of what Jessup calls 'the emerging model of VET' be that by which 'individuals will complete programmes of learning and will be awarded the appropriate qualifications' (Jessup, 1990a, p. 31)? I thought there were *no* NVQ programmes of learning!

All this confusion and equivocation may be explained by reference to a number of factors which are partly empirical, concerned with the implementation of NVQs discussed in earlier chapters, and partly theoretical, connected with the nature of learning processes. In the first place, whatever the NCVQ rhetoric tells us about the independence of competence criteria in relation to learning programmes, the actual *implementation* of NVQs across a wide range of vocational sectors has resulted in the modification and alteration of content and methodology, sometimes quite substantially, of existing VET provision. Smithers (1993) was particularly damning in this respect in his criticisms of the move from 'standard' City & Guilds courses for plumbers and electricians to NCVQ schemes. The City & Guilds schemes had much 'higher requirements for technical expertise' than the NVQs which were replacing them and also placed 'more emphasis on working relationships, public relations and environmental matters'. All in all, it is 'difficult to see how NVQs will improve the quality of British plumbers or maintain the present quality of British electricians' (pp. 23–4).

Although, as noted previously, the NCVQ does not technically award NVQs itself, but approves awards made by other bodies, the criteria laid down by the NCVQ are quite stringent. Awarding bodies or consortia must, for instance, 'agree to work with NCVQ and the lead bodies responsible for setting employment led standards in the development and implementation of the NVQ framework' and also 'agree to meet the conditions, regulations and guidelines specified or issued by NCVQ from time to time for accredited qualifications and awarding bodies' (NCVQ, 1991a, pp. 7–8). In practice, this has meant that existing bodies such as BTEC, CGLI and RSA have had to rewrite their syllabuses in order to meet NCVQ criteria, and, particularly in the case of BTEC (see Maclure, 1991, pp. 23–6, Smithers, 1993, p. 18)), this has led to disputes about course content, arguments between rival lead bodies (notorious in the area of catering; HCTC, 1991) and frequent changes of course outlines which can only be described as educationally counter-productive (for an account of such developments in the construction industry, see Callender, 1992).

The concerns of trainers and lecturers about the way in which NVQs were introduced into colleges in a top-down fashion were discussed in earlier chapters. Investigating the areas of agriculture, business studies, hairdressing and catering, Haffenden and Brown (1989) reported staff anxieties about competing notions of competence, frequent changes and a general lack of operational guidelines, and fears that NVQs had resulted in a loss of important theoretical content and knowledge. In the field of hairdressing, in particular, there was a concern that the new competence-based National Preferred Scheme (NPS) had resulted in a 'reduced curriculum' (p. 166). In catering the introduction of NVQs produced similar problems which still await a final solution (MSC, 1988; HMI, 1992), and in the coal-mining industry the 'confusion surrounding the disparity of meaning of the concept made it difficult to create a competence-based system' (Osborn, 1993, p. 186). Similarly, the Warwick University study of NVQ implementation in catering, business studies and hairdressing produced a picture of lecturers having to modify programmes and restrict learning contracts with students in order to meet the demands of a cumbersome assessment system (Hyland and Weller, 1994).

It may be the case that teachers and lecturers will always, to some extent, be resistant to change of any kind, particularly when it is externally imposed as in the case of the National Curriculum and NVQs. In addition, some of the changes, such as the increase in work-based assessment, may actually represent an improvement on certain pre-NCVQ areas of VET provision. The important point about the so-called NVQ 'revolution', however, is that the resultant changes in working practices on the part of trainers and lecturers do nothing to support the notion of the independence of NVQ assessment from learning programmes. Indeed, the existing available evidence indicates the exact opposite to be the case. It is highly improbable, even on a theoretical level, for an assessment system which requires the restructuring of content and methodology in terms of units and elements of competence measured by prespecified performance criteria and range statements to be introduced without altering the nature and rationale of existing learning programmes.

The new choices for learners and 'autonomous' learners referred to by Jessup need to be interpreted within the context of NCVQ guidelines and controls, none of which, as mentioned in earlier chapters, seems to have much to do with autonomy in the normal sense of the term. What Jessup really means by autonomy in this sphere is providing learners with 'far more exact information on the functions performed in occupations and professions' so that they will 'be able to explore the qualifications and units on offer, classified within the NVQ framework to clarify their relationship to each other' (1991, p. 115). The flexibility and freedom of learners extends no further than this. Once learners have opted for particular NVQ units, their subsequent learning and development must be subordinated to the gathering of evidence to satisfy predetermined competence criteria. Thus, CBET approaches (particularly, as I note later, behaviourist-inspired models) cannot help but circumscribe, delimit and restrict the experiences of learners. This makes nonsense of the claim that the NCVQ model is designed to provide the learner 'with more control over the process of learning and assessment' (Jessup, 1991, p. 115).

The case studies describing the impact of NVQs on existing programmes serve to confirm the fundamental connections between learning and assessment. Broadfoot's claims about the seminal role of assessment in determining the precise nature of educational systems was noted in the last chapter, and there are similar connections between specific forms of assessment and approaches to learning, teaching and views on education in general (these connections are well brought out in the differences between 'progressive' and 'traditional' approaches to education; see Meighan, 1981, pp. 161ff.). There is, moreover, a sense in which the connections between learning and assessment are, as Flew argues (1979), both necessary and complementary in that it is difficult to imagine a systematic programme of learning which did not (in some sense) include the monitoring of the learner's progress. Thus, given the nature of the connections between learning and assessment, the adoption of particular forms of assessment must inevitably influence the structure, operation and activities of learning programmes. This influence is, moreover, even more significant and decisive in the case of CBET strategies based on behaviourist foundations.

CBET AND BEHAVIOURISM

There can be no disputing the fact that the NCVQ model, both in terms of design and implementation, is based on and informed by behaviourist learning theory. The connections have been explored by a number of writers (Hodkinson, 1992; Norris, 1991; Ashworth and Saxton, 1990; Hyland, 1992a, 1993c), and it would be useful as a preliminary to cite some examples from the literature concerned with characterizations of the NCVQ model in terms of its learning foundations:

> The most prevalent construct of competence is behaviourist. It rests on a description of behaviour (sometimes called performance) and the situation(s) in which it is to take place (sometimes referred to as range statements) in a form that is capable of demonstration and observation. (Norris, 1991, p. 332).

> Competency-based vocational education – just appearing in the UK from the US – is a good example of a system using behavioural objectives. In behaviourist ideology a Stimulus (S) is associated with a response (R) and a Stimulus-Response (SR) bond formed. Competency-based vocational education involves students being trained to associate SR so that, given the proper job cue (S), the appropriate occupational task will be performed (R). (Bull, 1985, p. 74).

> The [NCVQ] procedure is unashamedly behavioural. It is the outcome of the training which is to be assessed and the overt behaviour of the Trainee is the significant variable. The requirements of the performance criteria set out the parameters and performance is judged against those parameters. This procedure clearly draws upon the work of the classical behavioural school of psychology. The work of Watson, Guthrie, Thorndike and Skinner is strongly represented. (Marshall, 1991, p. 61)

> . . . the rhetoric of the so-called competency-based movement . . . has spawned mounds of curriculum formats which are devoid of any significant inputs from adult learners and teachers. They are characterized largely by a myopic perspective on needs typically expressed in the form of simplistic behavioural objectives. (Collins, 1991, p. 90)

Smithers (1993) argues that the 'schematic framework derived from behavioural psychology' is 'ruthlessly applied' (p. 9) in the NCVQ approach to education and training. Before examining the specific criticisms levelled against the behaviourist thrust of the NCVQ model of VET, it is worth saying a little more about behaviourism as a learning theory and its place in contemporary educational psychology.

Bull's description of the behaviourist enterprise in terms of the establishment of S-R connections mentioned above, though telegraphic, is essentially correct. From its origins in the work of Watson, behaviourism has been concerned to make psychology 'scientifically objective' by concentrating its efforts only on observable phenomena and abandoning the 'examination of inaccessible and unobservable mental events' (Tennant, 1988, p. 107). The 'classical' behaviourists, drawing on the pioneering work of Pavlov, were interested in the reinforcement of our natural, instinctive responses (or reflexes) to various environmental stimuli so that, by constant association, they became 'conditioned' responses. Learning, on this account, takes place 'through acquiring responses through conditioned ties to these reflexes' (Child, 1981, p. 87). Watson's early experiments in the 1920s, for instance, succeeded in conditioning or extinguishing children's responses to various fear-provoking events.

At this level the S-R connections are predominant, but more recent exponents of behaviourism, notably Hull and Skinner, have been concerned to stress the greater efficacy of 'operant conditioning', which seeks to reinforce willed or intentional responses displayed by individuals (rather than their instinctive or reflex actions). For this reason, the theoretical position is symbolically expressed as S-O-R, to 'signify the importance of the intervening happenings in the organism O' (Child, 1981, p. 88).

Skinner's general theories, particularly his experiments with programmed learning and reinforcement techniques, are well known and, as Tennant (1988) notes, 'his views have had a direct impact on educational theory and practice' (p. 108). Although, as I explain below, behaviourism in general now has little acknowledged value as a learning theory in mainstream practice in either school or post-school education, its influence does remain in programmes utilizing behavioural objectives of one kind or another (see Curzon, 1985, pp. 88ff.), and, of course, in competency-based systems. Skinner's distinctive and unequivocal views still hold a central place in behaviourist ideology, not least because he provided what is perhaps the clearest philosophical account of the enterprise. For this reason, it is worth looking more closely at some of Skinner's key arguments as a preliminary to examining the main criticisms of behaviourism and the recommendations of alternative models.

Skinner was interested in human learning chiefly as a means of uncovering the empirical relationship between reinforcement and behaviour, with the ultimate aim of achieving a new 'science of behaviour' (Skinner, 1953) which would enable us to solve all manner of problems currently confronting the human race. The solutions to all such problems are, predictably, technical ones consisting in the changing of human practices by means of reinforcement and behaviour-modification techniques. Skinner suggests, for instance, that 'over-crowding can be corrected only by inducing people not to crowd, and the environment will continue to deteriorate until polluting practices are abandoned' (1973, p. 10). There is a certain compelling and commonsensical logic about all this (owing much, no doubt, to the common human preference for the immediate and concrete, what can be seen and touched!) which gives a certain plausibility to Skinner's talk about a 'technology of human behaviour'. Such a technology would be concerned only with the observable and would dispense with ephemeral 'mentalistic' phenomena. Perhaps the clearest statement of these principles is to be found in *Beyond Freedom and Dignity* (1973), in which Skinner makes the audacious claim that

> We can follow the path taken by physics and biology by turning directly to the relation between behaviour and the environment and neglecting supposed mediating states of mind. Physics did not advance by looking more closely at the jubilance of a falling body, or biology by looking at the nature of vital spirits, and we do not need to try to discover what personalities, states of mind, feelings, traits of character, plans, purposes, intentions, or the other perquisites of autonomous man really are in order to get on with a scientific analysis of behaviour. (p. 20)

The chief influences of behaviourist ideas on educational theory and practice have been in the use of behaviour-modification techniques and in the reformulation of curricula in terms of behavioural objectives. Broad behavioural approaches have been effectively employed in the areas of classroom management (Wheldell and Merrett, 1984) and in special education (Galloway, 1985). As long as such techniques are regarded, as Fontana (1984) suggests, as a 'useful tool' and not 'the total extent of knowledge' (p. 195), then such applications may be educationally justifiable, particularly in the case of the more recent 'cognitive behaviourist' formulations which attempt to provide a 'more coherent and humane analysis of behaviour' (Blackman, 1984, p. 12). Most applications of behaviourism in educational settings, however, do not fully satisfy the cognitive and 'humane' descriptions and have correspondingly less *educational* value (though they may still have some value as tools of instruction or training programmes).

General criticisms of behaviourism in terms of its circumscribed account of human thought and action, and its failure to account for reasoning, understanding and learning are common in the general psychological literature (see Gross, 1987; Radford and Govier, 1980). In terms of its applications to education, there is a large body of work within philosophy of education which points to the logical inconsistencies in behaviourist theory, the failure to distinguish adequately between voluntary and involuntary action, and the generally impoverished conception of human agency which informs most of the behaviourist approaches (Clark, 1979; Burwood and Brady, 1984).

Dearden (1984) provides perhaps the clearest account of these shortcomings and points to the 'absurd consequence of ignoring the understanding which accompanies and indeed importantly constitutes human behaviour' (p. 140). Human learning is unintelligible without reference to the context of learning and to the development of understanding, and this focuses attention on aspects of cognition and the nature of the learning process. Dearden goes on to argue that 'what someone is doing and why he [*sic*] is doing it are unintelligible without reference to certain of his beliefs, desires, intentions, experiences, imaginings, attitudes, sentiments, or in general his understanding' (p. 142). In so far as behaviourism is silent on these aspects of thought and understanding, it is, therefore, inadequate as an educational theory and, thus, a 'theory of cognitive learning' (p. 142) is required.

In terms of current research and knowledge about how students learn most effectively, particularly mature students, behaviourism simply does not seem to match up to the requirements. Examining work in the psychology of adult education, Tennant (1988) notes that a 'reservation commonly expressed about behavioural objectives is that they fragment learning into narrowly conceived categories of behaviour' (p. 117). Of particular interest within the context of the purposes of this discussion is Tennant's examination of behavioural objectives in terms of their suitability for the measurement of 'competence' (competence is evidently used here in a non- or pre-NVQ sense as a broad-based capacity or capability). In answer to the question, 'Do behavioural objectives offer us the best method for measuring competence?', Tennant outlines four main reasons for believing that they do not (pp. 117–20):

(i)   the behavioural indicators of competence can rarely be determined in advance;
(ii) the emphasis on terminal outcomes undervalues the importance of the learning process;
(iii) not all learning outcomes are specifiable in behavioural terms;
(iv) learning may be occurring which is not being measured.

All these considerations lead Tennant to conclude that behaviourism is 'incompatible with the ethos of adult education' (p. 120).

Similarly, discussing the impact of the CBET intrusion into initial teacher education and professional studies, Elliott (1993) has linked the behaviourist thrust with the 'social market' model of education and training which is underpinned by an 'emphasis placed on the atomistic specification of discrete practical skills (competences)' (p. 17) and has suggested more appropriate alternatives for teaching and learning in professional spheres.

LEARNING, EXPERIENCE AND NVQ OUTCOMES

It was observed in Chapter 3 that, according to Mansfield, there were at least six models of CBET in operation in different areas of education and training. Norris (1991) has additionally identified what he calls three 'constructs' of CBET: the generic, the cognitive and the behaviourist. Cognitive constructions stress the difference between competence and performance and insist that competence is about potential whereas performance relates only to actual situated behaviour. On this account, competence rests on the 'general ability to co-ordinate appropriate internal cognitive, affective and other resources necessary for successful adaptation' (Woods and Power, 1987, p. 414). Generic approaches favour 'empirical investigation to establish the competencies which discriminate between average and expert performers as opposed to the theoretical or logical requirements of a particular occupational function' (Norris, 1991, p. 332; this model has been utilized in recent approaches to professional education and will be discussed in more detail in Chapter 7). The most prevalent construct of competence, however, is the behavioural, which rests on a notion of competence as 'something a person is or should be able to do' and 'is a description of action, behaviour or outcome in a form that is capable of demonstration, observation and assessment' (p. 332).

Mansfield's (1989) own preferred 'job competence model' which encourages 'holistic analysis to derive broad work functions' is, as mentioned already, rather different from the mainstream NCVQ model which is (albeit implicitly and tacitly) criticized for its attachment to 'narrow and mechanistic tasks and skills' (pp. 29, 34). Similar criticisms are made by Marshall (1991) in his claim that the behaviourist-inspired NCVQ model tends to generate programmes which are 'one dimensional and prescriptive' (p. 62) and offer little scope for active and constructive contributions from learners. Although CBET strategies are meant to enhance precision and objectivity, they typically result in disembodied check-lists which are 'empty and uninformative' (Ashworth and Saxton, 1990, p. 19) and fail to capture significant aspects of human activity. Such approaches are 'atomistic, individualistic and unable to cover all types of relevant behaviour or mental activity' (p. 3) since, as Moss (1981) points out, the performance-related or observable parts of tasks describe neither their complete nor even their most significant elements in many cases.

The Skinnerian technicist thrust of CBET is picked out by a number of writers including Collins (1991), who argues that the 'simplistic behavioural objectives' of CBET approaches ensure that, though 'management interests are well served, education and training programmes are trivialized, while occupations are increasingly de-skilled through the deployment of narrowly defined prescriptions' (p. 90). Ashworth (1992) similarly argues that the 'competence notion has been inadequately specified in the TEED/NCVQ model' and that 'this view of competence entails an over-mechanistic way of thinking'. He concludes that the 'TEED/NCVQ model of competence provides solutions to the specification of learning outcomes which are normally inappropriate to the description of human action, or to the facilitation of the training of human beings' (p. 16). On this point Marshall (1991) simply states unequivocally that 'even the most radical behavioural psychologist would not now subscribe to the traditional view of learning so evident in the work of the NCVQ' and suggests that 'the NVQ model should now be refined and/or restricted to the training of basic skills' (pp. 61, 63).

These criticisms take on an added gravity when viewed against the current demands being made on the post-school system in terms of the urgent need to upgrade and enhance vocational studies and reform the 16 to 19 curriculum (Macfarlane, 1993; NCE, 1993). How can a behaviourist-inspired competence-based system possibly contribute to such a reform programme? For one thing, the upgrading of VET would seem to call for a re-evaluation of teaching/learning processes, whereas, as illustrated already, NVQs have either no relevance to such matters or, more commonly, tend to restrict and circumscribe learning through the imposition of predetermined competence outcomes. More significantly, the behaviourist thrust of the NCVQ strategy seems to be at odds with mainstream models of learning and teaching in post-school education which draw inspiration from cognitive psychology and the experiential tradition which has developed from this source (Hyland, 1993d).

Experiential learning theory – an umbrella term bringing together a wide range of perspectives from cognitive and humanistic psychology – has emerged as the preferred methodology within adult education (Mezirow, 1990) and, in a more practical form, is arguably the most influential model operating in the further education sector (Gibbs, 1988). It is unreservedly eclectic – drawing on the educational philosophies of Piaget and Dewey as well as the critical theory of Freire and Habermas – though a number of common and distinctive characteristics have emerged through its application in post-school settings of all kinds. Kolb (1993) offers a useful summary of the key features, noting significant emphases on learning as a continuous process grounded in experience, on the idea of a holistic process of adaptation through the resolution of conflicts and opposing viewpoints, and on the notion that learning needs to be regarded as a means of creating knowledge rather than merely the regurgitation and reinforcement of existing norms and traditions. Kolb aggregates all these ideas in his broad definition of experiential learning as the 'process whereby knowledge is created by the transformation of experience' (p. 155).

This conception of learning is on all fours with the 'reflective practitioner' (Schon, 1987) model which has been such a fruitful and influential source for the development of professional education over the last few years, particularly in the area of teacher education at all levels. Many of the basic texts on professional development in further and adult education are directly inspired by such a model of learning and development (see Minton, 1991; Kerry and Tollitt-Evans, 1992), as is the preferred FEU perspective on these matters (FEU, 1992a). For those who support such a conception of learning, behaviourist CBET strategies must be anathema, since they appear to be diametrically opposed to the fundamental tenets of the experiential tradition.

Instead of a holistic framework, CBET atomizes and fragments learning into measurable chunks; rather than valuing process and experience, NVQs are concerned only with performance outcomes; and, most importantly, instead of encouraging critical reflection on alternative perspectives, the NCVQ model offers a monocultural view based on the satisfaction of narrow performance criteria and directed towards fixed and predetermined ends.

A key problem resides in the nature of functional analysis and competence outcomes which, though clearly directly inspired by behaviourism, do not even appear to have the programmatic utility of standard behavioural objectives which, on Curzon's definition, indicate 'what a learner will be able to do on the completion of an instructional process' (1985, p. 89). Further education lecturers, for example, used to working towards VET objectives of various degrees of specificity, still complain of the excessive limitations of NVQs (Hyland, 1993d), and, according to Raggatt's (1994) most recent study, have commented that the 'narrowness of NVQs put pressure on employers who often wanted students on work placement to undertake a wider range of activities than was prescribed for NVQs' (p. 66).

If behavioural objectives (even those with practical value and use) are constructed in highly specific terms or are pursued to the exclusion of all else, they can easily become educationally counter-productive and vulnerable to all the weaknesses of behaviourism discussed earlier. Such objectives are thus open to the charge that they 'inhibit achievement', result in a 'limited model of teacher-student interaction' and, in extreme cases, 'may border on indoctrination rather than on education' (Bull, 1985, p. 79). Typically, programmes utilizing such objectives lead to a neglect of process, a reduction of content and a 'teaching to the test', and it is perhaps for this reason that, along with the demise of the Revised Code in the nineteenth century and the failure of the few attempts to apply behavioural objectives to the curriculum in this country (Kelly, 1982, pp. 99ff.), teachers have shown a reluctance to view their task solely in terms of the achievement of sets of prespecified learning outcomes. Moreover, competence outcomes, as already noted, are apparently even less concerned with process than mainstream behavioural objectives.

It is just this feature of CBET strategies which causes commentators such as Hodkinson (1992), for instance, to suggest alternatives to the 'behaviouristic NCVQ model of competence' in the form of models which focus on 'beliefs and how we think, as well as on performance', and which view the teaching/learning process as 'central in the development of intelligent practice' (pp. 35–5). Kolb's seminal writings on experiential learning stress the conception of learning as a continuous process grounded in experience by which knowledge is created through transactions between learners and the environments in which they operate. He is quite certain that outcomes approaches, by themselves, cannot be reconciled with such a conception; as he observes:

> When viewed from the perspective of experiential learning, the tendency to define learning in terms of outcomes can become a definition of non-learning, in the process sense that the failure to modify ideas and habits as a result of experience is maladaptive. (1993, p. 144)

On this account, CBET approaches seem to represent a paradigm case of 'non-learning' and, as such, it is difficult to see how they can do much to enhance the quality of learning and teaching either in VET or in *any* sphere of educational activity.

In discussing the development of learning strategies designed to increase professional effectiveness, Argyris and Schon (1974) note that 'the more an individual achieves goals that do not require learning, the more his [*sic*] behaviour becomes programmed, repetitive and routine' (p. 88). This 'routinization' of activities is a fundamental feature of the functional-analysis methodology of CBET systems (Field, 1991; Marshall, 1991), and this inevitably means that opportunities for positive and meaningful learning are severely restricted in programmes employing such strategies. Behaviourist strategies typically result in what Argyris and Schon (1974) refer to as 'single-loop learning' – 'learning to design actions that satisfy existing governing variables' (e.g., learning new techniques for suppressing conflict) – as opposed to 'double-loop learning' in which 'we learn to change the field of constancy itself' (p. 19), which can be illustrated in terms of the example by learning to be concerned with the surfacing and resolution of conflict rather than with its suppression.

Almost all intelligent action above the level of basic reflexes can be improved by using double-loop strategies, but, since this seems to be ruled out in CBET systems by the imposition of strict control over the governing variables (the competence outcomes), such approaches are necessarily limited and impoverished. This brings out in graphic terms the sheer folly of attempting to graft the NCVQ model on to programmes of professional study and development (this is examined at greater length in Chapter 7).

The criticisms levelled at NVQs by VET lecturers and trainers have been referred to already in earlier chapters. In the context of learning, such dissatisfaction could be interpreted as a consequence of the apparent mismatch between the processes favoured by lecturers, inspired broadly by the experiential/humanistic tradition, and the behaviourist orientation of the NVQ outcomes approach. The reduced curriculum, narrowness of focus and cumbersome assessment system were universal complaints noted in the Warwick survey, though, interestingly, this negative criticism did not unduly influence lecturers' comments on the changes in methods and course organization which had accompanied the introduction of NVQs.

In describing the methods actually used in programmes in relation to general course content and the teaching/learning environment, lecturers indicated overwhelmingly that they had maintained the commitment to process and individualized learning that had always characterized their approach to the task. In all three vocational sectors surveyed, references to 'student-centredness', 'individualized learning' and 'flexible environments' abounded, and allusions to 'workshops' and 'practical sessions' were littered throughout all the general descriptions and responses (Hyland and Weller, 1994). Of course, this perspective was undoubtedly influenced by the fact that 'real work environments' – in the shape of model offices, hairdressing salons, and college restaurants – had always been a feature of courses well before NVQ implementation, and, as already noted, the preference for 'student-centred' and 'flexible' learning environments seems to be well established generally in the FE sector.

In the light of the standard criticisms and perceived demerits of NVQs – such as the cumbersome assessment system, neglect of underpinning knowledge and the narrowness of focus – it would appear that lecturers were able to operate student-centred learning approaches in spite of (rather than *because* of, as the NCVQ might claim!) the introduction of NVQs. In the first place, it seemed to be generally the case that flexible and individualized approaches were already in operation in many areas before the introduction of NVQs in colleges. As one catering lecturer in our survey observed with admirable frankness, even though it was a 'nightmare running workshops' because of the heavy demands on tutor time, this approach 'did not start with NVQs . . . it has always been . . . workshops' (Hyland and Weller, 1994, p. 27). NVQs had, it appears, served to clarify and focus attention on industrial standards, but had not unduly interfered with existing approaches to learning and teaching. Of course, according to the NCVQ literature, NVQ assessments are supposed, in *theory*, to be independent of courses and learning programmes though, as already observed in earlier sections, this claim cannot be sustained in practice.

Moreover, it is clear that lecturers have had to struggle actively in many cases to maintain a commitment to process and to the broad vocational development of knowledge, skills and understanding in the face of the obsession with performance outcomes which characterizes the NVQ system. The resulting tensions emerge in the concerns expressed in research studies that 'possession of knowledge might be undervalued' (Haffenden and Brown, 1989, p. 149), that there was 'too little emphasis on theory' (MSC, 1988, p. 11) in the new NVQ schemes, and that NVQs inevitably led to a 'minimalist' approach to education and training (Raggatt, 1994, p. 66). In the Warwick study the lecturers in hairdressing and beauty interviewed were especially critical of the narrowing of the curriculum and the lowering of professional standards. As one lecturer in this area commented: 'I think the standards have gone way down . . . I really cannot think of any advantages of NVQs . . . the whole system is totally open to abuse' (1994, p. 31; on this point, see also Smithers, 1993, p. 21).

Even if we allow for a certain conservatism and inertia caused by innovation overload in FE, these criticisms and negative comments by lecturers (who are often also NVQ *assessors*!) must be a cause of some concern for anyone concerned with improving quality in VET. I would suggest that all this is the inevitable result of a mismatch between process and product. Even though lecturers in some areas may have adapted NVQs to fit their preferred learning approaches, this does little to reduce the clear tensions between process models of learning based on cognitive/experiential theory and the behaviourist outcomes approach which underpins NVQs. All the experience and evidence indicates that, with all the good will in the world, behaviourist strategies inevitably place restrictions on learning and lead to a 'teaching to the test' narrowing of learning objectives and experiences. Certainly this has proved to be the case in contexts in which behavioural objectives have been grafted on to existing cognitive development programmes (Collins, 1991, pp. 58–9 provides some American examples, and Taylor and Richards, 1985, pp. 63–5, 78–9 note some British instances). Furthermore, as Bull (1985) and Tennant (1988) have pointed out, competence outcomes are perhaps even more restrictive and circumscribed than standard behavioural objectives.

It is patently obvious that it is just not feasible, either educationally or logically, to claim that an assessment system can be simply tagged on to a learning programme without influencing the overall nature and purpose of that programme. Many schoolteachers committed to learner-centredness and process objectives are now acknowledging that the bureaucratically cumbersome nature of the National Curriculum assessment system has thwarted their initial intentions and attempts to assimilate the new framework. As the Chief Inspector of Schools noted in a recent report, the impact of the National Curriculum showed signs that it would 'lead to a distortion of the positive relationship between teaching, learning and assessment' (Spencer, 1993, p. 4). In relation to the arguments about the structure of the English curriculum in particular, many professionals thought that the 'combination of a shallow and reductive curriculum with oversimplified testing will destroy the spirit of intellectual enquiry which underpins good teaching and effective learning' (Whitbread, 1993, p. 35).

These observations serve to bring out the full implications of the tensions between process/outcomes and cognitive/behaviourist strategies. Lecturers in further and adult education may have been able to obviate the worst effects of trying to bolt on lists of competence statements to their existing programmes (Ecclestone 1993b), and, no doubt, this has helped to mitigate what Kolb refers to as the 'maladaptive' consequences of outcome approaches. What gets lost in such makeshift exercises, however, is the dynamic relationship and interaction between learning and assessment, in addition to a loss of coherence and fit between processes and products in learning schemes.

It is a quite serious educational mistake to isolate means and ends in this way, and the disembodied check-lists of competence units and elements typical of NVQs make the NCVQ model unequivocally culpable in this respect. The whole *raison d'être* of the 'learning by doing' strategy widely used throughout the post-school sector is its contribution to a 'cyclical sequence of learning activities' (Gibbs, 1988, p. 15) in which the evaluation of learning experiences is used to inform subsequent development through reflective observation (the 'double-loop' concept referred to earlier). All the empirical studies of the optimum conditions for effective learning in adult education and higher education (Richardson *et al.*, 1987) point to the importance of encouraging learning strategies in students, and paying attention to the conceptual structure of what is to be learned, so that what Bruner (1966) called the 'transfer of principles and attitudes' can be achieved. Such 'transferability' (now, of course, a popular slogan in competence talk and VET generally) consists, for Bruner, in learning 'not a skill but a general idea which can then be used as a basis for recognizing subsequent problems as special cases of the idea originally mastered' (p. 17). In this way the process becomes meaningful and significant for learners, and the idea of ongoing and progressive development is fostered. CBET strategies tend to frustrate and short-circuit this experiential process by giving primacy to behavioural objectives and outcomes.

Moreover, there is a sense in which this lack of attention to process, combined with a mechanistic and rigidly formal assessment system, can actually hinder or even *prevent* the growth and development of learning. Once an element or unit of competence is achieved on the can do/cannot do scale, there is no way for a student to develop competence further except by adding units or changing job or role functions. This is a serious shortcoming, and is emphasized by Chown and Last (1993) in their critique of the TDLB standards being used for training in the FE sector. They argue that the 'NCVQ model cannot acknowledge the growth of competence' since it 'does not admit a change in competence which is not allied to a change in organisational function' (pp. 21–2). In a similar vein, Eraut (1989), in criticizing the NCVQ model in terms of its applications in initial teacher education, points to the danger that, once trained, 'people might consider their competence as sufficient and ignore the need for further improvement' (p. 181). All this is certainly a very long way from fostering the widely canvassed ideal of 'lifelong learning'!

In addition to the importance of attending to the process of learning, rather than just its outcomes, the social and cultural context of learning, as Bruner's (1974) writings amply demonstrate, is also of cardinal importance. It is precisely the contextless nature of the NCVQ model which motivates Hodkinson's (1992) critique and his recommendation of an alternative 'interactive' model of learning. He is surely correct in noting that 'what you learn cannot be separated from the activity you are engaged in while learning, or from the context or culture in which the learning takes place'. Hodkinson stresses the importance of viewing learning as a 'dialectical process' and identifies the crucial role of 'schemas' (mental representations or sets of categories, rather like Bruner's transferable ideas, which play an indispensable part in the development of learning) in providing a foundation for the vital 'interaction between the learner and the learned' (p. 33).

Such considerations serve to highlight the vast gulf which exists between cognitive and behaviourist learning theories, in addition to illustrating clearly the limitations and pitfalls of attempting to bolt a behaviourist-inspired assessment system on to programmes informed by humanistic learning perspectives. Notwithstanding the best efforts of lecturers and students, the inherent tensions will inevitably surface and work to frustrate and distort the learning process. The NCVQ model is largely concerned with the generation and collection of evidence to satisfy performance criteria, and this is a very different enterprise from the fostering of learning and development.

COMPETENCE AND TEACHING

The work and role of the teacher in the learning process has thus far been mentioned only in passing, and it is interesting to note and explain why this is so. For one thing, it is fair to say that none of the currently influential models of learning in post-school education – concerned as they are with needs analysis, action planning, student-centredness and learning by doing – places much value on the traditional, didactic or teacher-centred approaches to education. Indeed, as noted in earlier sections, the NCVQ literature cleverly manages to align itself with these currently fashionable models by suggesting that NVQs are either independent of and have no impact on learning processes and teaching methods, or that they in some way encourage the autonomy and independence of learners (claims which it has been the purpose of this chapter to question).

Yet it is not quite correct to say that the new models leave little scope for teaching; it is more a case of changing the nature and functions of the teacher and moving these away from didactic purposes. After all, if the new models of learning (flexible colleges which provide learner services) have dispensed completely with the traditional teacher's role, it is still legitimate to ask what precisely those contractually employed as teachers, lecturers or trainers are supposed to be doing!

Hirst (1974) offers a formal definition of teaching as a broad label for 'those activities of a person A, the intention of which is to bring about in another person B, the intentional learning of X' (p. 109). Now, although it may appear that, in contemporary models of active and experiential learning, the A element of this triad has been displaced by B and X, this view could be rather simplistic and misleading. It seems more correct to say that the *activities* of A (i.e., the roles of teachers) have been altered radically so as to place more emphasis on self-directed learning and achievement. In this sense the new models are directly descended from and informed by the 'progressive' or 'open education' tradition (Nyberg, 1975; Hyland, 1978) which was influential in the school sector in the 1960s and early 1970s. The concept of so-called 'vocational progressivism' and the use of progressive methods by industrial trainers has already been touched upon and briefly criticized in Chapter 1. However, it would be worth saying something more about this in relation to the new models of teaching and learning, since it is important to show how the NCVQ approach fits into this framework.

Scheffler's analysis (1973) of three important and influential models of teaching will provide a useful background to the discussion here. The 'impression' model (pp. 68–70), associated with Locke's philosophy, pictures the mind of the learner as a *tabula rasa* upon which is to be imprinted the experience and knowledge of her cultural tradition. The teacher's task on this account is to exercise the mental powers of the student engaged in receiving and processing this information. Whereas the impression model supposes the teacher to be conveying ideas to be stored by students, the 'insight' model (which Scheffler associates with Plato and Augustine, pp. 71–5) denies that knowledge can be acquired in this fashion. The mind cannot simply store ideas, but must be stimulated and prompted into extracting order and meaning from the experiences which come before it. The notion of inert knowledge is thus replaced by a dynamic picture of active and experiential learning. Finally, the 'rule' model of teaching (attributed to the influence of Kant, pp. 76–9) stresses the fact that knowledge and insight must be understood as being acquired against a background of principles and reasons. The interaction between teachers and students is mediated by general principles of rationality to which all parties are bound and which determine and guide the development of understanding.

Like their earlier counterparts in the progressive tradition, the current models of experiential learning in post-school education all derive their meaning to some extent from a contrast with and a reaction to the impression model which is associated with traditional didactic teaching. Gibbs (1988), for instance, describes the replacement of a 'useless' approach based on 'conventional didactic knowledge-centred methods' with an 'experience-based programme' that makes use of such strategies as the 'experiential learning cycle', 'learning logs', 'problem groups' and 'learning reviews' (pp. 102–3) to illustrate the values of a learning-by-doing methodology. Similarly, the FEU (1992a) vision of the new 'flexible' FE college providing 'learner services' will involve changes to traditional college structures which include such new services as 'initial assessment, accreditation of prior learning/achievement (APL/A), action planning, individual learning programmes, 'top-up' facilities, roll-on roll-off, assessment on demand, records of achievement, credit accumulation, work-based learning and work-based assessment' (p. 2).

Leaving aside the veracity and legitimacy of this utopian vision for colleges, what needs to be said is that none of these essentially technicist procedures means a movement away from didacticism towards the experiential approaches discussed earlier. Traditional teacher-centred approaches are not necessarily changed by introducing needs analysis, action planning and roll on/roll off scheduling of programmes, just as, as Edwards (1993) noted, programmes for unemployed adults are not suddenly liberalized by the importation of progressive methods. Indeed, the British progressive tradition was notorious for its so-called 'procedural' openness (Hyland, 1978), that is, its employment and utilization of innovations such as the integrated day and open planning (Dearden, 1976) which introduced changes in approach without altering the ultimate ends and rationale of the educational enterprise. There was more than a hint of superficiality and even contradiction in this attempt to be open on means but closed on ends.

The NCVQ claims about learning present a rather different kind of contradiction which are well brought out in the FEU's endorsement of the alleged merits of NVQs within the context of making colleges more flexible. We are told that NVQs, which are 'independent of learning' and 'defined in terms of outcomes rather than inputs', are 'beginning to bring flexible learning centre stage for most FE colleges' (1992a, pp. 1–2). The tensions between, on the one hand, being independent of learning and, on the other, contributing to the promotion of autonomous learning have already been highlighted on a number of occasions. Autonomous learning is not just *any* sort of learning, and is not synonymous with providing needs analysis or roll on/roll off facilities. Learners are autonomous in so far as they are able to play an active part in the construction of their own learning experiences, and this, as experiential approaches are designed to facilitate, ought to inform all aspects of the educational enterprise, including means and ends, learning and the process of assessment.

NVQs are not conducive to this sort of autonomous learning in any normally accepted sense of the term. The links with so-called 'flexible' learning consist in the fact that, by offering pre-packaged programmes of outcomes independently of courses, they can (theoretically) be offered to any type of client at any time of the academic year. And even this putative advantage has been diluted as NVQs have been tagged on to already existing BTEC and RSA courses! It is a mistake to think that any purported 'flexibility' which may emerge from such approaches would be anything more than technical and administrative, and it is misleading nonsense to suggest, as the FEU account does, that the NCVQ version of flexibility leads to students becoming 'active learners' (p. 2). Moreover, in so far as NVQs may actually restrict-learning growth and development by identifying such development exclusively with the achievement of competences, the upshot, paradoxically, is the exact opposite of flexibility. Such restriction of growth has been suggested by Eraut (1989), Chown and Last (1993), and by Raggatt (1991, 1994). The Warwick study (Hyland, 1993d) reported views of some lecturers on the narrowness of focus and loss of theoretical underpinning in some vocational spheres, and in Raggatt's (1994) study the majority of respondents 'were doubtful that NVQs provided an adequate foundation for progression to higher level qualifications' (p. 66). This seems to militate against both flexibility of options and choice for students, and to circumscribe the continuity and growth of learning in education and training.

Programmes which are concerned exclusively with the satisfaction of predetermined competence criteria have nothing at all to do with the sort of active learning described by Kolb and Gibbs. Thus the concept of teaching which emerges from this approach is less rather than more likely to be informed by the non-didactic insight and rule models which are designed to facilitate learning rather than transmit content. The contradiction in CBET generally and NVQs in particular is that, in the last analysis, it is only 'content', the end-product in the form of competence outcomes, which actually matters. Thus, course tutors may offer lots of advice and counselling about the different options and routes available to students, but if all this eventually leads only to CBET programmes with prespecified outcomes and performance criteria, such tutors could not, without risk of logical contradiction or infringement of the Trades Descriptions Act, legitimately call themselves 'facilitators' or promoters of active learning. Competence outcomes are, in this sense, as traditionally restrictive and inhibiting as the three Rs of the nineteenth-century elementary school or the 'facts' relentlessly and doggedly inculcated in pupils in Mr Gradgrind's academy (Dearden, 1968)!

I would acknowledge that NVQs may have removed barriers to access and extended choices for learners in certain vocational spheres. However, the price that has to be paid for this is a complete loss of control over the direction and end product of learning. Once students have flexibly 'chosen' to follow a particular NVQ route, no further flexibility and choice (outside the normal option open to all students of changing courses) is possible. If a learner wishes to pursue business studies or catering, then certain competences, along with their associated performance criteria, must be achieved. Even the potentially liberating mechanism of APL/A (another fashionable notion 'borrowed' from contemporary practice by the NCVQ) is negated by the inevitable narrowing of all prior learning and experience of students to those particular elements which are relevant to the satisfaction of prespecified competences (NCVQ, 1989). Lecturers and trainers involved in such a process cannot help but be influenced, to a greater or lesser extent, by having to work towards ends which are narrowly circumscribed and assessed in a mechanical and inflexible fashion. In such circumstances, as many of the available studies show, teachers have to be especially determined and conscientious if they are to do anything but pay lip service to the ideas of experiential and active learning.

CONCLUSION

The NCVQ model of CBET is based on a behaviourist learning foundation which, though possibly adequate for lower-level tasks and skills, cannot meet the requirements for the upgrading of VET and the enhancement of the status of vocational studies currently being made by most people concerned with post-16 education (Whiteside *et al.*, 1992; NCE, 1993). Notwithstanding the confused and equivocal position of NVQs as to whether they are independent of learning programmes or conducive to particular kinds of learning, the upshot of implementing NVQs in practice seems to be a reduced curriculum, a narrowing of focus which marginalizes knowledge and theory, and, because of an administratively cumbersome assessment system, a serious delimitation of student–teacher interaction. The NCVQ rhetoric about active and autonomous learning is not matched by the reality of lecturers and trainers in the post-school sector striving to maintain a commitment to and emphasis on process in the face of strategies which seem to be exclusively concerned with products. Moreover, the segmented and compartmentalized assessment framework of NVQs seems to be inimical to growth, development and progression in learning.

The behaviourist-inspired learning foundation of NVQs seems to be utterly inappropriate in the light of the current needs of the post-16 system, for which experiential approaches informed by the cognitive/humanistic tradition are far more suitable. There is, moreover, a mismatch and potential conflict between NVQ procedures and preferred models of learning and teaching in mainstream further and adult education which assume active reflection on the part of learners and a dynamic interrelationship between learning, teaching and assessment along the lines of the 'learning by doing' model.

In the last analysis, NVQs are primarily (and even obsessively) concerned with producing evidence to satisfy competence performance criteria, and this is quite different from the development of learning. Thus, whatever NVQ proponents of the NCVQ literature may *claim* about the impact of the system on educational activities, the excessive concentration on *outcomes* cannot convince anyone that teaching and learning *per se* is either valued or encouraged by programmes leading to the award of NVQs.

Chapter 5

Knowledge and Competence

It was noted in earlier chapters that, along with the uncertainty about what competence actually is, there was an accompanying ambiguity and equivocation about the role of knowledge and understanding in the literature on CBET. From the original notions of competence as what a person can do rather than what a person knows, there was a growing and (in the case of certain CBET 'fundamentalists', see Black and Wolf, 1990, p. 13) a somewhat grudging acknowledgement that, certainly for anything beyond the most basic routine tasks, the assessment of competence could not be based solely on performance evidence but must take account of underpinning knowledge and understanding. The incorporation of knowledge and understanding was a function of the development of NVQs at higher levels at which the notion of 'sufficiency of evidence' (Jessup, 1990b, p. 32) was becoming a cause of concern. The changes were also linked to the growing popularity of the notions of core and transferable skills in the 16 to 19 curriculum, which seemed to require something more than the occupationally specific NVQ conceptions of competence (an evolution whose logical conclusion was the introduction of GNVQs).

It would be churlish to criticize the attempts of NCVQ to accommodate the new demands being made on its assessment system. Such evolution can be seen as a natural consequence of developing any educational innovation, and, moreover, it demonstrates a certain willingness to respond to criticisms and changing conditions. What is open to criticism, however, is what has been done with knowledge and understanding in the attempt to make it fit the particular requirements of the NVQ system. Knowledge is treated in an extremely cavalier fashion and accounts are (as with descriptions of competence itself) confused, ambiguous and, in some cases, downright bizarre and counter-educational!

For a system concerned principally with vocational qualifications, it is, arguably, legitimate for NVQs to interpret knowledge and understanding in a 'second order', instrumental way in terms of its practical implications for competent performance in employment. What is lacking in the NCVQ accounts, however, is any coherent account of what sort of knowledge is being referred to in the context of CBET and how precisely this knowledge is meant to be related to performance. Before examining examples of the NVQ literature on the topic, it would be useful to look at some basic distinctions within epistemology (theory of knowledge) so as to provide a background against which to locate the NCVQ perspective.

KNOWLEDGE AND EDUCATION

From the time of the ancient Greeks, the concepts of knowledge and education have been linked in the sense that the early Greek idea of a 'liberal education' – concerned with 'knowledge for its own sake' so as to 'free the mind from error' (Schofield, 1972, p. 150) – was closely allied to a search for the conditions which distinguished truth from falsehood and knowledge from opinion. Interestingly, the love of knowledge for its own sake (*philosophia*) was recommended by Plato as the surest way to intellectual freedom and rational behaviour and contrasted unfavourably with 'applied knowledge' which was thought to be prone to error (Schofield, pp. 152ff., traces the influences of these distinctions on the development of liberal and vocational studies).

Inheriting the Greek concern with knowledge as the pursuit of truth and certainty, contemporary philosophers of education have been particularly concerned with the exploration and characterization of knowledge as a preliminary to making recommendations for educational practice. Knowledge figures prominently in most lists of educational aims and objectives (see O'Connor, 1968), and Hirst and Peters (1970) give it pride of place, arguing that 'education suggests not only that what develops in someone is valuable but also that it involves the development of knowledge and understanding' (p. 19). Whitehead (1966) similarly asserts that 'education is the acquisition of the art of the utilisation of knowledge' (p. 6).

In this context, it is helpful to distinguish between knowledge as a body of ideas, facts or data (forms of knowledge, subjects or disciplines) and the 'conditions of knowledge', the criteria which have to be satisfied before any claim to knowledge can be confirmed or deemed justified. Scheffler (1965) sets out these conditions in schematic fashion as follows (p. 21):

X (any person) knows that Q (any item of knowledge) if and only if
1. X believes that Q
2. X has adequate evidence that Q
3. Q (is true)

This account is intended to reinforce the standard philosophical definition of knowledge as 'justified true belief' by insisting that belief, evidence and truth criteria must all be satisfied before any claim to know that something is the case can be confirmed. Ayer (1956) alludes to the same basic criteria in the claim that 'the necessary and sufficient conditions for knowing that something is the case are first that what one is said to know be true, secondly that one be sure of it, and thirdly that one should have the right to be sure' (p. 35).

At the level of organized bodies of knowledge, a number of architectonic principles and systems of classification have been adopted in epistemology generally and philosophy of education in particular. The medieval curriculum was based on the 'Trivium' of grammar, logic and rhetoric which were regarded as the 'essential instruments of knowledge which would enable pupils who aspired to university education to study the more difficult subjects of the Quadrivium' (Curtis, 1965, p. 145). Such constructions of knowledge, still based to a large extent on the writings of Plato and Aristotle, eventually came to inform (suitably tempered by the Reformation and the Renaissance) the notion of a classical education and the aristocratic 'gentleman ideal' (Wilkinson, 1970) which dominated the development of state schooling in Britain. As I suggest in later chapters, it is this conception of education which is at the root of the damaging vocational/academic divide in contemporary studies.

The standard classical curriculum derived its rationale and prestige, not so much from any content thought to be intrinsically worthwhile, but from its endorsement by and association with the most powerful political and economic groups in Britain (Hyland, 1993b). This is not to say that such a curriculum was incapable of independent justification on educational or epistemological grounds. Although Marxian theorists would claim that no system of education can be divorced from its political and economic context (e.g., Bowles and Ginitis, 1976), it does seem possible to offer an educational rationale for curriculum planning which – while acknowledging the claims of critical theorists that all knowledge is in a sense socially constructed and a product of particular forms of socio-economic arrangements (Gibson, 1986) – gives due weight to *epistemological* rather than social or economic considerations.

Perhaps the most influential (though also controversial and contested) recent attempt to offer an epistemological rationale for curriculum organization within philosophy of education is to be found in Hirst's work on 'forms of knowledge'. Hirst (1974) claimed originally that over the years the domain of knowledge had been progressively differentiated into a number of distinct forms which are distinguishable from each other by virtue of their central concepts, their distinctive logical structure, their truth criteria (ways of testing claims to knowledge) and their particular methodology (pp. 43–4). Furthermore, it is argued that these distinct forms of knowledge – initially they were listed as mathematics, physical sciences, human sciences, history, religion, literature and the fine arts and philosophy (though in later versions the terminology is altered, see Hirst and Peters, 1970, pp. 63–4) – form the basis of that development of knowledge and understanding which is at the heart of a liberal education. Although curriculum-planning has been influenced by a wide range of epistemological models over the last two or three decades – such as Phenix's notion of 'realms of meaning' (1964) and Skilbeck's ideas on school-based curriculum development (Reynolds and Skilbeck, 1976) – Hirst's writings still play a prominent part in mainstream discourse on the organization of the curriculum (if only as a position to be contended with; see Kerr, 1968; Taylor and Richards, 1985).

Thus far the discussion of knowledge, both in terms of its conditions and its organizational features, has been concerned with propositional knowledge, or 'knowing that'. Although Hirst does refer to 'fields of knowledge', such as geography or economics, which consist of a combination of forms and of theoretical and practical elements (Hirst, 1974, p. 46), the domain of knowledge was 'essentially the domain of true propositions or statements' (p. 85). But the domain of knowledge is surely far wider than the domain of true statements or knowledge *that* something is the case, for we also speak generally of people knowing *how* to, for example, ride a bicycle, read a technical drawing or understand and speak a foreign language. Although this domain is, of course, recognized in mainstream philosophy of education, it has perhaps received less emphasis and attention than it merits.

Pring (1976) characterizes the knowing that/knowing how distinction as one between a 'belief-type and procedural-type knowledge' and argues that 'so much of the school curriculum is concerned with knowing that [yet] . . . so often primacy ought to be given to procedural knowledge or knowing how' (p. 18). This may have been true of the curriculum in the 1970s, but, following the vocationalization of the system which has been increasing apace from the early 1980s, it is no longer the case (except, of course, in terms of elitist 'gold standard' A-level perspectives which persist in the ranks of the 'old humanists'!). Indeed, it is fair to say that, not only have the procedural or practical versions of knowledge had rather more than their fair share of attention in the form of the curriculum developments described in earlier chapters, but also that an element of 'throwing the baby out with the bathwater' has occurred in the sense that valuable theoretical or propositional knowledge has been removed from programmes in the interests of utilitarian or work-related efficiency and relevance (Smithers, 1993). The upshot is, in many cases, an impoverished programme of VET which now has to be supplemented by core skills and GNVQ initiatives!

However, the idea of the practical, the procedural or knowledge how is clearly of special importance in the context of VET since, whatever theoretical versions of knowledge are involved in vocational pursuits, it is the practical applications of this knowledge which take priority. In view of this, it is surprising that the knowing that/knowing how distinction, and the domain of practical knowledge, has not been given greater attention in the NCVQ and CBET literature. Indeed, it seems to be the case that all such theoretical or philosophical concerns with definitions and distinctions are completely submerged in the esoteric discourse surrounding standards and performance!

KNOWLEDGE AND NVQs

Black and Wolf (1990) admit that the 'problems associated with the lack of consensus on what we mean exactly by "knowledge and understanding" are compounded in the "Standards" context by the commitment in the programme as a whole to *performance*' (p. 13). Such a lack of consensus is, indeed, difficult to overlook since it reveals itself throughout the NCVQ literature in the unsystematic and cavalier handling of the idea of knowledge and, in order to make the concept fit the NVQ framework, the tendency to invent new stipulated and seemingly arbitrary definitions of knowledge to serve the purposes of the CBET assessment system.

Although the earlier interpretations of competence stressed the primacy of performance, with an insistence that competence refers to what people can do rather than with what they know, this did not, of course, imply an assumption that competent performance was totally independent of knowledge and understanding. It was considered, rather, that 'if a person performs competently we need not be concerned with what he or she knows' (Jessup, 1991, p. 121). Later formulations introduced the notions of 'range statements' and 'second order measures' to check and ensure the transferability of competence to different contexts, and this entailed the testing of knowledge and understanding, provided that it was directly related to the competence being tested.

It cannot be stressed too often that competence strategies are concerned only with measurement, assessment and accreditation, not with learning and education *per se*, and the discussion of knowledge in the literature reveals this most forcefully. Mansfield's (1990) claim that 'to perform competently, we need knowledge, understanding and skills' (p. 15) serves to remind us of the unequivocal instrumentalist thrust of the debate in this area. The primary concern is not with learning or the development of understanding, but with identifying 'what people need in their heads to perform effectively with their hands, feet, voice, eyes, and so on'. Moreover, there is 'no justification for assessing knowledge for its own sake but only for its contribution to competent performance' (Jessup, 1991, pp. 121, 123).

This no-nonsense instrumentalism would, of course, delight behaviourists and appal advocates of liberal education (see Bailey, 1984). Recognizing all this, however, what I want to concentrate on is the confusion, incoherence and ambiguity which character-izes conceptions of knowledge in this sphere. Even if we accept the overriding practical concern with assessment and the measurement of standards and performance, advocates of competence still need to explain what sort of knowledge is meant to underpin competence and just how the connection between knowledge and compet-ence is to be conceived. The confusion about the precise nature of competence itself, compounded by the determination to pick out only those items of knowledge thought to be directly related to elements of competence, has resulted in a position which is epistemologically equivocal and theoretically suspect.

Although there is a rich and varied field of different formulations to choose from, the literature on competence reveals no clear consensus about what knowledge is or how it is meant to underpin competence. Wolf (1989) tells us that knowledge and understand-ing are 'constructs which have to be inferred from observable behaviour, just as much as competence itself' (p. 45). But this rather strange assertion glosses over the fact that there is a world of difference between assessing the knowledge and understanding we hope to develop in, say, history or science, which needs to take account of a wide range of cognitive abilities, skills and values, and concentrating only on that knowledge which is thought to underpin competent performance. Even if we accept that some sort of 'inference' is going on in these different cases of assessment, the criteria and evaluation techniques are surely vastly different according to whether we are interested in historical knowledge, scientific understanding, vocational competence, or even the knowledge and understanding which is said to underpin competence. Because all these various achievements need to be 'inferred' in some way, this does not mean that they are similar either in kind or degree.

Although Jessup (1991) is commendably critical of the 'black box' behaviourism of early competence assessment, a residual attachment to the early fundamentalism is reflected in his subsequent treatment of knowledge. After quite correctly noting the existence of 'cognitive skills' such as problem-solving and perceptual skills, he goes on to assert that skills 'refer to a process that leads to an outcome, while knowledge may be elicited as an abstraction from behaviour (e.g. facts, principles, theories)' (p. 121). Talk of 'skills' (an earlier counterpart and forerunner of competence in the 1980s process of vocationalization) is as loose as talk of competence, but the interesting aspect of Jessup's claim is that it still betrays an attachment to functionalist behaviourism which leads to a complete mis-characterization of knowledge and understanding. We are mistakenly led into thinking that skills are practical and active whereas knowledge is theoretical and passive. On this account it would be difficult to understand how someone could be a 'skilled historian' or a 'knowledgeable footballer'! Knowledge is not always an abstraction from behaviour, nor are skills always practical or outcome-orientated (Barrow, 1987).

Mansfield (1990) further defines the knowledge relevant to the assessment of competence in terms of 'outcome evidence', 'content evidence' and 'process evidence' (p. 19), and Bartram (1990) wants to distinguish between 'declarative knowledge', knowledge as a 'body of facts', and 'procedural knowledge' which 'can be inferred from one's actions' (p. 55). But if, as Wolf claims, both knowledge and competence are to be inferred from behaviour, how is it possible to distinguish between procedural and declarative knowledge on the grounds of inference from actions? For that matter, if both knowledge and competence are said to be behavioural constructs, how can it make sense to mark a division between 'first order measures' which look at performance only, and 'second order measures' which examine performance under-pinned by knowledge and understanding (Wolf, 1990, p. 34)?

All this confusion and equivocation seems to be the result of attempting to capture and describe, in behaviourist terms, something which is essentially non-behaviouristic, namely, the development of knowledge and understanding. In order to maintain the desired direct contact with behaviour and observable performance, competence theorists have clearly been forced to manipulate knowledge so that it fits the preferred framework. The upshot is a conception of knowledge, understanding and human behaviour which is not just viciously reductionist, but also utterly naive and simplistic.

KNOWING HOW, PERFORMANCE AND COMPETENCE

The sort of epistemological considerations which seem to be suggested by the literature on knowledge and competence are those raised by Ryle (1973) in his well-known discussion of the differences between 'knowing how' and 'knowing that'. Ryle's project was to explode the myth of the 'intellectualist legend', the 'dogma of the ghost in the machine' which led people to the mistaken belief that 'the intelligent execution of an operation must embody two processes, one of doing and another of theorizing' (p. 32). The following passage from *The Concept of Mind* – which, with its reference to 'competences', might easily be taken by NVQ apologists as an early philosophical justification of their position (if only they ever sought such a justification!) – neatly summarizes the central arguments and Ryle's alternative thesis: 'In ordinary life . . . as well as in the special business of teaching, we are much more concerned with people's competences than with their cognitive repertoires, with the operations than with the truths that they learn' (p. 28). Ryle's thesis, and related discussions about 'knowing how' and 'knowing that', have spawned a large literature within philosophy of education, and it is worth picking out some points and arguments which have a bearing on the examination of competence.

The tendency to a simplistic view of knowledge in the competence literature was noted earlier and, in examining Ryle's version of intelligent action, Gribble (1969, pp. 59ff.) warns us of the dangers (caused, admittedly, by an over-simple reading of Ryle) of assuming that 'knowing that' is to be equated with the passive storing of 'facts' or 'information'. He points out that even a knowledge of simple propositions involves such things as an awareness of the differences between facts and values, and between truth and falsehood, and entails the making of judgements and the appeal to evidential conditions. Thus, knowing that Paris is the capital of France is not reducible to the performance of saying 'Paris' whenever the question, 'What is the capital of France?' is asked. If this were the case, parrots could be said to have 'knowledge' about all sorts of subjects!

The key mistake here is to equate knowledge with public *tests* for knowledge. One way of determining a person's knowledge of history would be to devise some sort of public examination to assess this knowledge, but it would be a gross error to conflate the examination performance and the person's knowledge of history. Similarly, in spite of what Hare once said (1964, p. 1), we do not make decisions and judgements about a person's moral beliefs or character solely on the basis of observing that person's behaviour.

The tendency to over-simplify in this area has led to various attempts (in spite of Ryle's warning against such reductionism; 1973, pp. 57–8) to reduce propositional to practical knowledge with the claim that 'knowing that' something is the case is equivalent to 'knowing how' to satisfy certain performance criteria. Roland Martin (1961), for instance, discusses Ryle's distinction in a way which suggests an attachment to such a position when she observes that 'know is a dispositional term' and that 'knowing that' can be translated into 'knowing how to answer a question or to state a fact' (p. 62).

Although it is possible to analyse some cases of propositional knowledge is this performance-linked dispositional way, these cases do not exhaust the domain of propositional knowledge and involve far more sophisticated skills than Roland Martin allows for. J. L. Austin's examination of 'performative utterances' is relevant here, particularly his identification of ritual phrases such as 'I warn', 'I order', 'I promise', etc., which were deemed to be not descriptions but performances of certain sorts of acts. In the process of examining such acts, Austin (1970) makes the intriguing observation that 'stating something is performing an act just as much as giving an order or giving a warning' (p. 251). Elsewhere, Austin spoke of the 'fallacy' of supposing that 'I know' is a descriptive phrase and argued that 'if you say you *know* something . . . you must undertake to show, not merely that you are sure of it, but that it is within your cognisance' (pp. 100, 103, author's italics).

Austin's main concern here was to demonstrate the fuzziness of the descriptive/performative distinction by identifying a peformative dimension of making statements. Over and above this, he was simply drawing attention to the evidential conditions of knowledge, and there was no implication that the whole domain of knowledge could be covered by the idea of performances. In addition, it should be noted that Austin's primary concern here was with a certain special class of formal speech acts (usually made in the first person), and not with knowledge claims in general. Thus, 'I know' and 'I state' become suitable candidates for performative analysis but, of course, propositional knowledge (and, indeed, practical know-how) exists outside and independently of such constructions. Indeed, it seems to me that claims to knowledge are not typically made in this personal and direct way and that the assessment of knowledge in educational contexts rarely involves an evaluation of performance in Austin's sense of the term (see Scheffler, 1965, pp. 25–9).

It is important for our discussion to be clear about what is being claimed in the analysis of knowledge as performance, so that we are not misled into simplistic and misguided reductionism. All that is being said is that, if I make a claim to knowledge, such a claim needs to be publicly justified; this does not mean, however, that knowledge only exists in public acts of justification. To conflate knowledge and its justification would be to make the mistake referred to earlier of equating knowledge with public tests for knowledge.

The significance of evidential conditions referred to in Austin's account helps to bring out the rather naive and simplistic thrust of thinking that propositional knowledge can be interpreted solely in terms of knowing how to state facts or answer questions. Such a view not only seriously underestimates what is involved in knowing facts, but also provides ammunition for those who wish to portray knowledge and understanding as inert and passive against the apparently active and dynamic business of ensuring that we try to 'assess the knowledge required to underpin and extend competent performance' (Jessup, 1991, p. 127). Bailey demonstrates clearly how those proponents of the 'economic utility model' of education have managed to belittle the knowledge and understanding characteristic of liberal education by means of stock phrases such as 'knowledge without skill' and 'able to understand but not to act'. As an antidote, Bailey (1989) points to the 'rich evidential sense' of coming to know and to understand and argues that

> To know and to understand in this sense is to be able to follow and to practise particular kinds of investigative procedures, weigh evidence, make judgments and decide what to believe and what not to believe; to decide how to see things and how not to see things. Being able to explain things to oneself in this kind of way, with attention to consistency and coherence, is the first step to being able to explain them to others. (pp. 233–4)

KNOWLEDGE IN THE NCVQ SYSTEM

Against this background, it is now possible to pick out a number of significant weaknesses in the epistemological position of the NCVQ model of CBET.

1. There is a bewildering range of conceptions of knowledge in the competence literature, and confusion over what kind of knowledge is meant to be related to competence, and how exactly it is so related. In so far as it is possible to identify any commonality, there seems to be an attachment to some version of Ryle's thesis (though Ryle is not cited in justification) in the sense that performance is given a central position and knowledge is allowed to enter the picture only on condition that it is directly relevant to competent practice. As Debling (1989) maintains: 'Where knowledge is a specific requirement it has to be demonstrated' (p. 88).

This view of knowledge is both incomplete and over-simple. Ryle's observation that when we evaluate competent performance we are evaluating one thing (doing), not two things (thinking then doing), needs to be placed in context. Ryle was concerned with the evaluation or *appraisal* of action and, in this area, stressed the need to appraise the action as a whole, not its separate mental and physical aspects (in this sense, the NCVQ method of trying to identify relevant knowledge to support performance for assessment purposes is in conflict with Ryle's account). Ryle did not want to claim that the mental components of behaviour were of lesser importance; his intention was 'not to deny or depreciate the role of intellectual operations, but only to deny that the execution of intelligent performances entails the additional execution of intellectual operations' (1973, p. 48).

On this account, competence strategies are guilty of two cardinal errors: first, they separate the mental and the physical components of performance and attempt to appraise these separately, and, second, they mistakenly give performance pride of place in evaluating competence and seriously underestimate the role of knowledge and understanding.

2. Even if we allow that, for competent performances in the area of VET, the relevant knowledge will typically be of a 'knowing how' or practical kind, the descriptions of this underpinning knowledge in the literature are undiscriminating and one-dimensional. The position here is very similar to that in respect of the recent emphasis on 'skills' in education (see Barrow 1987; Smith, 1987), in that we have a central concept of something claimed to be definite, measurable and observable, yet the conception is both dangerously simplistic and overestimates the importance of the physical at the expense of the intellectual aspects of activities.

It was noted above that Roland Martin's account of 'knowing that' was based on a number of misunderstandings about propositional knowledge. Notwithstanding this, the description she offers of 'knowing how' is much more discriminating and provides some fruitful ideas. In particular, she makes a distinction between two types of knowing how which can be usefully applied to the examination of the connections between practical knowledge and competent behaviour. Dispositions to act that are picked out by knowing how claims can refer to knowledge based on practice or knowledge derived from experience and understanding (1961, pp. 62–3). Learning how to swim or speak a foreign language, for example, are typical cases of skills developed through practice. The ability to deal with problems in science or examining moral questions, on the other hand, demands a level of understanding and experience which (though not ruling out elements of practice completely) clearly requires long-term fostering and development (hence the folly of using the term 'skill' to cover activities as wide apart as riding a bicycle or doing history; see Barrow, 1987, p. 189).

What makes the 'experience-dependent' cases of knowing how different from the 'practice-based' ones is that the former (but not the latter) involve the exercise of intellectual capacities of the kind labelled by Geach 'mental acts'. Against Ryle's tendency to reduce psychological states to hypothetical dispositions to act in certain ways, Geach (1971) points out that there are 'acts of judgment' (pp. 8–9) which are independent of behaviour and dispositions but which need to be incorporated into descriptions and explanations of conduct and action. On this account, it is not possible, for instance, to characterize the differences between the states of mind of two people by saying that there are circumstances in which one person would act differently from the other. As Geach observes, when two people differ in their behaviour 'we look for some actual, not merely hypothetical, difference between them to account for this' (p. 5). We are thus led to an investigation of the mental character of dispositions and behaviour, and Geach picks out the ability to perform acts of judgement as a typical illustration of such traits. Moreover, these acts of judgement presuppose the possession of a wide range of other capacities of a logical, linguistic and conceptual kind.

3. Geach's subtle critique of aspects of Ryle's thesis serves to remind us of the dangers of reductionist behaviourism and the naivety and inadequacy of competence-based education in its reliance upon such a foundation. It was suggested earlier that one consequence of such a position was the tendency on the part of competence proponents to manipulate the concept of knowledge so that it fits the behaviourist mould. Not only does this tend to minimize the extent to which theoretical knowledge is required to generate practice, it also implies that there are some routine activities which need little or no underpinning knowledge for their performance.

Such a position is implicit in the attempt to distinguish 'first order' measures which look solely at observable performance from 'second order' measures which examine performance underpinned by knowledge and understanding. Thus, NVQ level 1 competences which are described as being 'routine and predictable' can be assessed by watching people engaged in activities, whereas at NVQ level 4, concerned with 'competence in a broad range of complex, technical or professional activities' (NCVQ, 1991a, p. 4), observers would need to undertake the separate evaluation of underpinning knowledge and understanding.

However, outside the pragmatic framework of instrumental expediency, there seems to be little justification for this differential approach to assessment. Consider, for instance, a lower-level routine element of competence drawn from the Building Society Sector which requires employees to 'promote the sale of associated products and services to customers' (Mitchell, 1989, p. 59). Now, although such a competence-statement can be simplified by *stipulating* fairly simple criteria, the achievement of satisfactory performance in this area is clearly not so simple, and could involve a good deal of experience, knowledge and understanding of a factual, theoretical and interpersonal kind. This could not be achieved by just mimicking the requisite behaviour, nor could it be assessed by simply observing performance then looking around for bits of knowledge to support this.

The follies of behaviourism are clearly evident here, and are well brought out in Dearden's (1984) critique of behaviour modification which was mentioned in Chapter 4. In a similar way, Giddens (1984) demonstrates, in examining the bases of social interaction, how we evaluate the 'competence of actors' by utilizing that 'practical consciousness' which is founded on 'mutual knowledge . . . not directly accessible to the consciousness of actors'. In our relationships with others and judgements of actions we 'routinely and for the most part without fuss maintain a continuing "theoretical understanding" of the grounds of their activity' (pp. 4–6). Just as NVQ competence-statements are misguided in their conception of performance as active and knowledge as passive, so the minimalist and generally atheoretical conception of activity in the competence literature leads to an emasculated and impoverished view of human behaviour. Eraut (1989) is right to take the NCVQ to task for advocating such a position, and correct to assert that 'people use theory all the time . . . it is their personal theories which determine how they interpret the world and their encounters with people and situations within it' (p. 184). Whether such theoretical underpinnings can be brought into the sphere of assessment through something called 'capability evidence', as Eraut has recently suggested (1993, p. 15), is rather more problematic. Certainly, capability (as the Royal Society of Arts project has demonstrated, Burgess, 1986) can be a useful term in the discussion of higher level and professional learning and knowledge (this is referred to again in Chapter 7). However, it cannot (no more than the more dubious construction of 'meta-competence') be asked to carry the full weight of the efforts to integrate theory and practice, particularly when this is conceived purely in terms of evidence.

4. Another consequence of the behaviourist manipulation of knowledge in writings on competence is its undiscriminating treatment by NVQ practitioners (the imprecision and confusion about the concept of competence is also a feature of references to knowledge and understanding). This treatment is based on erroneous assumptions, not only because knowledge is consistently downgraded in value against practice or performance, but also in its suggestion that knowledge and understanding (often given stipulated definitions and labelled in bizarre ways) are optional extras which can be brought into play, constructed and deconstructed as required, in order to service the assessment of competence. As Elliott (1993) notes in his critique of CBET in teacher education, the behaviourist thrust means that 'the significance of theoretical knowledge in training is a purely technical or instrumental one'. He goes on to observe that, according to this approach to education and training, 'Knowledge belongs to the realm of inputs rather than outputs. Its introduction can only be justified if it is a necessary condition for generating the desired behavioural outcomes of learning' (p. 17).

The false picture of knowledge which emerges from a reading of the competence literature has certain similarities to that offered in Bloom's (1956) taxonomy of educational objectives for the cognitive domain, in that we come across the same contextless and disembodied statements. Bloom's six levels of cognition – ranging from knowledge of specifics through comprehension, application, analysis and synthesis to the evaluation and comparison of theories and generalizations – are, in fact, strikingly similar in layout and design to parts of the NVQ framework. Gribble (1969) has criticized all such attempts to subdivide knowledge in this way and, in particular, has expressed serious doubts about Bloom's postulated hierarchical progression from 'knowledge of facts' to 'knowledge of principles'. For Gribble, 'knowing something involves judging that something is so, and judgment is a complex mental operation'; the 'appropriate standards and criteria for judging performances which indicate a particular mental ability are those which characterise the various forms of knowledge' (p. 58). Wilson (1972) makes a similar point when he criticizes those educators who are 'bewitched with the common idea that knowledge is like a physical object which can be broken down or built up into a hierarchy of component parts' (p. 106).

Bloom's approach to knowledge was mechanical and atomistic, but it was, at least, systematic and consistent. The same cannot be said about the knowledge prescriptions found in writings about NVQs. Instead of a coherent account, we are offered stipulated categories, such as 'outcome' or 'process' knowledge, which are, without much explanation, utilized at will to pick out 'relevant' items to serve as supplementary evidence of performance. It is simply outrageous, even in a vocational context, to suggest that the pursuit of knowledge is valuable only to the extent that it helps 'to ensure competent performance' or is 'required to facilitate transfer of skills' (Jessup, 1991, p. 123).

5. Finally, advocates of competence-based education are clearly guilty of mistaking and confusing the assessment of x with x itself (a mistake similar to that of identifying 'intelligence' with IQ, see White, 1974). Moreover, this confusion is compounded by the fact that it operates on two levels. Not only is there a tendency to equate the assessment of competence with competence itself, there is also a conflation of the

performance criteria (occupational standards) which determine competence with the performance itself.

This error (already mentioned at various stages in the earlier sections above) is revealed in a number of ways in the competence literature, but is, perhaps, most clearly demonstrated in the tendency to reduce all talk of knowledge, skills, competence, and the like, to talk about *evidence*. Thus, an element of competence such as 'mount and store exposed radiographs', along with certain performance criteria, comes to represent and *instantiate* competence in a particular sphere for dental surgery assistants (Mansfield, 1990, p. 19). In this way, otherwise, 'empty and uninformative' (Ashworth and Saxton, 1990, p. 19) competence statements are given some vestige of meaning by reference to the all-encompassing notion of evidence. As Mansfield (1990) asserts, we begin to 'recognise and locate knowledge in its rightful place' when we come to regard it 'as a source of evidence, together with performance evidence' (p. 21).

Jessup (1990b) provides what is, perhaps, the clearest and most definitive NCVQ account of these matters when he asserts confidently that it is

> not necessary to define what we mean by 'knowledge and understanding' or to distinguish it from other attributes . . . Along with, and in combination with, other basic skills . . . it comprises the repertoire of attributes a person might possess which underpin competent performance. Occupational competence is being able to *apply* these attributes in various combinations to the successful performance of work functions. (p. 39, author's italics)

CONCLUSION

The examination of the treatment of knowledge, understanding and cognate terms in the NVQ literature serves to confirm Jessup's admission that 'the relationships between knowledge, skills and competent performance are not well understood' (1991, p. 132). There is no coherent account of knowledge in NVQ writings, nor is there any adequate distinction between the theoretical (knowing that) and the practical (knowing how), apart from a persistent downgrading of the former in favour of the latter.

The obsession with evidence in the development of NVQ assessment has served to restrict the discussion of the place of knowledge and understanding to purely technical questions which, by themselves, will never add up to a clear and coherent account of the relationship between knowledge, understanding and intelligent behaviour. Moreover, this narrow instrumentalism is compounded in the NCVQ model of CBET by the fact that, as the leading NVQ apologists are constantly reminding us, the system is concerned only with accreditation and is independent of the mode of learning. Having such a remote connection with learning, there has been no incentive for CBET to develop a systematic and coherent VET framework in which the questions about knowledge, skills, theory and practice are connected with the activities of learners. What remains, therefore, is an impoverished knowledge framework linked with a mechanistic and reductionist conception of evidence and standards which cannot provide an adequate foundation for the upgrading of VET and the promotion of a learning culture currently being called for by employers and educators.

Chapter 6

Competence and Vocational Education and Training

More has been written about VET in recent years than perhaps any other single aspect of post-compulsory education. However, as Esland (1990) notes, although VET issues have 'remained high on the political agenda' since the 1970s, the state's response has generally been one of 'crisis management . . . giving rise to schemes and initiatives designed to limit the social damage which followed widespread de-industrialization' (p.v.). Many of these schemes and initiatives formed part of the so-called 'new vocationalism' of the 1970s and 1980s which was discussed in the first chapter. Since the NCVQ had its origins in this background, it was quite natural that NVQs should come to be identified with attempts to upgrade VET and solve the persistent problems of British industrial training with a view to improving economic performance and prosperity.

The official government endorsement of the NCVQ framework in the 1991 White Paper *Education and Training for the 21st Century* (DES, 1991) and the subsequent establishment of NETTs could be regarded as the logical conclusion of the process of VET reform, though (as will be noted in later chapters) the reform of the qualifications system and the 16 to 19 curriculum is still ongoing and the subject of lively debate. I want to argue that this official reform policy and the faith placed in NVQs is, in view of the weaknesses and shortcomings of CBET already outlined, seriously mistaken and misplaced. However, in order to elaborate this position and locate it within the framework of contemporary trends in VET, it would be useful to examine what are considered to be the key problems and the proposed solutions in this area before going on to look at the role of the NCVQ in all this.

THE PROBLEMS OF VET

A number of different strands of argument and debate need to be disentangled in relation to the so-called problems of VET. There is a tendency to conflate the alleged weaknesses of Britain's education and training system with a whole range of different industrial and economic problems. This leads to a confused and distorted picture of our VET provision and, more seriously, tends to result in dangerous one-dimensional views of both educational and economic problems. Thus it becomes natural to move from claims that 'Britain's education and training system is an inefficient and confusing mess' and that 'most of our young people finish formal schooling earlier than in most other industrialised countries' to the assertion that 'successful economies have developed a high-skills, high-value-added industrial and commercial strategy. For Britain, the economic implications of not doing so are painfully obvious' (Bennett *et al.*, 1992, p. 2).

This message – which has the advantage of being clear and easy to understand – is echoed on all sides of industry and education and, expressed in various CBI reports and recent government policy statements, is now an established feature of contemporary educational folklore. However, this interpretation of the problems of VET is far too simplistic and can be misleading in a number of important respects. First, it suggests that Britain's relative economic decline has been *caused* solely by the problems of VET (and the corollary notion that in remedying these problems we also halt the economic decline!) and, second, it relies too heavily on simple, quick-fix solutions to VET which tend to be excessively technicist and superficial, and leave untouched the underlying problems in both the educational and economic spheres.

Since the period of the so-called Great Debate and the beginning of new vocational initiatives in the 1970s, there has been an increasing tendency to correlate VET and economic/industrial performance in a direct and often causal manner. As Whiteside (1992) notes, this sort of interpretation was encouraged by analyses of the problems of British society such as Barnett's *Audit of War* and Wiener's *English Culture and the Decline of the Industrial Spirit* which 'contributed to the development of a set of beliefs among politicians and industrialists that one of the central causes of Britain's prolonged economic decline lay in its education and training system' (p. 4). Raggatt and Unwin (1991) in a similar context suggest that the 'rationale for the structural and curriculum developments in VET in recent years has been the increasingly single-minded pursuit of a vocational education and training system that will enable Britain to contend more effectively in the international competition for world markets' (p. xi).

For all sorts of political, financial and generally prudential reasons, educators and industrialists from all sides have backed the diagnosis and prognosis implicit in this perspective. However, the links between educational change and industrial and economic activity are far more complex and indirect than this rather simplistic version allows for. In the first place, in spite of commonsensical beliefs that investment in education has both individual and social benefits, there are few straightforward or unequivocal proofs of this thesis. As Dore (1976) explains, it 'would be hard to make out a case for believing that the economic growth of Britain was a consequence of improved or expanded education' (p. 14). Although Britain was the first industrial country, it 'was not the pioneer in educational change, whereas many of the less industrialized nations in Europe reacted much more speedily to bring education in line with the needs of developing economies' (Green, 1990, p. 309). Similarly, McMaster (1991) argues that the 'economic miracle' in Japan actually preceded the establishment of its distinctive national education system rather than the other way around, and Wadd (1988) finds little connection between educational change and periods of economic boom and recession. It is at least plausible, he suggests, that 'instead of higher standards (of education) securing prosperity, it is the rich countries that can afford higher standards' (p. 28). Dore expresses similar sentiments through the graphical illustration: 'rich men have Cadillacs; therefore we should get some Cadillacs in order to be rich' (1976, p. 88).

Of course, there must be *some* connection between education and industrial and economic development, it is just that the links are not as simple and straightforward as the standard arguments and slogans would have us believe. On the level of individual investment in education, graduates tend to earn more than non-graduates in most countries (Dore, 1976), and Anderson's '40% literacy threshold' (1965) – the thesis that a 40% school enrolment appears to be a precondition of economic growth – seems to hold good for all the major historical and contemporary cases of economic development. On the other hand, the links between educational achievement and economic benefits are becoming blurred in modern post-industrial states, and both 'manpower planning' and 'human capital theory' (Woodhall, 1990) are both less certain and more ambiguous than in former times. It is indeed ironic that the rather simplistic slogan 'Learning Pays' (Ball, 1991) should have such currency in these confused, troubled and not so simple times!

The consequence of holding to a direct and one-dimensional link between education and the economy is the generation of misleading nostrums about the need for educational change (such as the new vocational initiatives) coupled with a one-sided view which neglects other important features of the situation. As Esland (1990) puts it, the

> displacement of responsibility for economic failure and decline from political and economic arenas to the educational and training institutions (and the individuals within them) has had the effect of distorting public policy debate about the relationship between economic change, education and employment. (p.v.)

Not only does this narrow focus overlook key aspects of Britain's recent economic history – the failure and incoherence of investment and industrial policies, the dominance of finance capital and the erosion of our industrial base and share in world trade – it also produces a one-sided and distorted perspective on the requirements for educational reform in the light of all this. The history of short-lived schemes during the period of the new vocationalism – YTS, TVEI, school compacts, and the like – is symptomatic of this misguided reliance on the promotion of an 'enterprise' culture and a market-forces model of VET as a panacea for all our industrial and educational ills.

THE SOLUTIONS

The main strategic solutions to the problems of de-industrialization, economic recession and spiralling youth unemployment in the 1970s were 'the growing involvement of the state in training, epitomised by the creation of the MSC, and the increasing pressure on schools to be responsive to the needs of industry' (Finn, 1990, p. 47). Both planks of this policy were to be progressively modified, substantially transformed and subsequently abandoned as their irrelevance to the economic climate and requirements of VET came to be questioned during the 1980s.

The role of the MSC and the 'New Training Initiative' were described in Chapter 1. Evans (1992) reports that this experiment in state interventionism really came to an end following the Conservative election victory in 1987, when, worried by the charges of imperialism being levelled against the MSC, a mission was launched to 'roll back the state' (p. 42) in this area. The tensions between a powerful centralized quango committed to interventionism in VET and a government overtly pledged to free-market policies became too embarrassing and, towards the end of its life, the MSC was maintained by the government mainly to deal with high youth unemployment through YTS schemes. As soon as demographic and economic trends made the need for YTS less urgent, the MSC was phased out through its conversion to the Training Commission (later the Training Agency) in 1988.

The 1989 CBI report had established an agenda which eventually resulted in the proposals for change contained in the White Paper *Employment for the 1990s* (DES, 1990). After visiting Boston to investigate the operation of Private Industry Councils (PICs), the then Employment Secretary, Lord Young, became convinced that the PIC model could provide a foundation for the future planning and development of VET in Britain (Evans, 1992). The new policies which emerged from this – the establishment of 82 TECs in England and Wales and the subsequent introduction of Training Credits through which training could be bought by consumers – were heavily influenced by the free-market philosophy of the 'neo-liberals' (Whitty, 1990) in government think tanks such as the Centre for Policy Studies and the Adam Smith Institute.

Although it is perhaps too early to make final judgements, there is little evidence that either the TECs or the training credit mechanisms which they control are achieving any more success than the abortive schemes tried out in the 1970s and 1980s. Both employers and training providers have found difficulty in understanding and operating the training credit scheme; more than half of employers were unaware of the new scheme, and 44 per cent of the young people involved in the credit scheme said that it had not influenced their attitudes towards training (ED, 1992a). A NATFHE report on the pilots concluded that the new system had failed to expand choices and opportunities for young people, and that credits were a high risk and unreliable source of funding for further education colleges (NATFHE, 1993).

Perhaps a large part of the problem lies in the ambiguous status of TECs, which, in spite of all the market rhetoric, actually function as semi-private companies working under state supervision. Certainly, there is little sign that the ultimate aim of making TECs self-financing, funded as well as directed by employers, will be achieved. The budgets and activities of TECs are, in fact, subject to strict government control; as Evans observes, the 'desire to control public expenditure . . . coupled with the need for annual parliamentary scrutiny and control ensured that the eighty-two TECs would never be allowed to float free' (1992, p. 170). TEC directors were quick to point out this lack of autonomy in responding to the highly critical Youthaid report which accused the government of failing to meet the pledge of training places and condemning young people to poverty and poor quality training (Youthaid, 1992). Sir Geoffrey Holland (then at the Employment Department) noted at the time that 'not all TECs are delivering' and that they 'clearly need to develop rapidly and professionally their partnership with education', though 'few had made much progress in this area' (Nash and Prestage, 1992, p. 4).

Evans concludes his analysis of TECs by describing them as 'fascinating, experimental but flawed organisations' (1992, p. 157), and argues that 'too much faith is placed by Conservatives . . . on the impetus of a free training market' (p. 225). Unlike their counterparts in Germany and Japan, British employers, outside a few notable large companies, have shown little interest in investing in VET (even in times of relative prosperity), and the failure of voluntarist schemes in the past does not inspire confidence in current arrangements. Although TECs have stimulated an interest among employers and VET providers at a local level (often through goal-directed and NVQ-linked funding), there is no necessary connection between employers' interests and the national interest in this sphere. British employers have an appalling track record in this area, and there is no evidence that their traditional short-termism will be changed simply through piecemeal tinkering with funding mechanisms for VET. As Maguire (1992) argues, 'by placing employers in control of the TECs, there is no guarantee that their attitude to training will suddenly change and result in their adopting a longer-term perspective'; all in all 'there can be little confidence in the expectation that employers alone can provide the appropriate means to bring about change in the VET system' (p. 103). I would suggest that this observation applies equally to employers' role in the NVQ system as well as to their position in relation to the planning of VET through TECs!

In terms of the VET curriculum and qualifications system, the fostering of 'enterprise' and the attempt to change the motivations and attitudes of students and teachers eventually gave way in the late 1980s to a consideration of the specific content and organization of vocational studies. Certainly, there was something strangely pathetic about the pairing of enterprise with the sort of low-level skills training associated with YTS. Moreover, vocational initiatives of the 1980s tended to 'individualize' or 'personalize' the issues (Esland, 1990) by suggesting that the problems of the British economy were in some sense a reflection of the poor motivation and lack of skills of school leavers. However, as Ainley (1988) points out in his critique of the YTS initiatives, this approach to vocationalism was 'based on the false premise of transition from school to work', whereas 'the problem is not one of transition but of work itself'; 'training, even if it were all training in real skills, cannot of itself produce jobs' (pp. 116–17). In a similar vein, Stronach (1990) has described much of the vocationalism of this period as 'a kind of contemporary magic' (p. 155), a form of reassurance that, because the problems could be individualized in the form of the characteristics of school leavers, solutions were readily available in the form of VET reforms.

More rational approaches to VET following the 1989 CBI report tended to focus on the failures of the system picked out in the comparative studies by Finegold and Soskice (1988) and Jarvis and Prais (1989). The 'low skills–low quality equilibrium' identified by Finegold was linked with our low post-school participation rates, lower levels of qualifications and generally poorer educational attainment levels compared with Germany and other competitors. A view of the problem began to emerge which picked out the early selection and low participation traits of the education system as central to the British malaise, combined with the idea that 'the English system of post-16 education and training is too much influenced by the prestigious academic route designed to meet the needs of an academic elite' (Whiteside, 1992, p. 9). As Whiteside suggests, there is now a powerful 'alliance' of interests (including significant groups in the Labour, Liberal Democrat and Conservative parties, in addition to the CBI, the Employment Department, the Department of Trade and Industry and powerful groups in different sectors of the educational system) with a general consensus on the 'definition of the problem' and broad agreement on an 'agenda for action' (pp. 5–7) which includes:

- the need to increase participation and attainment rates post-16;
- the need to devise a coherent curriculum and qualification system in which 'academic' and 'vocational' elements are equally valued and carry credit transfer;
- the need to improve the quality of teaching and learning;
- the need to develop co-ordinated approaches at all levels to the delivery of 16 to 19 education and training.

This agenda is now a powerful force in educational reform (though there are tensions and conflicts about strategy which will be referred to in later chapters in discussions about schooling and the 16 to 19 curriculum), and was clearly influential in informing the 1991 White Papers on further and higher education leading to the Further & Higher Education Act 1992 which reinforced official support for the NCVQ framework and proposed that the national targets based on NVQs were the answer to all our main problems in the area of VET.

NVQs AND THE REFORM OF VET

It was mentioned in the first chapter that the NVQ framework and the status of NVQs were given a boost through the provisions of the Further & Higher Education Act 1992. Not only was there a commitment to the NVQ framework as a means of reforming VET and upgrading education and training generally, there was a clear message that schools and colleges would be encouraged through financial arrangements 'to offer only NVQs to students pursuing vocational options' (DES, 1991, vol. 1, p. 19). This strategy has subsequently been reaffirmed in official announcements which bring the new GNVQs into the picture, and by the pressures on higher education institutions to consider NVQs at levels 4 and 5 (Tysome, 1993b).

For reasons implicit in the criticisms of NVQs in terms of their implications for learning, assessment and knowledge described in the earlier chapters, I would suggest that this reliance on the framework is misguided and quite radically mistaken – whether the objectives are the reform of VET, enhancing the quality of education and training, upgrading the skills of the workforce, or some other agenda linked with making general education more responsive to industrial and economic needs. In order to elaborate on earlier arguments, it would be useful to explain this case further by looking at issues in three main areas: 1) what employers want from VET; 2) what educators and industrialists seek from a national system; and 3) what seems to make rational educational sense in the light of historical and present requirements given current demands and the recent experience of Britain and other countries.

1. The demands of employers in terms of the education system are notoriously capricious and ambiguous. Employers are often keen to criticize general schooling in broad terms (lack of basic skills and irrelevance to working life), but are less forthcoming with either specific ideas for reform or with the means to bring about such

reform (NCE, 1993). Employers have been complaining about our system of vocational training since at least the time of the Paris Exhibition in 1867, when, even then, we seemed to be falling behind our industrial competitors (Musgrave, 1966). The resurgence of employer interest in education following the Great Debate of the 1970s is simply the continuation of a perennial theme.

A promising line is suggested in the research designed to discover what employers actually want from the system. However, much of this research has produced some strange results which seem rather remote from mainstream issues and requirements. A number of surveys in the 1980s indicated that employers were less interested in academic or occupational achievement than they were in basic skills, personal effectiveness and desirable character traits (Guy, 1991). Indeed, if we were to take seriously the results of some of these surveys – such as the one by Wigan Youth Opportunities Unit in which local employers placed keenness, honesty and reliability at the head of sixteen qualities sought in young workers (Wigan Metro, 1980), or the Bristol Youth Award Survey in which reliability, punctuality and willingness to learn headed the list (Bristol Youth Award, 1989) – then we would concentrate all our attention in VET on values and personal and social education and abandon any specific skills training! The MSC survey which noted that employers were looking 'for a greater willingness and a better attitude to work from young people' (MSC, 1977, p. 17) was representative of this overriding concern with attitudes and values.

Employers' requirements are, it turns out, 'extremely ambiguous', and can in fact be 'contradictory, confused or simply unknown' (Finn, 1990, p. 48). This in itself is worrying, but it takes on greater significance when we reflect that just about everything in the VET field is now meant to be employer-led, from NVQ specifications through to the planning of youth training in regional TECs and the control of governing bodies in the newly incorporated FE colleges. In the context of the reform of VET, this employer dominance takes on a special significance when viewed against the background of employers' poor record of involvement and interest in the nuts and bolts of the vocational curriculum.

The claims made by the NCVQ about the benefits of NVQs to employers were questioned in Chapter 1. Not only is there little evidence of active employer interest and participation in NVQs (outside the large company representatives on lead bodies), there is also genuine doubt that the system is really employer-led (Field, 1993b). The widespread ignorance and indifference might conceivably be overcome by the NCVQ public relations campaigns, though there is very little indication of this at present. What is more problematic, however, is the evidence that, when employers do learn exactly what NVQs mean, many of them seem to like them a lot less than pre-NVQ qualifications, in spite of all their flaws and inadequacies (Smithers, 1993). The evidence cited in earlier chapters on these issues is well summed up in Callender's (1992) report on NVQs in the construction industry which found, alongside the appalling ignorance, apathy and confusion of employers, NVQs which were

> unduly limited in terms of the breadth of the activity they refer to and the demands they make on skills, knowledge and understanding. They are tending to squeeze out general job knowledge because of their emphasis on performance. This narrowness may therefore encourage rigidity rather than the flexible application of skills. Consequently, some training providers feel that standards are dropping. (p. 21)

In a similar vein, a recent survey on NVQs in relation to training credits noted that some 'employers saw training in ways diametrically opposed to an NVQ approach', which was often thought to be 'only loosely related to the workplace' (ESRC, 1993, p. 2). At another level, representatives of some occupational sectors have reacted to the unstoppable expansion of NCVQ activities by adopting a pragmatically offensive stance designed to wrest control from the quango. As the assistant secretary of the Institute of Electronics and Electrical Incorporated Engineers stated recently: 'NVQs have great potential, but the system is too bureaucratic-led. Not enough people from the sharp end of industry are being involved' (THES, 1993, p. 5).

Even if we had a more full-blooded employer commitment to NVQs and education and training, there is very little evidence to justify the claims that an employer-led system will result in the desired reforms in VET. As mentioned earlier, voluntarism in this area has not produced the goods in the past, and there is no reason to believe that the initiatives surrounding training credits and NVQs will do so in the future. Moreover, there is every reason to doubt that regional employer interests will coincide with national requirements for VET.

In addition, there is a clear mismatch between what NVQs are designed to do and what educators and industrialists claim is required if we are to achieve a quality system of education and training. The emerging consensus (the alliance's 'agenda for action' mentioned earlier) seems to be that our system needs a general upgrading to achieve the highly skilled workforce recommended in the various CBI reports and by the National Commission on Education (NCE, 1993). Not only have NVQs failed to meet requirements in this respect, but, arguably, they are structurally incapable of fostering the high-level education and training implicit in the reform programme (Smithers, 1993). As the 1993 National Commission report observed, NVQs place 'emphasis on jobs as they are currently organised, with no regard to how they might develop in the future'; such an approach 'emphasises practical capability at the expense of underlying principles and knowledge' (p. 280).

Apart from the evidence of de-skilling and loss of broad theoretical perspectives as a result of the implementation of NVQs, there is the brute fact that most NVQs thus far achieved are at levels 1 and 2, with 37 per cent at level 1 (Field, 1993a). Even if the NVQ system were concerned with education and training (rather than the accredita-tion of outputs), this would mean that most of it fell way below the most basic requirements of education for 16-year-olds – hardly suggestive of a move to a highly skilled workforce! But the significant point here is that, even if more of the NVQs thus far developed had been at higher levels, the mechanistic and circumscribed nature of the system would still be a long way short of the perceived requirements of VET reform and the upgrading of skills in the workforce.

Comparisons between different occupational groups in terms of skills requirements in Britain, France and Germany (Steedman and Wagner, 1989; Hayes, 1989; Smithers, 1993) have indicated consistently that NVQs are too narrow in outlook, and too concerned with low-level task-based standards to raise the general level of workforce skills and training. The study by Jarvis and Prais (1989) of training for retailing in France and Britain concluded that the NVQ's approach was

> narrowly job-specific ('competence-based'); their exclusion of externally marked written tests of technical knowledge and of general educational subjects will, we fear, lead to a

certificated semi-literature under-class – a section of the workforce inhibited in job-flexibility, and inhibited in the possibilities of progression. (p. 70).

Leaving aside the technical disputes about the relative value of written as opposed to practical skill tests, the key points here about general educational attainment and 'flexibility' – echoed in all the critical studies of NVQs cited – fly in the face of the current demands and programme for reform of the British system. What is required is a *broadening* of the general educational base, rather than a narrow concentration on occupationally specific skills. As White (1990) has observed, purely technical or vocational training will not provide people with the sort of flexible and transferable skills required in post-Fordist economies; the 'flexibility required by this occupational context can only be supplied and accredited by *educational* means' (p. 11, author's italics). GNVQs and the development of core skills can be seen as a belated attempt to remedy some key shortcomings of CBET in this respect, though whether this will be sufficient to achieve the desired goals is still a contentious issue (discussed further in Chapter 8).

The narrowness of focus and mechanistic assessment of occupational tasks associated with NVQs are by no means the only handicaps of CBET approaches in terms of the requirements of VET reform. There is a sense in which a system based on the functional analysis of occupational tasks, combined with an insistence that assessment must be work-based or at least work-related, can never produce general transferable or future-orientated skills at any level. First, as mentioned already in other contexts, by tying NVQ accreditation to workplace roles, mobility and opportunities for occupational development are severely restricted. In NCVQ terms, such change and development becomes possible only by changing work roles and functions. How can this cater for people who want to train for *different* roles in the future?

Second, the obsession with performance outcomes characteristic of the NVQ system does not allow for the development of learning and thinking skills, two key areas (particularly in relation to understanding systems and technology) identified in recent American studies of 'What Work Requires of Schools' (Kelsey and Cushing, 1992). The satisfaction of performance criteria, or the generation of evidence to satisfy such criteria, is simply the recording of *present* skills and abilities (often in narrowly circumscribed contexts), and this is quite different from the fostering of capacities and understanding for use in *future* education or work situations. Thus, without quite radical modifications, NVQs fall some way short of providing a programme of education and training.

3. All members of society have a stake in (and, as taxpayers, carry the burden for) our national systems of education and training, and, for this reason alone, it seems unbalanced and socially unjust to give employers full control and responsibility for a VET system which is still funded primarily out of the public purse. In France and Germany, where employers shoulder much greater financial responsibility for VET provision, there is far greater education/industry consensus and collaboration in the delivery of national systems of education (though different models are used; a school-based one in France and a firm-based one in Germany, Noah and Eckstein, 1990; Green, 1992).

Moreover, there are sound educational reasons why VET provision should be designed by educationalists as well as industrialists. The short-term and parochial interests of employers already referred to are most unlikely to add up to a blueprint for the national system of education and training currently being called for. The solutions lie, not in the provision of generally lower-level occupationally specific skills of the sort that NVQs are concerned with, but with the development of generalizable skills in the areas of literacy, numeracy, problem-solving and interpersonal communication. All of these depend upon the provision of sound general education for 14- to 19-year-olds of the sort being recommended by the all-party alliance referred to earlier and by the National Commission on Education (NCE, 1993).

In addition, fundamental *educational* (as distinct from specifically vocational) reform will have to take place if VET is to be improved and upgraded in the desired ways. On the continent the much higher status of training is coupled with a solid theoretical foundation and breadth of knowledge which is not matched in our system (and certainly not by NVQs or even GNVQs!). As Prais (1991) has noted, in Germany, France and the Netherlands 'breadth is demanded on all approved training courses in the interests of nationwide standards and the transferability of skills; the British approach emphasises the tailoring of qualifications to meet as far as possible the varying needs of employers' (p. 88). This consideration, therefore, adds to the list yet another reason why VET should not be exclusively led by employers. The 1992 National Commission on Education report *Towards a Well-qualified Workforce* usefully summed up many of the issues in this sphere in observing that

> Education and training for 16–18 year olds should not be purely employer- or market-led. The employer-led or market-led approach would not succeed in overcoming Britain's 'low skills equilibrium', in which many enterprises staffed by poorly trained managers and workers produce low quality goods and services . . . Moreover employers' needs are inevitably much shorter-term than those of young people with a lifetime of work ahead. (NCE, 1992, p. 7)

CONCLUSION

The employer-led and occupationally specific nature of NVQs makes them unsuitable and inappropriate for the tasks assigned to them of enhancing the status of VET in Britain and upgrading the skills of the workforce. Moreover, the CBET system based on functional analysis cannot provide the necessary *educational* foundation for the development of the skills which are by common consent now thought to be crucial to the establishment of a sound and coherent 16 to 19 system of education and training in this country. Chown (1992) correctly observes about NVQs that

> a system which is claimed to provide flexible, qualified, skilled, confident, problem-solving, autonomous and quality-conscious employees for economic success in the future appears, in fact, to be based on an inadequate and outmoded, hierarchical model of the past. (p. 56)

The NCVQ volte-face represented by the introduction of general NVQs in 1992 can be interpreted as a response to these deep-seated and seemingly intractable problems. In Chapter 8 I will go on to examine the issues surrounding the development of GNVQs against the background of the developing 'core skills' movement and the attempt to bridge the vocational/academic divide. However, before that I want to examine the impact of the expansion of CBET approaches on teacher education and professional studies in further, adult and higher education.

Chapter 7

Competence, Post-School and Higher Education

As mentioned in earlier chapters, although the original and natural home of NVQs and CBET is work-based VET, in recent years the NCVQ model has displayed a marked tendency to extend its remit into new spheres of educational provision. In this chapter I will examine the impact of CBET on adult, continuing and higher education and, taking post-school teacher education as an illustrative model, attempt to demonstrate the inadequacies of the NVQ framework for professional studies in general. These criticisms will be supplemented by recommendations for more appropriate alternative models of vocational/professional education and development in adult and higher education based on the concepts of 'expertise' and 'reflective practice'.

POST-SCHOOL EDUCATION

There are two main ways in which the expansion of NVQs and the increasing influence of the NCVQ model have had an impact on education and training in this sphere of work. First, as described in the early chapters, lecturers and trainers in this sector have had to cope with considerable changes in assessment practices linked to the introduction of NVQs. Reactions to and attitudes about such changes have been mixed, but there is enough evidence to suggest that, in spite of NCVQ claims about the system being independent of the mode of learning, lecturers and tutors have had to work hard to accommodate the move to CBET assessment. Related to these developments has been the increasing marginalization of traditional 'liberal' or 'non-vocational' adult education. The massive expansion of NVQs, coupled with the vocationalizing implications of Schedule 2 of the Further & Higher Education Act 1992 (NIACE, 1992), has resulted in a serious threat to this traditional provision. There has certainly been a reduction in non-vocational provision and, as significant and potentially disastrous for those adult educators who fear the loss of the 'liberal' tradition, a damaging restructuring of courses so that they satisfy new accreditation criteria (Ecclestone, 1993b).

Table 7.1 *The TDLB qualifications framework*

The TDLB Qualifications Framework describes levels 3, 4 and 5 of the NCVQ framework as follows:
Level III:
deliver training specified and designed by others, assess the outcomes of that training and from identified learning needs, design training which facilitates learning and meets objectives at operational level
Level IV:
design, deliver, manage delivery and evaluate training and development programmes and learning experiences to meet individual and organisational objectives
Level V:
contribute to the formulation of strategic objectives and the identification of future capability requirements; design and implementation of HRD systems to meet those objectives and design and operate procedures for the evaluation of outcomes

(*Source*: FEU, 1992c, pp. 1–2)

The second major impact of NVQs in this sector has been on post-school teacher education and staff development. Reference was made in Chapter 1 to the more immediate origins of CBET in the performance-based teacher education movement which was popular for a time in the 1960s in America. Given this background, I suppose it was only a matter of time before the NCVQ system was extended to incorporate the professional preparation of teachers and lecturers. Although CBET strategies for schoolteacher education were reported to have been ruled out initially by the former DES (Jackson, 1991), the consultation document on the reform of initial teacher education issued in early 1992 contained ominous references to criteria which would 'place more emphasis on the achievement of professional competence' (DES, 1992, p. 3). More recently the DFE has been considering the sponsoring of research on competences and teacher training in the wake of Circular 9/92 which required 'schools and students to focus on the competences of teaching' (DFE, 1992, p. 1).

In further and adult education, CBET strategies have been around for some time and are now well established. The City & Guilds 730 Further and Adult Education Certificate course – the nationally recognized preliminary route into further and adult education teaching – has been experimenting with competence-based elements for the last few years, and modifications along these lines continue in spite of unsuccessful experiences in the sector (Chown, 1992; Hyland 1992b). Similar strategies for the Certificate in Education (FE) for further education lecturers – an inservice course which follows on from the City & Guilds 730 – are now in operation in a number of regions (McAleavey and McAleer, 1991) in spite of criticisms and the absence of a lead body for education (Chown and Last, 1993).

Indeed, in this latter area the establishment of CBET approaches as an acceptable and legitimate foundation for the education, training and development of FE staff has been considerably aided by the FEU, which piloted and publicized widely its work with standards developed by the Training and Development Lead Body (TDLB). The upshot of the FEU field trials is a range of competences to cover the assessing, lecturing, staff development and management functions undertaken by staff in the FE sector. Competences in the various areas will be accredited at levels 3 and 4 (assessor/lecturer) of the NCVQ framework, with a level 5 category to cover staff development and management roles (FEU, 1992c, see Table 7.1).

The TDLB was set up in 1990 to develop 'national standards . . . which span all industries and occupations' and was designed to be 'accepted nationally by all parties having an interest in training and development'. These national standards are, in fact, based on the same model of functional analysis as the NCVQ model of CBET and 'describe the expected performance of an individual in a work role' (ED, 1992b, p. 1). As Chown rightly observes, 'the TDLB standards are about instruction and the supervision of training; they are not about teaching and education' (1992, p. 56). The fact that such significant and far-reaching changes in the professional preparation and development programmes for post-school staff can be arbitrarily imposed in such a top-down manner with minimum consultation and negotiation (Chown and Last, 1993) is a further indication of the power of the underlying political and ideological forces driving these developments which have been touched on throughout this examination of the expansion of NCVQ influence.

Similar influences have now penetrated the work of higher education institutions in a number of strategic areas, though in this sphere the impact has been much more subtle and oblique. Barnett (1990) has catalogued the 'growing clamour from industry for the graduates it employs to have more work-related skills' (p. 158), and has described the attempts to achieve this through such schemes as the Higher Education for Capability (HEC) project and research on the development of transferable skills by the Council for Industry and Higher Education. This engagement with the world of work was, according to critics in the industrial camp, considered to be long overdue, though it has to be said that the emergence of the NCVQ on the scene has served to quicken considerably and alter radically the pace and process of change in higher education.

In 1989 the Committee of Vice-Chancellors was expressing astonishment at the idea of allowing the NCVQ to determine standards at higher degree and professional levels (Jackson, 1989), whereas, by the end of 1992, the same committee was seriously considering the establishment of a consortium of universities which would function as awarding bodies for NVQs at levels 4 and 5 (Griffiths and Tysome, 1992; the NCVQ viewed this move with suspicion and disapproval). On this matter the Open University's vice-chancellor commented that the 'education profession has dragged its heels longer than anyone else over the NVQ movement' (THES, 1992, p. 6) and announced that the OU would be making its own bid to take a lead in the development of higher level NVQs (the OU now has a centre for VET specifically concerned with NVQ developments).

As the resistance to vocational cultural changes weakens in these increasingly utilitarian times (and especially in the new post-binary atmosphere of increased competition for students of all kinds!), the interest in the potential market in relation to NVQs grows proportionately. Within the general framework of seeking to emphasize 'outcomes' in higher education, a research project funded by the Employment Department, involving the universities of Nottingham and Sheffield in conjunction with Rolls-Royce and Boots, reported favourably on the feasibility of developing 'generic guidelines for academic accreditation of work-based learning' (ED, 1992c, p. 3). In a similar vein, the universities of London, Glasgow and Sussex have been involved in a joint project (also funded by the Employment Department) designed to 'explore the delivery of the National Standards for Training and Development within Masters degree programmes' (Glasgow University, 1992, p. 2). These 'National Standards' are, in fact, nothing more nor less than the TDLB standards based on NCVQ competence criteria outlined earlier. If we add to this picture the recent intensification of activity since GNVQs came on stream, with various NCVQ schemes designed to persuade universities to interview GNVQ candidates for entry in 1994/95, it is little wonder that there is talk of a 'fundamental review of university provision' as the NCVQ 'spreads its influence into higher education' (Tysome, 1993b, p. 3).

Since a major theme of this book is that the NCVQ model is less than entirely successful even in its original home of work-based VET, it is necessary to view these forays into new spheres of activity with seriousness and concern. I intend to offer specific criticisms of the CBET model in relation to teacher education and general higher education before going on to consider alternative strategies.

COMPETENCE, PROFESSIONALISM AND TEACHING

There is one particular strand of argument in this area which needs to be disposed of at the outset. This is the utterly spurious claim that, because students (or course members) in the post-school sector now have to follow programmes based on the NCVQ model, then their teachers should also follow suit. Often this view is simply insinuated in sweeping quasi-prophetic statements about the 'changing face of FE' (see, for instance, Bees and Swords, 1990), but sometimes the claim is put forward openly and directly. In correspondence between the DFE and the FEFC, for example, we come across the following statement:

> The government envisages that the education service – and particularly the FE sector – will play a major role in delivering NVQs. FE colleges are well placed to explain to employers the value of competence based qualifications. It would be helpful if the FE sector could be seen to be supporting the implementation of such qualifications for its own staff. (DFE, 1993a, p. 3)

This is a none too subtle expression of a pragmatic or *prudential* reason why FE staff should have qualifications based on the NCVQ model, but there is no *logical* and certainly no *educational* connection between the states of affairs being appealed to. Does this mean that school teachers should undergo training based on the principles of the National Curriculum or A level syllabuses simply because this is what their students will be experiencing? And what about staff working in the areas of basic skills or training for the unemployed; will they need to enlist on programmes designed on the same principles as the courses their students are following?

The 'argument' amounts to no more than an assertion or an expression of preference, and is utterly devoid of rational or educational justification. Even if NVQs had proved to be successful in the areas they were originally designed for – and there is ample evidence that they have not – it would still be preposterous to suggest that the education and professional development of FE staff should be based on a model designed for the work-based accreditation of vocational skills! Moreover, there are more than enough straightforward educational arguments which indicate the inappropriateness of the NCVQ model of CBET (in the guise of 'national standards') for either the professional preparation of teachers or continuing professional studies in higher education.

It has been argued throughout this book that CBET is conceptually confused, epistemologically ambiguous and based on largely discredited behaviourist learning principles. How could the use of such a model possibly enhance the quality of teaching in FE or contribute to the enhancement of professionalism for lecturers, tutors and trainers? In order to examine this question further it would be useful to inspect the notion of professionalism in this sphere more closely, before looking at the implications of introducing CBET models for preparation and staff development.

Langford (1978) offers one of the clearest accounts and picks out six key features of professionalism – payment; knowledge and skills; responsibility and purpose; the professional ideal of service; unity; and recognition (p. 5) – for particular attention in relation to teaching. However, although this philosophical analysis and other (mainly sociological) investigations by Flexner (1915) and Larson (1977) provide some interesting descriptive material about the nature of professionalism in general and teaching in particular, they pay too little attention to the interrelationships between the various elements of professionalism. Whether professionalism is defined as a 'peculiar type of occupational control' or as an expression of the 'inherent nature of particular occupations' (Johnson, 1972, p. 45), it is important to note the differences and connections between the internal mechanisms of professionalism (knowledge base, education, certification) and the external arrangements made to secure public acknowledgement of professional status (links with other bodies, state agencies and the public).

In criticizing the process of increasing professionalization in adult education, Collins (1991) seeks to distinguish this from 'professionalism', which is defined as a 'serious commitment to the task at hand' (p. 87). This comment points towards what is clearly the crucial distinction to be made in this sphere between what Hoyle (1983) describes as 'professionalism', concerned with the 'improvement of status', and 'professionality' (or professional development), which is concerned with the 'improvement of skills' (p. 45). Over and above this, the overarching process of 'professionalization' may, and in the case of teaching, nursing and social work, often does involve both enhancement of public status and improvement of knowledge and skills. However, as Hoyle correctly points out, it 'cannot be taken as axiomatic that professionalization is invariably accompanied by professional development' (p. 45).

It is probably true to say that, until quite recently at any rate, teaching in general has undergone considerable professional advancement both in terms of its knowledge/ skills base and also in respect of its public status. Admittedly, the position and status of schoolteachers, particularly with the movement towards an all-graduate profession and the extension of the period of training underpinned by the growth of educational studies as an academic field, is perhaps rather different from that of teachers in adult and further education. In this latter area, teaching has tended to have a 'Cinderella' status as a result of its large number of unqualified and part-time staff, in addition to its lack of clearly defined legislation and funding mechanisms. However, the education and training of adults has expanded considerably in recent years (Stephens, 1990) and, coupled with the growth of vocational and certificated courses for teachers of adults, this has been accompanied by the expansion of specialized research and academic studies in the field (Bright, 1989). It is indeed deeply ironic that over the last few years many of these benefits have been overshadowed by the growth of impoverished conceptions of professionalism linked to the expansion and influence of CBET strategies throughout the system.

Until the recent widespread vocationalizing trends and the rise to prominence of the economic utility model of education, the professionality (knowledge/skills) elements of teaching were more or less in balance with the professionalism (public status) ones. Since the 1970s and 1980s, however, especially in the light of the centralization of control over education systems both in Britain (Whitty, 1990) and across Western Europe (Moon, 1990), there has been a narrowing of academic focus at all levels of the profession, a de-skilling of the teaching role, and a corresponding loss of autonomy and status (not to mention morale!) on the part of teachers in general (Simon, 1992). The attempt to introduce CBET strategies into the education of teachers – combined with proposals to take teacher training, professional studies, research and funding out of the hands of higher education institutions and to centralize control in a new quango, the Teacher Training Agency (Griffiths, 1993) – can be regarded as the logical conclusion of these de-professionalizing trends.

Edwards (1993) has suggested that, in order to avoid being labelled as regressive Luddites, teachers in further and adult education need to formulate creative responses to CBET in the form of programmes which refer to competence criteria but still maintain a commitment to experiential learning and reflective practice. Educators in initial teacher education seem to be achieving this quite successfully in the form of school-based mentorship models (Dunne and Harvard, 1992; Everton and White, 1992) which were already developing well before and independently of the CBET onslaught. Post-school teacher education will need similar creative responses in the light of the introduction of TDLB standards into the sector.

POST-SCHOOL TEACHER EDUCATION

In suggesting alternatives to the CBET model for education and development in this sector, it is important to be specific about the shortcomings and inadequacies of the NCVQ approach to education and training. The experience of implementing NVQs in certain vocational areas such as retailing, catering and construction, as noted already, has been less than entirely successful, resulting in a narrowing of focus and a loss of significant theoretical content. In her report on NVQs in the construction industry, for instance, Callender (1992) noted that NVQ programmes were 'limited and too mechanistic' and that often 'their educational content has been squeezed out along with pedagogic concerns' (p. 27). This is extremely worrying in the case of applying similar strategies to teacher education, within which matters of educational and pedagogic concern are quite naturally and properly of central importance. Marshall (1991) has suggested that, though the NVQ framework may be suitable for 'training basic skills', it becomes 'less effective as the level of skill and cognitive requirement increases', and it would be 'ludicrous to apply the same model to all levels of training' (p. 63). Certainly it would be ludicrous, and extremely damaging, to try to apply this model to areas of professional development such as teacher education for which it is ill-designed and almost entirely inappropriate.

Referring to the behaviourist foundation of the NCVQ model described in Chapter 4, Hodkinson (1992) attacks such an approach for its attachment to 'narrow and mechanistic tasks and skills' and its obsession with performance at the expense of the 'schema . . . and complex intellectual processes' (p. 34) needed in order to generate and sustain educational activity. He recommends instead an 'interactive view of competence' which would serve to 'refocus attention on the learning process and encourage meaningful reflection on performance' (p. 37). These criticisms and recommendations for alternative practice are timely and useful, for they pick out key weaknesses of the CBET approach in relation to the learning process and the development of intelligent practice through reflection on experience.

The model of experiential learning described in Chapter 4 is completely at odds with the operation of CBET systems. The mismatch between the behaviourist foundation of NVQs and the stress on products and the cognitive/experiential emphasis on process favoured by many FE lecturers was described in order to repudiate the NCVQ claims about NVQs and learner autonomy. In much the same way there exist glaring paradoxes in the attempt to apply CBET strategies to post-school teacher education. The experiential learning approach based on Kolb's theories is not only influential in the teaching methods widely employed in further and adult education (Gibbs, 1988), it also informs and connects with the 'reflective practitioner' (Schon, 1987) model which has been so influential in recent years in teacher education and professional studies at all levels. Arguably, this is now the dominant model of education and development in all professions, and clearly informs many of the influential notions and basic texts for teachers in further and adult education (see Minton, 1991; Kerry and Tollitt-Evans, 1992).

Now, as in the case of NVQs and student learning in FE, CBET strategies are in direct conflict with the basic tenets of experiential learning and reflective practice. The NCVQ model has nothing at all in common with the creation of knowledge through the transformation of experience which is at the heart of the experiential approach to learning. It is concerned primarily with products, whereas experientialism also values the process of learning. The whole *raison d'être* of the 'learning by doing' approach widely used in FE teacher education is intended to 'help learners to reflect on experiences they have had; to obtain full accounts of what took place, to make value judgments about those events, to categorise experience and to move on to analyse the experience and draw out learning points for the future' (Gibbs, 1988, p. 40). This cyclical process of learning and development is totally negated by an approach which is concerned only with collecting evidence to satisfy competences based on a functional analysis of work roles.

There are also clear mismatches between the cognitive thrust of experiential approaches and the behaviourist foundations of CBET. All the evidence indicates that bolting competences on to existing learning programmes will inevitably lead to a narrowing of focus and a loss of theoretical content. This would be particularly damaging in an area such as teaching which is a 'complex and dynamic process' and in which 'interaction and context are crucial aspects of practice' (Chown, 1992, p.53). The development of knowledge and skill in teaching needs to be a continuous process in which there is a dynamic relationship between learning processes and reflection on the goals of intelligent practice. This is not compatible with a strategy based solely on TDLB standards in which the generation of evidence to meet predetermined outcomes has pride of place. As Chown and Last (1993) note, the TDLB model cannot account for the 'crucial relationship between competence and context, because it lacks the dimension of the perceptual, analytical, critical process which relates the two' (p. 21).

Another serious shortcoming of the NCVQ model in relation to teacher education is its failure to account for the important collaborative and collegial aspect of the work of staff in FE. A major part of the enterprise of lecturers and tutors involves working with colleagues to plan, deliver and evaluate programmes. Effective teamwork is essential in this sphere. Yet the NCVQ model adopts a radically 'individualistic orientation by emphasising personal competences' (Ashworth, 1992, p. 8), and this militates against the development of teamwork skills and experience that are so vital in educational institutions. Ashworth goes on to observe that

> the idea of competence assumes that it is an individual's personal property, so to speak; an individual has the competence which will be certified in an NVQ . . . So the whole way of thinking is focused on the individual. This ignores the *truly collective aspects of teamwork*. (p. 12, author's italics)

This 'individualism' is a serious hindrance to professional development since, although all teachers naturally function as autonomous individuals as part of their professional practice, it is not possible to develop *professionally* on the basis of purely personal theories. An effective model of professional development needs to incorporate 'a process of change and transformation . . . which combines both personal and professional values into theories of action' (O'Hanlon, 1993, p. 245).

Of crucial concern also is the lack of transferability of competences based on the NCVQ model and the restrictions placed on the development and growth of competence. In criticizing the applications of the NCVQ model in teacher education, Eraut (1989) stressed this particular shortcoming. There is the danger that, once trained, people might 'consider their competence as sufficient and ignore the need for further improvement' (p. 181), and this would clearly be disastrous in the rapidly changing world of post-school education. Chown and Last (1993) sum this weakness up well in their comment that

> the NCVQ model cannot acknowledge the growth of competence. It does not admit a change in competence which is not allied to a change in organisational function. There is, it would seem, no place for formally recognising the continuing development of teachers as competent practitioners unless they change roles – moving into management, mentorship or staff development. (pp. 21–2)

This last comment brings out not just the rank inappropriateness of the model for teacher education and staff development, but also the rather more sinister implications of the mechanical and hierarchical nature of the NCVQ framework noticed by Field (1991) and mentioned in the earlier chapters. Certainly, it could be said that the TDLB system is the embodiment of a 'crude, political, five-level, perception of people, power, roles and functions' (Chown, 1992, p. 56), and it is in the separation of functions of FE staff and the differential allocation of levels to different functions that there lurk perhaps the greatest dangers to professionalism in the sector. It might well be that the career structure and development of staff is controlled by management through assigning institutional functions to staff at the three TDLB levels (which might also be used for staff appraisal!). This would indeed be a crude manipulation of the system for ulterior and anti-educational motives, but the point is that functional analysis allows for this perspective to gain credibility and prominence.

The roles of staff in post-school education add up to rather more than a list of occupational functions, and the use of the TDLB competences can quite easily serve to de-professionalize teaching is this respect through its functionalist methodology. Such de-professionalization would be in the interests of nobody; it would weaken the standing of teaching as a profession and would weaken the knowledge and skill base of FE staff. This is precisely what Collins (1991) was getting at in describing CBET as a strategy in which 'though management needs are well served, education and training programmes are trivialized, while occupations are de-skilled through the deployment of narrowly defined prescriptions' (p. 90). Programmes using such limited criteria as TDLB standards are likely to produce staff who are uncritical of change yet well able to perform the circumscribed and restricted tasks and duties required of them by institutional management. Moreover, the linking of specific functions (assessing, lecturing, managing) and types of work in FE with three different NVQ levels is bound to be divisive and offensive to professional ethics.

The pace of change in the post-school sector in recent years has resulted in a fluid and uncertain state of affairs in which lecturers are required to be flexible, critical, reflective and knowledgeable about a vast range of curricular and organizational matters. Added to this are the increased expectations outlined in the 1991 White Papers, and Further & Higher Education Act 1992 and the NETTs. In order to cope with all these different demands, staff in the sector will need a good deal more than the ability to satisfy occupational work roles. They will need, in the words of the 1991 HMI survey on further education teacher-training, to 'develop a more independent and critical perspective on educational matters' (HMI, 1991, p. 7).

HIGHER EDUCATION

In considering the impact of CBET strategies on higher education, all the weaknesses outlined earlier count heavily against the efficacy and suitability of the NCVQ model for work in this area. If the model is less than effective in the area of work-based VET, how can it possibly make sense to try to apply it at higher levels? At least the Open University vice-chancellor, in welcoming the expansion to higher education of interest in NVQs, was honest enough to admit that 'although the driving test approach of NVQs does make sense, there are problems as you try to apply it to higher and higher levels of learning' (THES, 1992, p. 6). Against the background of the weaknesses and radical shortcomings of NVQs already discussed, this must be counted as a quite magnificent understatement!

Perhaps a part of the explanation for the recent interest of higher education in the NVQ framework (that is, apart from the overt ideological/political pressures now driving the spread of CBET) can perhaps be found in Barnett's (1990) claims about the current 'undermining of the value background of higher education' (p. 8). The idea is that contemporary higher education is being undermined epistemologically, through relativistic theories of knowledge, and sociologically, through the loss of academic freedom and autonomy as a result of the increasing influence of the state, industry and other agencies over what goes on in higher education institutions. The vulnerability of universities in such an intellectual and ideological vacuum leaves higher education wide open to attack from all sides, perhaps especially from the 'industrial training' lobby. Against this background the persuasive appeal of competence talk and CBET strategies is not difficult to understand.

Barnett argues that there is a twofold danger in recent trends in this area: the developments are 'likely to lead to the curriculum being dominated by technique' and the 'techniques in question are imported from the outside world and are imposed arbitrarily upon, and unconnected with, the curriculum' (p. 159). Both these threats are in fact clearly revealed and realized in the introduction of TDLB standards into staff training at FE level and into higher education through the 'research' on outcomes and the use of 'national standards' in postgraduate courses. Barnett elaborates a reconstituted and 'emancipatory' concept of 'liberal' higher education which – incorporating such things as critical perspectives, open and self-directed learning – would seek to 'neutralize the effects' (p. 203) of the forces currently undermining theory and practice in this sphere.

The fact that higher education is considered to be what Barnett calls a 'contested concept' is now a distinctive theme in many current discussions, and commentators such as MacIntyre (1990) and Bloom (1988) have offered perceptive diagnoses of the current malaise. In an examination of these recent critiques of the modern university, Mendus (1992) observed that an element common to all such accounts was the 'myth of the fall', the suggestion that there has been a 'loss of integration in modern society' which is contrasted unfavourably with some prior era 'when wholeness and coherence were the order of the day' (p. 177).

Mendus quite rightly challenges both the accuracy and utility of such a perspective and in the process notes that, although the new visions of higher education derive from a variety of different philosophical and political traditions (from neo-conservative to postmodernist), a unifying element is the general belief in the importance of fostering criticism and self-reflection. Prescribing a compatibilist position between Bloom's suggested return to the 'great tradition' and MacIntyre's idea of a diversity of institutions to mirror the contemporary plurality of values, Mendus argues that students should 'be presented with different and competing traditions' in order to enable them to become 'critical creators as well as critical discoverers' (p. 182). This comment links well with the experiential tradition mentioned earlier in the context of FE practice; it is concerned with the *activity* of learning and the need, as Kolb (1993) explains, for 'active experimentation at one extreme and reflective observation at the other'. In this way the learner 'moves in varying degrees from actor to observer, and from specific involvement to general analytic detachment' (p. 148).

This account is broadly similar to those offered by contemporary adult-education theorists seeking to offer renewed visions for adult learning and development in what they regard as deeply troubled times. Collins (1991), for instance, has criticized the 'technicist obsession' which characterizes the current professionalization of adult education, and recommends a return to an 'emancipatory, critical practice' and a 'transformative pedagogy' which would allow teachers to 'envisage themselves as intellectual-practitioners rather than technicians' (p. 118). In a similar vein, Usher (1992) outlines a 'postmodern' perspective on adult education which, remembering 'its history as an oppositional discourse', can help us to 'open ourselves, through critical dialogue, to the humanistic tradition' (pp. 212–13).

Such perspectives are on all fours with Barnett's preferred model of higher education practice which makes use of the reflective practitioner model mentioned earlier in connection with teacher education and professional development. Barnett (1990) suggests that 'every student is or should be a reflective practitioner' and that this will require sufficient 'self-reflection' to enable students to develop beyond interest and immersion in a form of knowledge and, through 'critical self-evaluation', begin to question its 'epistemological validity . . . and its possible ideological strains' (p. 160).

Having outlined the utter irrelevance and appalling inadequacy of the NCVQ model of CBET for work in adult, further and higher education – and the serious threats it poses to rational practice in those fields – it now seems appropriate to offer some alternatives to this model for theory and practice.

ALTERNATIVES TO CBET: EXPERTISE AND REFLECTIVE PRACTICE

In criticizing the NCVQ approach, Eraut (1989) recommends instead a model of professional development, based originally on the work of Dreyfus and Dreyfus (1984), which consists of a five-stage description of knowledge and skill acquisition in professional contexts: novice, advanced beginner, competent, proficient and expert (p. 182). Unlike the NCVQ approach involving the assessment of competence at five discrete (and not clearly interconnected) *levels*, competence on this model is just one *stage* of development, and a 'competent' practitioner would only be around half-way to the realization of full potential in any particular professional sphere.

This model of professionalism has been used successfully in the field of nurse education by Benner (1982), and Elliott (1989) has described a similar approach to the training of police officers. In more recent work Elliott (1993) has attempted to codify the basic tenets of this strategy for professional education and offers ideas for a 'practical educational science'. Using the work of Dreyfus and Schon, Elliott attempts to provide a model which steers between and offers an alternative to the 'teacher as researcher' paradigm on the one hand, and the 'social market' model (performance indicators, competence outcomes, the TDLB approach) on the other. Using the original Dreyfus categories, Elliott describes a four-phase model of 'experiential professional learning' (pp. 75–7):

1. *From Novice to Advanced Beginner*: in which learners need to develop an ability to discern, on the basis of observation and analysis, a wide range of aspects, both situational and non-situational, which are potentially relevant to intelligent action.

2. *From Advanced Beginner to Competent*: in which the learning emphasis shifts to choosing a course of action (or goal) and discriminating all those aspects of a situation which have to be taken into account in reaching a decision about how to implement that course of action.

3. *From Competent to Proficient*: based on experience gained, learners are now in a position on the basis of intuition to discern potentially relevant aspects of situations, to discriminate in the light of their goals which are salient, and to synthesise saliences with a view of the situation as a whole.

4. *From Proficiency to Expertise*: in this phase the extent and range of experience accumulated by the learner is so vast that learners begin to make even intelligent decisions on the basis of intuition rather than conscious deliberation in the light of evaluation data gathered around past decisions. The 'reflective space' between interpreting a situation and deciding what to do in it gradually disappears as learners progress through this phase.

It should be noted that, though 'competence' does appear in this model, the general strategy is light years removed from the NCVQ model of CBET. Indeed, this is only to be expected, since the NCVQ model technically has nothing to do with learning or development, whereas the whole *raison d'être* of experiential professional learning is that development is *incremental* and *career long*. This idea could not be further removed from the chasing of competences to satisfy performance and accreditation criteria. In so far as this notion of professionalism is competence-based at all, it could be linked to the 'generic' notion identified by Norris which was discussed in Chapter 3. This strategy 'favours empirical investigations to establish competencies which discriminate between average and expert performers as opposed to the theoretical or logical requirements of a particular occupational function' (Norris, 1991, p. 332) and has been utilized successfully in contrast and opposition to 'more behaviourist models which identify competence as an ability to produce certain pre-specified behavioural responses to situations' (Elliott, 1993, p. 77; as in the NCVQ and TDLB models!).

The 'experiential' model of professional development – which is broadly similar to the approaches recommended by Eraut, Kolb and Hodkinson already discussed – uses a concept of 'expertise' which draws heavily on the pioneering work of Argyris and Schon (1974) which was concerned with 'theories of action' and 'theories-in-use' employed by expert professionals (pp. 12ff.). The concept of expertise – defined by Tennant (1991) as the 'knowledge and skill gained through sustained practice and experience' (p. 50) – has attracted wide attention in recent years and there is now a substantial body of empirical work recording investigations in professional and occupational fields of all kinds.

Summarizing a range of such studies, Chi *et al.* (1988) were able to identify a number of common characteristics of expertise evident across different spheres of activity. Experts were found to have a considerable amount of domain-specific knowledge (which again seems to count against the notion of broad generic competence or 'meta-competence'), perceived meaningful patterns in their professional activity, were faster and more economical in judgement and decision-making than novices and had strong self-monitoring skills. All these qualities seem to match well with the characteristics of the reflective practitioner which go beyond the 'dominance of technique' to develop a 'theory of action' (Argyris and Schon, 1974, p. 149) which relates specifically to professional practice.

There are now well-defined examples of development work in specific professional fields such as nurse education, teacher education, medical education and social care which have attempted to interpret the NCVQ criteria within a framework which remains faithful to professional principles and practice. Challis *et al.* (1993), for instance, recently completed a project which looked at ways of integrating competence outcomes within undergraduate medical training courses. The importance of using a wide range of assessment techniques and of maintaining a primary emphasis on the specific professional content rather than the demands of the NCVQ framework was clearly brought out in this research, and confirmed in the project by Kelly *et al.* (1990) which looked at the implementation of NVQs in the field of social care. Criticizing the 'mechanistic' nature of standard NVQ implementation, the researchers urged professionals to secure 'ownership' of the change process and to emphasize the principle that 'NVQ needs to work for social care; not the other way around' (p. 94).

A particularly well-documented example of sound practice in this general area is the work done by Winter (1992) on the ASSET programme, a competence-based degree-level qualification in social work developed by Anglia Polytechnic University in conjunction with Essex Social Services. Picking out weaknesses in the 'orthodox format' of the NCVQ approach (as represented by the competences specified in the Management Charter Initiative) such as insufficient attention to 'critical thinking' and lack of 'reference to any ethical dimension' of professionalism (pp. 107–8), Winter seeks to demonstrate that these deficiencies may be remedied by the incorporation of 'core assessment criteria' which give due emphasis to the knowledge, principles and values characteristic of the work of professionals in the field. He concludes that the success of the programme derives from the fact that 'competences are not treated as product specifications but as learning goals; and instead of "quality standards" derived from an organisational mission statement there are educational criteria derived from an elaborated theory of the reflective practitioner' (p. 114).

Winter's mention of the lack of reference to the ethical dimension of professional practice in the NCVQ model is worth stressing, since it is a major shortcoming of all CBET approaches based on functional analysis. The obsession with technique typical of behaviourist-inspired strategies leaves out the important place of human values in educational and professional activity. This important value foundation of professional practice is well brought out in Carr's (1992) description of 'extended professionalism' in which, like other professions, teaching is 'to be understood in terms of the provision of an ethically grounded, essentially consultative, public service' (p. 22). The NCVQ and all the other 'social market' and technicist approaches cannot account for this value dimension of intelligent professional practice. Little wonder that Elliott (1993), after explaining how his experiential model of professional learning naturally gives rise to considerations of 'the nature of educational values' (p. 76), goes on to observe that the approach recommended 'would radically differ in its conception of teaching competence to the behaviourist conception embedded in the "social market" perspective and the model currently promoted by the NCVQ' (p. 79).

The failure to engage with the ethical dimension of learning and education – in conjunction with the patent inadequacy of a behaviourist-inspired functional-analysis model for programmes concerned with critical reflection – also counts heavily against the validity of the NCVQ model for work in higher education in either general or professional/vocational areas. Aside from the many shortcomings already referred to, how can a system rooted in the functional analysis of work roles provide the educational foundation for a developing system of mass higher education grappling with complex problems such as the failure of modern universities to offer a 'distinctive visage to the young person' (Bloom, 1988, p. 337) or to offer a coherent response to the 'conflict of traditions' described by MacIntyre (1990, p. 228)?

A behaviourist model concerned first and foremost with employer-defined outcomes does not recognize and has no need for moral or philosophical issues of this kind. More to the point, CBET systems reduce all such value questions to questions about 'production technology . . . the citation of performance indicators to measure . . . technical efficiency and effectiveness' (Elliott, 1993, p. 67). We should not be too surprised at this, since it is well known that behaviourism, finding values a troublesome feature of the human condition, has always preferred either to overlook them or to reduce them to measurable units (Dearden, 1984). Well might Elliott (1993) observe wryly about the behaviourist (technicist, CBET) approach to professional education that

> although now somewhat discredited in the academic domain it continues to linger in the political domain as an ideological device for eliminating value issues from the domains of professional practice and thereby subordinating them to political forms of control. (p. 68)

Bearing in mind the 'political' forces driving the expansion of the NCVQ framework into further and higher education, such comments are worthy of serious attention.

CONCLUSION

It is self-evidently desirable that all lecturers, tutors and trainers in post-school education are 'competent' practitioners, just as it is justifiable to provide higher education graduates with 'capability' skills for working life. But these aims are basic minimum, lowest common denominator ones, and leave just about everything else to be said about VET, adult and higher education. Moreover, there is enough evidence to suggest that, even at the level of accrediting occupational and vocational competence, the NCVQ model leaves much to be desired.

When we come to teacher education, staff development in post-school education and continuing professional education, it has been argued that the NCVQ model of CBET has nothing of value to offer. Not only does it patently fail to provide what is required in the areas of learning, knowledge, experience and values, there is every indication that it thwarts and militates against the basic principles of experiential learning and the ongoing development of professional practice. In the light of all this, teachers should eschew all CBET models of professionalism and – should it be necessary to engage with TDLB standards in adult and further education or higher-level NVQs in graduate programmes – should draw on the creative alternatives which are to be found in the new models of professionalism concerned with developing expertise and reflective practice.

In the last analysis, a system concerned only with the accreditation of outcomes cannot provide the necessary foundation for the ongoing improvement and enhancement of educational and professional practice. The satisfaction of competence outcomes using programmes based on NVQs or TDLB standards is often nothing more than the recording and reporting of *current* skills. This is not the same as learning and professional development, which is necessarily concerned with *improving* practice with an eye to *future* situations. As Argyris and Schon (1974) observe: 'Whatever competence means today, we can be sure its meaning will have changed by tomorrow. The foundation for future professional competence seems to be the capacity to learn how to learn' (p. 157). The NCVQ model of CBET and the TDLB standards have nothing at all to do with this activity of 'learning how to learn'.

Chapter 8

General NVQs and the Vocational/Academic Divide

In Chapter 6 it was noted that a key element in the 'agenda for action' advocated by the contemporary 'alliance' is the 'need to devise a coherent curriculum and qualification system in which "academic" and "vocational" elements are equally valued' (Whiteside *et al.*, 1992, p. 7). I think Whiteside's description of the programme is broadly correct in this respect, but it should be noted that this is a highly complex and contested arena. It will be important to make relevant distinctions between the various demands made in this area for a unified 16 to 19 (or indeed a 14 to 19) framework, a bridging of the vocational/academic divide, and a common core (or core skills) for the 16 to 19 curriculum, since there are different and competing educational prescriptions involved in the recommended programmes for action. However, before examining the current scene and assessing the role of GNVQs in all this, it would be useful to provide some historical background to the debate by examining the origins of the so-called vocational/academic divide in education.

THE ORIGINS OF DIVISION

Maclure (1991) has referred to the 'historic failure of English education to integrate the academic and the practical, the general and the vocational' (p. 28). Although there is a tendency to view this educational divisiveness as a relatively recent phenomenon, perhaps developing in the years after the 1944 Act, the roots of the division need to be traced further back. As Silver and Brennan (1988) note, 'education and training, theory and practice, the liberal and the vocational – the polarities have centuries of turbulent history' (p. 3). It is, for instance, feasible to locate the origins of the different perspectives in the rival views of the ancient Greek philosophers, Plato and Aristotle, especially in their disagreements about the nature and purpose of the pursuit of knowledge (Schofield, 1972, ch. 8). However, although some of these issues will be touched on in the next chapter, which is concerned with contemporary issues surrounding liberalism and vocationalism, for present purposes it is legitimate to begin the search for the divide in the nineteenth century, since it was in this period that the blueprint for the state schooling system was worked out.

The cultural and socio-economic factors which underpin what has come to be labelled as the vocational/academic divide predate the establishment of compulsory schooling and are present in perhaps their starkest form in the public-school tradition and the ideal of the gentleman. Owing something to the Confucian conception which associated a particular style and etiquette with a hierarchical social system, the 'gentleman ideal' emerged as the approved form of education for the public schools and universities which fed the civil service (Wilkinson, 1970). The standard form of classical education central to this ideal gained its prestige, not from any particular content thought to be intrinsically valuable, but from its endorsement by and close association with the most powerful political and economic groups in British society. As Wilkinson observes:

> The gentleman was taught to consider himself above specialisation, whether in the sense of regional style or that of technical know-how . . . technical specialisation was the mark of one who had to use knowledge to earn a living and not for the leisured pursuit of wisdom and beauty . . . (p. 133)

The developments in technical education in the late nineteenth century were to demonstrate just how powerful the influence of this non-instrumental conception of knowledge could be. As Green (1990) observes, unlike developments in France and Germany, the new industrial bourgeoisie in England were to a large extent assimilated by the landed aristocracy, which meant that the schooling system 'favoured gentry values and maintained a rigid hierarchy of rank' (p. 168). Stemming from this there developed deep-seated divisions and fissures between the educational values of the manufacturing classes and the aristocratically inclined liberal professions. Demands for the improvement and expansion of technical education and training gathered force after Britain's comparatively poor performance at the 1867 Paris Exhibition and eventually led to the passing of the Technical Instruction Act 1889 (Musgrave, 1966). The concept of training which emerged, however, was highly theoretical – 'instruction in the principles of science and art applicable to industries' (Musgrave, 1970, p. 68) – and completely inadequate to the industrial requirements of the time.

The pervasive influence of the theoretical can be discerned in much of the major educational legislation from the turn of the century to the 1944 Act and beyond, and this was typically accompanied by the ascription of an inferior status to practical pursuits. Vocationally relevant training was invariably subservient to a 'good liberal education' which would easily enable students to 'acquire any technical knowledge which they might need' (Wardle, 1976, p. 120). During the inter-war years, as more recruits to industry were drawn from higher education, it was still mainly general knowledge and attitudes which were sought more often than specific vocational skills.

Investigating the origins of vocational schooling in Britain, Shilling (1989) chose to characterize the post-1945 period as one in which 'education–industry relations shifted from a collective to a corporate strategy and schools became subject to greater industrial influence' (p. 39). The academic/vocational divide and the higher prestige of theoretical pursuits was, however, maintained even during this period as bodies such as the Federation of British Industry and the Institute of Mechanical Engineers sought to enhance the recruitment of abler pupils from schools rather than pressing for a general upgrading and restructuring of vocational education. The technical schools, established under the 1944 Act as a strand of the proposed tripartite system, withered and declined as employers looked to the grammar schools to provide high-level professional recruits (McCulloch *et al.*, 1985). It is arguable whether even the intensive activity of the period of new vocationalism in the 1970s and 1980s really did much to break down the differences and divisions between vocational and academic pursuits (Macfarlane, 1993).

THE REFORM OF 16 TO 19 EDUCATION

Although the bridging of the so-called vocational–academic divide is a key element in the 'agenda for action' currently being canvassed by a powerful 'alliance' of employment, industrial and educational interests, this objective is ambiguous and covers a broad area of distinctively different and competing proposals. The broad agreement on the need to improve post-16 participation rates is not particularly contentious or controversial (and this now seems to have been achieved by default as a result of high youth unemployment!). However, once youngsters have been persuaded to remain in education beyond 16, there are different versions of the curriculum that they should follow.

Within the broad commitment to coherence in the curriculum and support for the national targets, there are disagreements about means and ends. For those who favour a 'market' approach to reform (e.g., CBI, Employment Department), the necessary changes can be brought about incrementally by providing official support for the value of vocational studies, and encouraging take-up through training credits and TECs. On the other hand, other groups doubt whether this tinkering with the system – especially in a society which has always lacked a pro-training culture, whether at the level of employer investment or student motivation – is enough to overcome the legacy of past mistakes and prejudices. Thus, in place of the market-orientated voluntarism favoured by the government, there are more radical calls for systematic change and legislation ending employment under the age of 18 which is not connected with education and training (e.g., Labour Party, 1991; Finegold *et al.*, 1990). The 1993 National Commission report aligned itself squarely with this latter group in its recommendations for fundamental changes in the system, including VET 'traineeships' of two or three years (very similar to the German system favoured by the Labour Party), the merging of the DFE and the Employment Department and, most radical of all, the introduction of the General Education Diploma (GED) (not unlike the system favoured by Finegold), which would 'replace the range of qualifications, including GCSE, A levels, BTEC and both general and more specific vocational qualifications' (NCE, 1993, pp. 67ff.).

The official government line was established in the 1991 White Paper which outlined reforms designed to 'promote equal esteem for academic and vocational qualifications' (DES, 1991, vol. 1, p. 3). This objective was to be achieved by means of a range of measures including the extension of the training credit scheme to all 16- and 17-year-olds, and the introduction of ordinary and advanced diplomas which would record achievement in both vocational and academic areas (though this particular aspect of the proposed reforms has not yet been followed up). However, alongside the commitment to 'remove the remaining barriers to equal status between the so-called academic and vocational routes' there was the equally firm commitment to 'maintaining A levels and the standards they represent' (pp. 20, 24). This general approach has been consistently affirmed by the DFE, most recently in reaction to the NCE proposals through the announcement of new 'starred' A levels (Pyke, 1993).

The follies of this half-hearted approach to 16 to 19 reform have been pointed out by critics who favour more radical solutions to the problem. Perhaps the most forthright of these alternatives was that put forward in the report by the Institute of Public Policy Research, *A British Baccalaureat* (Finegold *et al.*, 1990), which proposed a new unified system of education and training – modular in structure, with mixed vocational and academic core and option modules which would lead to a single qualification, an 'advanced diploma' or 'British bac'. In a similar vein, the Labour Party is committed to a unified qualifications structure – the Advanced Certificate for Education and Training – which would replace the present jungle of qualifications (Labour Party, 1991). As mentioned above, all of these proposals were codified and endorsed in the 1993 NCE report.

However, in spite of the cogency of some of these arguments and the attractiveness of starting again with a clean sheet, it would be mere wishful thinking to suppose that such 'revolutionary' programmes would find favour over the mainstream 'incrementalist' plans. As Maclure (1991) points out, the fact is that we do not start with a *tabula rasa* in this area, since our 'educational scene comprises the institutions and the curriculum structures of 150 years of history and these institutions and structures have been endowed with great and mysterious significance within the culture' (p. 44). The force and power of such cultural inertia goes some way to explaining the relative failure of the AS level experiments, the resistance to modular A levels, and the determination of neo-conservatives to maintain the A level 'gold standard' at any cost.

Against this background the more moderate 'incrementalist' vision of a unified post-16 framework seeks to place greater emphasis on vocational studies in the hope that this will redress the balance and bridge the divide by raising the status of VET generally. Although some of the leading players in the alliance clearly believe that, following the failure to reform A levels in the 1980s, the current strategy will lead to piecemeal and gradual reform, there is certainly little evidence to suggest that the desired ends are any nearer to achievement. For one thing, the key elements of current strategy – the introduction of GNVQs and the attempt to establish core skills across the 16 to 19 curriculum – may actually compound the main problems by adding yet another layer of potential confusion. In place of the twin-track vocational/academic routes, we now have three routes, with GNVQs offering a 'third middle route . . . providing a broadening dimension to the vocational route' (Sutton, 1992, p. 37).

GENERAL NATIONAL VOCATIONAL QUALIFICATIONS

The policy process through which much of recent educational reform has been effected – top-down, non-consultative, backed by assertion rather than research, and spread through funding controls and powerful public relations – was criticized in earlier chapters. Whatever their eventual merit and educational potential, the introduction of

GNVQs into the system offers a paradigm example of the way in which contemporary policies are developed and established in practice.

The impromptu process of reform described by Gipps (1993) began in the case of GNVQs with references in the 1991 DES White Paper to the need for qualifications which would 'cover broad occupational areas and offer opportunities to develop the relevant knowledge and understanding, and to gain an appreciation of how to apply them at work' (DES, 1991, vol. 1, p. 19). More specifically, GNVQs should:

(a)　offer a broad preparation for employment as well as an accepted route to higher level qualifications, including higher education;

(b)　require the demonstration of a range of skills and the application of knowledge and understanding relevant to the related occupations;

(c)　be of equal standing with academic qualifications at the same level;

(d)　be clearly related to the occupationally specific NVQs so that young people can progress quickly and effectively from one to the other;

(e)　be sufficiently distinctive from occupationally specific NVQs to ensure that there is no confusion between the two;

(f)　be suitable for use by full-time students in colleges and, if appropriate, in schools, who have limited opportunities to demonstrate competence in the workplace. (p. 19)

The reference to the need to avoid 'confusion' in e) is both well placed and vital since there is indeed scope for considerable confusion over the precise objectives of GNVQs and their links with other qualifications!

Following the initial reference in the White Paper, the NCVQ carried out a consultation exercise between October and December 1991 which resulted (perhaps not unexpectedly!) in the finding that there was 'strong support' for the GNVQ model which would help to contribute to the 'speedy introduction of GNVQs' (NCVQ, 1992a, p. 4). This introduction took place in September 1992 with pilot GNVQs in five vocational areas – Art and Design; Business; Health and Social Care; Leisure and Tourism; and Manufacturing – at levels 2 and 3 (now referred to as Intermediate and Advanced levels) in around a hundred centres (NCVQ 1993c, p. 4). Even before the first pilots had been introduced the NCVQ was issuing 'news releases' incorporating statements of support for GNVQs by leading figures. John Patten, for instance, was quoted as saying that 'GNVQs will build on the strengths of existing provision to offer young people a good general education', and the BTEC Chief Executive suggested that the 'GNVQ will play a vital role in widening access to higher education' (NCVQ, 1992b, pp. 1–2). In similar fashion, there seemed to be no great need to wait for the results of the evaluations of the pilots before expressing messages of 'overwhelming support' for GNVQs (RSA, 1992, p. 2), and outlining plans to 'speed up the development of GNVQs' (Tysome, 1993a, p. 9).

In autumn 1993 three further GNVQ pilots – in the Built Environment, Hospitality and Catering, and Science – were introduced and six more (Distribution, Engineering, Information Technology, Land Based Industries, Management, and Media and Communications) are due to come on stream in 1994, in addition to the development of GNVQs 'corresponding to levels 4 and 5 of the NCVQ framework' (NCVQ, 1993c, p. 5). The pace of change and development has been matched by intensive (not to say feverish!) public relations activity and by the introduction of new terminology to effect the new blueprint and master plan of qualifications which is meant to supersede previous frameworks and complement the NETTs (see Fig. 8.1).

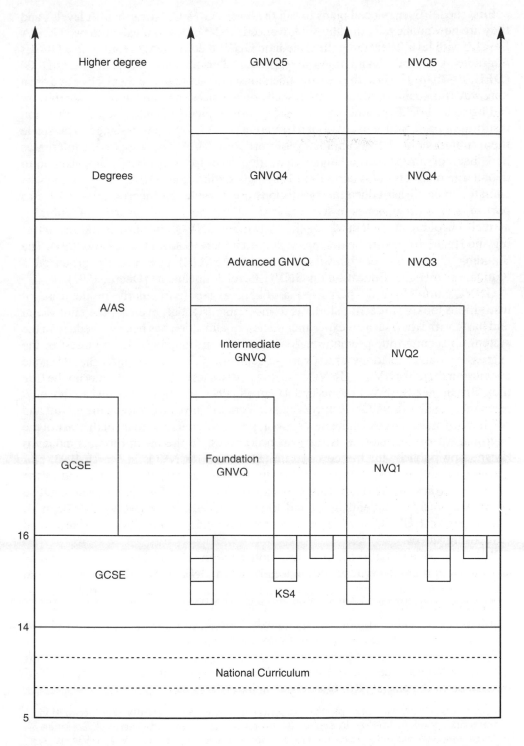

Figure 8.1 The national qualifications framework (*Source*: NCVQ, 1993c, p. 17)

First the DFE announced plans to call the level 3 GNVQs 'vocational A levels', and they are now publicized officially as 'Advanced GNVQs . . . equivalent to two GCE A Levels', with level 2 becoming 'Intermediate GNVQs equivalent to four or five GCSEs at grades A–C' and 'Foundation GNVQs equivalent to four GCSEs at grades D–G' (DFE, 1993b, p. 1). Since the new qualifications have yet to prove themselves and are a long way from being tried and tested, such equivalences can only, at best, be arbitrary claims and should presumably be taken with a pinch of salt. Higher education institutions have been actively wooed by various NCVQ schemes designed to persuade them to interview GNVQ candidates for entry in 1994/95, and a spate of conferences have been organized by the Higher Education for Capability (HEC) organization to debate the place of NVQs and GNVQs in higher education (HEC, 1993). In the new climate, some higher education institutions are considering incorporating NVQs as part of degree programmes in science (Irwin, 1993), and the University of Salford is actively encouraging students doing the 'Advanced GNVQs' in Business, Manufacturing and Health to apply to do degrees at Salford in 1994 (Salford University, 1993). The Standing Conference on University Entrance (SCUE) has recently produced a 'Guidance to Higher Education on GNVQ Level 3' document (Deere, 1993).

GNVQs are obviously perceived as filling a gap (particularly in the case of institutions looking to recruit students to meet quotas!), but, even so, the enthusiasm and haste with which such an experimental new qualification has been embedded in the system do seem a trifle premature. As mentioned in Chapter 1, in the midst of the aggressive public relations and overt sloganizing we can recognize the foregone conclusion that, like NVQs, GNVQs are *doomed* to succeed. It may or may not be true that 'Britain needs GNVQ to succeed' (Fennell, 1993, p. 13), but in any case it would seem that, again like NVQs, lecturers and trainers will have no choice in the matter and will have to make the best of the new system, just as teachers had to do in the case of the National Curriculum and its assessment procedures. In the mean time, as money is lavished on publicity for the new system (£1 million for NVQs in March 1993, plus another £1 million for GNVQs in November 1993; Targett, 1993, p. 6), and as the awarding bodies, RSA, BTEC and City & Guilds compete for slices of the lucrative new market, 65,000 students in around 1500 accredited centres (NCVQ, 1993c, p. 4) are hoping that GNVQs live up to the promises made in the glossy brochures and advertising videos.

What few commentators seem to have noticed in the midst of all this hectic and *ad hoc* innovation are the crucial differences between GNVQs and their more occupationally specific counterparts, especially in so far as these indicate a discernible retreat from cherished foundational NCVQ principles and practice (for critics such as Smithers, 1993, these are not nearly enough, though, in fairness, this report fails to mark important differences between NVQs and GNVQs).

Apart from the emphasis on broad vocational goals rather than occupationally specific outcomes, just what are the differences between GNVQs and NVQs? According to the official NCVQ account, unlike NVQs the

> award of a GNVQ will *not* imply that students can perform competently in an occupation immediately on qualifying. Students will, however, have achieved *general skills, knowledge and understanding which underpin a range of occupations*. (NCVQ, 1993c, p. 7, author's italics)

Ashworth (1992) has commented that GNVQs 'do not appear to be based on the notion of competence used by NCVQ hitherto' (p. 10). I would suggest that this is slightly understated, since it seems more accurate to say that GNVQs are not based on *any* notion of competence in the sense in which this is interpreted and understood in CBET and mainstream NCVQ literature. Competence is, in fact, rarely mentioned at all in the context of GNVQs. Instead we come across references to 'statements of attainment' which are deliberately used to mark a contrast with the 'statement of competence' of NVQs (NCVQ, 1992b, p. 9). In addition, as competence fades into the background, talk about a 'good grounding in occupational concepts' (RSA, 1992, p. 2), 'breadth of knowledge and understanding' (BTEC, 1992, p. 5) and 'well-integrated experience' (Deere, 1993, p. 6) gains prominence. It is noticeable also that the new occupational qualifications are meant to ensure 'relevance in the workplace' (BTEC, 1992, p. 5); GNVQs are, at best, 'work-related', they are not 'work-based', as NVQs, at least in theory, are supposed to be.

All this is a long way from the original NCVQ aims and principles. A more radical departure still is indicated in the approach to assessment in GNVQs. The new awards are made up of mandatory and core units – typically eight mandatory and four core for the Advanced level – and, providing students satisfactorily complete all their units, 'merit and distinction grades are awarded to students who demonstrate a level of performance above the basic GNVQ requirement' (NVCQ, 1993c, p. 13). The assessment is to be based on a 'portfolio of evidence' accumulated throughout the course. Moreover, '*different* forms of assessment', other than 'assessing performance' are to be utilized, and 'it is suggested that evidence gained as a result of a project or assignment carried out by a student will need to be supplemented by *written* tests linked to each unit' (NCVQ, 1992a, p. 85, my italics).

If we add to these changes the fact that these 'written' tests will be 'externally set' and that the 'pass mark on the tests is high as students must demonstrate that they have mastered the knowledge, understanding and principles underpinning each unit' (NCVQ, 1993b, p. 10), then the departure from CBET and basic NCVQ principles is complete. In the development of GNVQs the vocational wheel has turned a full circle; with the abandonment of work-based competence, and the introduction of grading and externally set written tests, the NCVQ has moved about as far away from basic foundational CBET procedures as it is possible to move while still retaining the NVQ label. It is little wonder that awarding bodies such as BTEC are offering such enthusiastic and full-blooded support for GNVQs (BTEC, 1992); the new qualifications are nothing more than reworked and reconstituted BTEC courses! (and, what is more, are seen as such by many teachers, see Smithers, 1993, p. 32).

These radical developments raise a whole host of important questions, not least of which is the future of occupationally specific NVQs in the new world of broad-based vocational qualifications. And what must the 'fundamentalist' NVQ supporters think about all this? Concerns were voiced during the GNVQ consultation phase about these very issues, with some vociferous and unequivocal opposition to key GNVQ proposals being expressed by representatives from a wide range of agencies. The Building Employers Confederation was adamant, for example, that grading was 'contrary to the NVQ concept' and the Pitmans Examinations Institute similarly did 'not support the grading of units' (NCVQ, 1992a, pp. 26, 29). The notion of centrally administered written tests was also opposed as 'contrary to the spirit of NVQs' (Paston Sixth Form

College), and the Association of Principals of Colleges stated firmly that 'centrally set and administered tests or examinations are not supported' (pp. 36–7). One of the most telling comments of all came from an (unnamed) LEA which roundly criticized centralized testing and observed that 'It is unfortunate that such manipulation of the NVQ system will be necessary to move into line with the procedures for academic qualifications, but it is realistic to consider doing so' (p. 35).

These observations and criticisms serve to remind us not just how far GNVQs represent a movement away from NVQs and NCVQ principles and procedures, but also correctly characterize the chief motivation for doing so, namely, the drive for parity of esteem with academic qualifications and the achievement of legitimacy in higher education. The NCVQ justification of GNVQ written tests and grading is quite clear in this respect; in order

> to achieve credible parity in relation to A and AS levels there should be a requirement that the written tests in general NVQs should both form a very significant part of the final assessment and that this part should be centrally set and administered. (p. 86)

This is clearly one of the chief ways in which GNVQs are being sold to higher education as possible entry qualifications, though much progress will have to be made to answer criticisms of the 'bizarre and unsatisfactory compromise' (Smithers, 1993, p. 10) of GNVQ assessment in this respect. Again, Malcolm Deere of SCUE puts the case for GNVQs with just these considerations in mind when he comments that

> the confidence within users, such as higher education, in the judgments based on the relevant evidence that may exist will depend upon the quality assurance features that will be applied centrally. The three Awarding Bodies have now agreed an assessment Code of Practice, endorsed by NCVQ. For each mandatory unit there will be a single test specification, setting out the scope of the knowledge, concepts, principles and relation-ships that will be subject to external tests. The three awarding bodies will jointly produce a model external test, clearly signalling the format and style that will be used and keyed to an agreed number of items (between 30 and 40). In 1993/94 the tests will be available four times a year, in future years testing will become more frequent. (1993, p. 9)

Before examining the implications of all this for NVQs, VET and post-16 education generally, there is one remaining feature of GNVQs which needs to be discussed – with potentially far-reaching ramifications for the vocational/academic divide and the alliance's programme of reform – and that is the incorporation of 'core skills' in the new vocational qualifications.

CORE SKILLS AND COMMON LEARNING OUTCOMES

There is nothing particularly new in the recommendation for some sort of core skill element in 16 to 19 education and training. Following on from the 1959 Crowther Report's recommendation of more broad-based general studies in the late secondary stage, a 'liberal studies movement' was taken up in the FE sector (Macfarlane, 1993, pp. 53–4), admittedly, concerned not with general education *per se*, but with adding a liberal dimension to mainly technical studies. With the curriculum and qualifications developments of the 1970s and 1980s – in particular the development of BTEC cross-modular assignment work and the growing emphasis on resource-based and student-centred project work through the post-16 vocational schemes – the general studies movement was transformed into a common skills or core knowledge programme. As Lawson (1992) has observed, the contemporary emphasis can be seen in a sense as a logical development of the National Curriculum and a 'vindication of the idea that there ought to be a core of educational experience . . . and the extension of the idea to the 16–19 phase' (p. 85).

The FEU document *A Basis for Choice* (FEU, 1979) had recommended a core entitlement of knowledge and skills for all FE learners (now an established part of theory and practice in the sector), and various core-skills projects were funded by the MSC in the early 1980s as part of the New Training Initiative (Lawson, 1992, p. 86). However, core skills really became a key element of the reform agenda after Kenneth Baker's 1989 speech to the Association of Colleges of Further & Higher Education, and the subsequent publication of the influential CBI report *Towards a Skills Revolution* (CBI, 1989). At about the same time, other bodies began to move in a broadly similar direction and a 'core of related knowledge, skills, qualities and attitudes has featured in the requirements of BTEC, the TVEI, and the CPVE' (Maclure, 1991, p. 38). The 1989 HMI paper on post-16 core skills included ten elements – knowledge about information technology, using information technology, knowledge about industry and commerce, knowledge about society and the environment, communication, numeracy, problem-solving, practical skills, working co-operatively and adaptability – and the CBI added 'values and integrity' and 'positive attitudes to change' (p. 39). Building on these initiatives, the NCC, working closely with the FEU and NCVQ, agreed a joint strategy in support of the idea of 'a common set of core skills which could be incorporated in both A/AS levels and post-16 curriculum in school on the one hand, and in NVQs or as units within the NVQ framework, on the other' (p. 39).

The inclusion of core skills in GNVQs, therefore, can be seen as a natural development and reassertion of ideas which have been put forward by a wide range of different bodies and agencies over the last twenty years or so. Whether all these agencies mean the same thing by core skills – and whether the GNVQ version matches up to and satisfies these requirements – is an entirely different matter. There are obvious differences of emphasis even in the terms used to recommend core elements. Common skills is the favoured BTEC term, the CBI refers to common learning outcomes, general skills was the SEAC preference, and personal, transferable skills are favoured in higher education applications of the term (ED, 1993b, p. 8).

In the original documentation, GNVQs were meant to have six core units – problem-solving, communication, personal skills, numeracy, information technology and an optional foreign language unit (1992a, p. 78) – and this specification was based, precisely and exactly, on the jointly agreed framework for post-16 education published by the NCC in 1990 (Lawson, 1992, p. 88). Two groups of core skills – Group 1: communication, problem-solving, personal skills, and Group 2: numeracy, information technology, and a modern foreign language (Macfarlane, 1993, p. 56) – were outlined in the NCC scheme, but, for reasons not altogether clear, only three core skills came to be incorporated into GNVQs. Selecting 'communication' from Group 1 of the original NCC formulation and 'application of number' (rather than numeracy) and 'information technology' from Group 2, these three become 'mandatory core skills units' and 'form part of the requirement for the GNVQs which will be offered by BTEC, City & Guilds and the RSA Examinations Board' (NCVQ, 1993d, p. 2).

Table 8.1 *Example of a GNVQ core skill*

Communication Level 2
Element 2:1: Take part in discussions with a range of people on routine matters
Performance Criteria:
1. own contributions are clear and appropriate on the subject matter
2. own contributions are made in a tone and manner suited to the audience
3. contributions from others are listened to attentively
4. own understanding of points made by others is actively checked and confirmed

Range: Subject matters: routine matters (e.g. responding to day-to-day enquiries; discussing routine tasks)
Mode: face to face; using the telephone
Audience: people familiar with the subject matter and in frequent contact with the individual (e.g. supervisors, colleagues, peers, tutors); people familiar with the subject matter but not in frequent contact with the individual (e.g. some customers/clients)

ASSESSMENT

Core skills units levels	National Curriculum Levels
1	4 and below
2	5 and 6
3	7
4	8 and 9
5	10 and above

(*Source*: NCVQ, 1993d, pp. 3–4)

Although the other core skill units in the original list of six may be taken as options (stressed notably at the advanced level), there is no rational explanation of why these seemingly basic and eminently justifiable core units were left out of the final specifications. Stranger still is the assessment procedure for the three core skill units. Although all GNVQ candidates must complete the core units – which 'should be integrated in the vocational activities which make up the learning programmes' – the units are assessed separately and by means of criteria which are *different* from those used in mandatory and core vocational units. Thus although the three core skills units are set out in the standard NCVQ format – broken down into elements with performance criteria and range statements – the assessment criteria are linked with National Curriculum levels 4 to 10, with core skill level 1 being equivalent to National Curriculum level 4 or below and core skill level 5 equated with level 10 on the National Curriculum framework (NCVQ, 1993d, p. 3; see Table 8.1). There is no adequate explanation of why this system was adopted or, indeed, the role it plays in furthering the aims and principles of GNVQs.

The core skills movement was a response to perceptions by employers and educators that there was an urgent need to improve basic skills, particularly literacy and numeracy, among young people (NCE, 1993, p. 327; interestingly, Smithers, 1993, claims that these issues have been 'sidelined' (p. 43) in the NCVQ core skills developments). A second purpose and thrust of core skills implementation is directed towards the broadening and integration of vocational studies and, of special significance currently, of supplying students with the all-purpose transferable skills so highly valued by trainers and employers. In Chapter 2 it was suggested that, although the notion of core skills such as communication and numeracy did make sense in the contexts of generalizability and integration of learning, there was little evidence (either philosophical or empirical) to support the notion of broader generic skills and competences. It would be useful to link these claims about generic competences with the core skills and GNVQ strategy.

A report by the Employment Department's Methods Strategy Unit on these issues begins by endorsing the view outlined above, that

> the core skills movement is based on beliefs about transfer. It assumes that it is possible to identify generic skills that are transferable across education and work contexts and that the acquisition of such skills will enhance learner flexibility, adaptability and autonomy. (ED, 1993b, p. 9)

Although correct in some respects, this statement is almost certainly claiming much more than is justifiable by the evidence. For one thing, there is no *necessary* connection between core skills and transferability. The core skills of communication and numeracy, for instance, may be used in many different sorts of learning activities, but this does not make them *transferable* to all learning activities. At most, it means that such skills have a broad and general relevance and applicability. And even here we have to be careful, since there is still a context-specific element in relation to such foundational skills as language and number. Mastering communication and understanding language and concepts in, for instance, a GNVQ Art & Design assignment, does not mean that any linguistic skills acquired therefore become automatically transferable to, say, GNVQ Science, BTEC Leisure & Tourism, or A level History.

The Employment Department report concentrates most attention on the ubiquitous 'problem-solving' skills (ironically, since these were ultimately omitted from GNVQ mandatory units!) and correctly cites Larkin's argument that 'there is a lack of empirical evidence' to support the 'idea that developing general problem solving skills could result in improved problem solving across a wide range of domains' (p. 10). This is indeed the case, and the more nebulous 'personal skills' have even less credibility in this respect. In addition to the deep philosophical difficulties surrounding these putative 'general powers of the mind' (Dearden, 1984; Powell, 1968), it was noted in Chapter 2 that the empirical evidence – for example, the work on professional expertise by Chi *et al.* (1988) – tended to support the notion of domain-specific knowledge and skills. The 1993 National Commission report also seems to favour this notion as applied to education and training. The report makes much of the 'knowledge revolution' and the need to develop 'applied intelligence' to cope with current demand, but, instead of the once popular ideas about general intelligence, there is a distinct preference for Gardner's concept of 'multiple intelligence' based on seven separate domains: 'linguistic, logical-mathematical, musical, spatial, bodily-physical, interpersonal and relating to internal self-knowledge' (NCE, 1993, p. 41).

Certainly this notion of distinctive domains does appear to be more in keeping with commonsense knowledge which indicates that there is a significant difference between problem-solving in science and problem-solving in art and design, and between operating effectively in catering management and managing successfully in the performing arts. There will, of course, be areas of overlap and common elements, but this is rather different from the claims made about wide-ranging transferable skills. Perhaps the most important point of all concerns learning itself, or rather the context of learning, and this is something which is given prominence in a number of recent reports and studies, including the Employment Department project on transferable skills and the National Commission document.

The Employment Department report rightly stresses the importance of attending to learning styles and the nature of learning situations in order to 'create a facilitative physical environment' (p. 18) which fosters positive attitudes to learning and motivates achievement. This is summarized neatly in the National Commission report slogan 'learning to succeed' (pp. 41ff.), based on the simple notion that achievement in education and training ultimately depends on self-perpetuating patterns of success and failure inculcated throughout a person's educational development, a view supported by the evidence of years of adult education practice and experience (NIACE, 1991) and by the employer experiments in the field of promoting learning such as the Ford EDAP scheme (EDAP, 1992).

The lesson of all such experience is that, granted the importance of core skills or common learning elements in providing a foundation for post-16 studies, the most important 'core' skill is not just learning *how* to learn, but learning *that* learning is itself worthwhile, valuable and (as Bennett *et al.*, 1992, claim) may also be financially profitable. Experiential learning strategies which were outlined in Chapter 4 have a key role to play in this process, since their whole *raison d'être* is to maximize learners' effectiveness, and this entails giving due attention and emphasis to the *process* of learning, and not just its outcomes.

CONCLUSION: GNVQs AND BRIDGING THE DIVIDE

There is a sense in which the introduction of GNVQs may be described as 'putting learning back into VET' (Hyland, 1993e, pp. 10–11) in that the new qualifications entail a return to more systematically planned courses, learning assignments and broader assessment procedures (though, as already indicated, there is still much progress to be made in this area). Whether they will be successful or not depends upon a number of factors, and also on the particular goals and targets being considered.

In terms of take-up, the success is almost a foregone conclusion. Given the massive exposure, enrolment rates are likely to increase exponentially, particularly if the links with higher education are consolidated. Added to this, the ongoing reform of the National Curriculum under Sir Ron Dearing has progressed from an initial preference for three key stages and a 'coherent curriculum from 14 to 19' (Dearing, 1993, p. 32), to a recommendation for the inclusion of GNVQs as optional elements in the post-14 framework (Nash, 1994).

However, whether GNVQs turn out to be educationally worthwhile, and conducive to high-quality education and training, is still an open question and a matter for empirical investigation. There are, it has to be said, some early teething troubles. A report issued by the Office for Standards in Education (OFSTED) in Autumn 1993 was highly critical of work produced by GNVQ students, particularly at intermediate level, and the NCVQ responded by alerting schools and colleges to potential problems in new vocational A levels (Utley, 1993b). The survey conducted by Smithers (1993) also highlights a number of worrying features of the new qualifications, and there is heated debate among the awarding bodies and real concerns are being expressed about the viability of the multiple-choice assessments in GNVQs (Utley, 1994). In addition, since many students are still having to do conventional qualifications such as GCSEs and A levels alongside GNVQs (presumably to satisfy league-table requirements and admissions tutors), problems of curriculum planning and coherence concerning the organization of timetables are causing a number of centres to request 'half GNVQs', since full programmes are found to be too burdensome (Dean, 1993).

Even if all these problems are overcome and the new courses prove popular and successful, there is still the question of whether they will help to improve the 16 to 19 curriculum and help bridge the vocational/academic divide. The signs are not promising in this respect. For one thing, there is now a hopelessly confused three-track curriculum instead of the original dual system, and if, as seems likely, GNVQ programmes come to replace NVQs in certain vocational sectors, those students working for NVQs are placed in a difficult position. A GNVQ/A level duopoly is likely to leave NVQ candidates out in the cold, and might reduce the status of the occupationally specific route to that of the old CPVE or low-grade TVEI programmes. This would be disastrous both for vocational students and for the future of VET, and would make the NETTs pointless and meaningless.

Predictions are always difficult against the background of rapidly changing policy shifts, but all the signs are that the incrementalist approach to reform represented by GNVQs will not bring about the sort of foundational changes necessary to upgrade vocational studies and bridge the vocational/academic gulf. Another strand of the incrementalist reform programme is the use of core skills (or common learning elements) to underpin all 16 to 19 courses, thus (particularly with modular A levels, Young, 1993) encouraging flexible and greater integration between the different routes. However, as Coates (1990) has commented, perhaps the most that can be hoped for from this strategy is some minor modifications of A levels. Indeed, there is a case for arguing, with Lawson (1992), that core skills developments have actually *polarized* positions in the 16 to 19 debate and that, against the alliance's objectives, the 'implementation of core skills tends to highlight the division between vocational and academic approaches' (p. 91).

This more pessimistic perspective on the current reform programme is perhaps justified by the official DFE rebuttal of the radical plans put forward in the 1993 National Commission report (Nash, 1993d). It could well be that those who oppose reform and favour the *status quo* know only too well that they are safe so long as fundamental reforms like the merging of the DFE and the Employment Department and the replacement of the present differentiated system with a common GED framework (or something similar) are kept at bay. This in itself tends to support the claims of those on the radical side of the alliance who argue that nothing short of such foundational change is likely to succeed.

If we push all this to its logical conclusion and take seriously the lessons of the past, I would argue that only a programme of radical reform can achieve the goals and targets being sought. Such a programme would entail:

1. Adopting the Dearing proposals and establishing a coherent 14 to 19 curriculum for *all* students;
2. Insisting on a 'common core' for all from 14 to 16 (Dearing suggests English, maths, science, physical education, a modern foreign language and technology, Blackburne, 1994) in order to provide a broad foundation of general education;
3. An 'education for work' component (described in more detail in Chapter 9) as a mandatory component and unifying theme of the 14 to 16 stage;

4. An abolition of A levels and the establishment of something like the GED recommended by the National Commission, which could be awarded at ordinary (around the age of 16) and advanced levels (18 or 19) and would 'replace the range of qualifications, including GCSE, A levels, BTEC and both general and more specific vocational qualifications' (NCE, 1993, pp. 67–8);

5. A post-16 stage in which 'vocational' and 'general' elements are available for specialization, but in which (as Dearing recommends) overlap and transfer are possible and, in order to ensure parity, all elements (especially the vocational ones!) are underpinned by the knowledge and breadth of learning which characterize the technical and vocational French Baccalauréat and German Abitur (Smithers, 1993, pp. 10ff.). Specific 'occupational' preparation could then build on this foundation, perhaps in the form of the 'traineeships' recommended by the National Commission (NCE, 1993, pp. 273ff.);

6. Since all this would require considerable administrative and bureaucratic change and development, the logical corollary would be the adoption of the Dearing and NCE proposals for a new body with overall responsibility for both vocational *and* academic studies (both education and training), so as to ensure that vocational studies is 'seen as part of the mainstream of educational provision from age 14 onwards' (NCE, 1993, p. 54).

All this would mean quite fundamental changes in the structure and organization of both vocational and general education awards and, probably, the abolition of the NCVQ rather than the 'reconstitution' recommended by Smithers (1993, p. 42). However, given our present aspirations and requirements, it seems to me that nothing less will suffice. And if all this seems far too radical and remote from reality, it would be well to remember the number of U-turns on policy in relation to the National Curriculum and youth training over the last five years or so. Nothing, it now appears, is unthinkable in the world of education and training!

Chapter 9

Vocationalism, Liberalism and General Education

In the last chapter it was noted that the NCVQ was strongly supportive of certain aspects of the general alliance programme of 16 to 19 curriculum reform. Firmly in the 'incrementalist' camp, the general strategy favoured is the development of GNVQs to achieve parity of esteem with academic qualifications, and the use of core skills to build bridges between the different routes. However, this policy of different but equal may be no more effective than the failed experiments which characterize past tinkerings with the system. Moreover, just as higher-level NVQs may be manipulated so as to satisfy higher education requirements (Tysome, 1993b, p. 3), there is every indication that GNVQs will undergo so much change to gain parity with A levels that NVQs will lose even the minimal and uncertain status they now hold, and vocational studies in general will suffer in the downgrading.

Over and above all these dangers, it is possible to suggest that the whole enterprise concerned with enhancing vocationalism through upgrading VET and leaving the academic route intact is fatally flawed because it is based on and tacitly endorses the fundamental vocational/academic dichotomy in the first place. This acceptance has meant that dualist and polarized views have pervaded all the debates and reform programmes. Certainly, the 'new vocationalism' initiative out of which the NCVQ enterprise grew in the 1980s could be described as being counter-productive in this respect. Not only did it patently fail to produce the coherent and upgraded VET system which everyone agrees is necessary for future development, the vocational/academic gap was actually 'widened as the work of the NCVQ emphasised the assessment of job-specific competence' (Whiteside *et al.*, 1992, p. 132). Moreover, much of the basic grounding on the general or academic 'liberal' side was lost through the misguided notion that occupational practice could manage without it. As Bailey rightly points out, the 'belittling of knowledge and understanding' (1989, p. 233) by the industrial trainers and supporters of the 'economic utility model of education' was both fallacious and disastrous for education in general and vocational education in particular. There can be no doubt that vocational studies has suffered a serious loss of status and impetus as a result of developments in the 1970s and 1980s (as the Smithers, 1993, survey clearly confirmed).

The introduction of core skills and GNVQs can be regarded as an attempt to put things right in this respect, though there is little indication that these most recent tinkerings will bring about lasting changes and reforms in the system. By introducing a third track, the current policy actually *accentuates* the vocational/academic division and, as part of this process, the incorporation of core skills is having 'significantly different effects on the academic and vocational curriculum' (Macfarlane, 1993, p. 57). Moreover, with the 'integration of core skills into examined courses the vocational curriculum has abandoned its separate non-examined general studies component and with it the liberal education ideal' (p. 57). Whether or not Macfarlane's trust in 'non-examined general studies' is justified or not is debatable, but he is certainly correct in pointing out the disappearance of the liberal ideal from vocational education.

The impact of the NCVQ approach to VET, in conjunction with the narrow skills training and hopelessly woolly attempts to change attitudes and motivations in line with the 1980s enterprise culture (Hyland, 1991a; Esland 1990), has produced an utterly impoverished and dehumanized approach to vocational education. As Ashworth (1992) has observed about the general NCVQ approach:

> . . . this view of competence entails an over-mechanistic way of thinking. It assumes that all difficulties in education and training can be overcome by the application of some simple technical solution . . . the TEED/NCVQ model of competence provides 'solutions' to the specification of learning outcomes which are normally inappropriate to the description of human action, or to the facilitation of the training of human beings. (p. 16)

In order to remedy these failings we need to construct a revitalized account of VET which does justice to the 'general' or 'liberal' aspects of vocationalism and which is located firmly within a coherent framework of general education. The foundations for such a strategy need to be built on a reconstituted concept of education in which the vocational and liberal are reconciled, and I would suggest that the building blocks for such a foundation can be found in John Dewey's theory of vocationalism (Hyland, 1993b). Before looking at Dewey's ideas and their implications for contemporary VET, it is worth examining the basic concepts in this area more closely.

LIBERALISM, VOCATIONALISM AND GENERAL EDUCATION

Reference was made at the beginning of the last chapter to the origins of the vocational/academic divide in the nineteenth-century gentleman ideal based on a classical education. Wiener (1981) has suggested that this 'gentry ideal' ensured that, alongside the Industrial Revolution in England, there emerged a suspicion of technology and a distaste for and evasion of the realities of manufacturing and commerce. It was this ideal which was associated until quite recently with exclusively academic and professional pursuits in the classical tradition, with technology, business and even science struggling for admission to privileged status. There is some justification for the comment by Silver and Brennan (1988) that it was the persistence of such 'gentrified' notions which fuelled prejudice and 'public ignorance' (p. 23) about the nature of industry at the root of current dualisms (in contrast to the rather different historical developments and traditions in France and Germany).

The prejudices associated with the gentry ideal of classical studies can be traced back to ancient Greek notions, particularly Plato's ideas about the nature of knowledge and the purpose of education. The original meaning of 'liberal' education as the 'freeing of the mind from error' can be traced to Plato's distinction between 'genuine' knowledge (knowledge acquired through rational reflection' and mere 'opinion' (knowledge acquired through practical activity for specific purposes; Schofield, 1972, p. 151). The former concept of knowledge, disinterested knowledge, came to be thought of as intrinsically valuable (knowledge for its own sake), whereas the latter, instrumental knowledge, came to be associated with more practical and less valued vocational pursuits (see Lewis, 1991).

However, this differential value basis for vocational and academic studies has nothing more than historical association to support it. Beyond the contingent fact that the classical gentry ideal came to be associated with the most powerful political and economic groups in Britain, there are no intrinsic or logical reasons for the liberal/vocational dichotomy in education. Certainly, there are epistemological and moral criteria to be satisfied before a process can be legitimately called 'educational' in Peters' 'normative' sense which is associated with a 'liberal education' (Peters, 1966, pp. 144ff.). However, Peters' justification of education in terms of involvement in 'worthwhile activities' can apply as equally to so-called vocational as it can to academic activities.

Hirst's (1974) concept of liberal education based on the evolved and historically developed 'forms of knowledge', for instance, is concerned broadly with 'the comprehensive development of mind in acquiring knowledge . . . aimed at achieving an understanding of experience in many different ways' (p. 47). Certainly, the development of knowledge and understanding at the heart of this conception of education will be subject to certain formal criteria (concerned with breadth, means of transmission, and so on), but there is nothing here which necessarily legislates for hard and fast distinctions between vocational and other legitimately educational endeavours.

The distinction between 'instrumental' and 'non-instrumental' (or between 'practical' and 'theoretical') activities tends to break down when applied to concrete cases, since, as Peters (1978) observes, both theoretical and practical activities can be pursued 'for their own sakes' (p. 9). It is often the context of learning and the ends to which it is directed which are decisive. As Dearden (1990) notes in discussing the vexed questions surrounding the differences and relations between education and training, there are no a priori reasons why they should not in some circumstances be compatible; a 'process of training could be liberally conceived in such a way as to explore relevant aspects of understanding, and in a way which satisfies the internal standards of truth and adequacy' (p. 93). A similar point is made by Peters (1966), who, in citing 'cognitive perspective' as one key feature of educational activity, would 'not deny value to activities which have a limited cognitive content'. Thus, although 'cooking . . . is obviously an activity which is necessary for the maintenance of a way of life', it can be 'done just as a tiresome chore, or it can be delighted in for the opportunities for skill and ingenuity which it affords' and can 'become an extremely absorbing and worthwhile pursuit' (pp. 176–7).

All this is not to deny that there are, of course, real distinctions to be made between 'liberal' and 'illiberal' processes and between intrinsic and instrumental value. The point is that it would be a mistake to think that these sets of terms can be applied in a way which rigidly demarcates liberal and vocational education. Moreover, when we come to consider the ultimate ends of educational activity, the notions of intrinsic and instrumental value tend to merge for, as Bailey (1984) reminds us, 'it is precisely its *general and fundamental utility* that provides part of the justification of a liberal general education' (p. 28, author's italics).

In addition to the general utility of liberal education – 'its capacity to liberate a person from the restrictions of the present and the particular' – Bailey provides a range of supplementary reasons for the provision of education which is 'fundamental and general' (p. 29). There are, for instance, cogent moral duties incumbent on any legislation for compulsory education. If we are to impose *any* education system on others, this, at the very least, ought to be shown to be in their best interests and to promote rather than restrict their capacity for autonomous personal development. Being autonomous and making choices depends both on knowledge about all the options on offer and also on possessing the wherewithal to reflect on these options and to make rational choices. And, since 'autonomy' is here being used in a sense which is rather broader than the sense it has in some of the NCVQ literature (where it often means the freedom to achieve competence outcomes!), it requires a good general educational grounding for its realization. As White (1973) argues in looking at arguments used to justify the compulsory curriculum in terms of helping students to make choices, if choices are to be genuine and rational, then a person 'must know of all the possible things he [*sic*] may want to choose for their own sake, and he must be ready to consider what to choose from the point of view not only of the present moment but of his life as a whole' (p. 22).

What all this implies is that a good general education is a prerequisite, no matter what choices are made or forms of life chosen. In practice, of course, the realities of life, particularly working life, mean that none of us has absolutely open and free choices, but the point is that our choices would be even less free and open without access to the knowledge and skills provided by general education. This also serves to remind us that vocational education – 'initiation into work as part of a worthwhile form of life' (Corson, 1991, p. 178) – needs to be integrated with and not separated from the general objectives of education. Dearden (1990) expresses this point well when he observes that

> Work is an extremely important part of the lives of those who have work to do. It not only provides material rewards; it also structures time, choice and activity. It modifies the worker in all sorts of ways; in his [*sic*] skills and sensitivities, in his knowledge and attitudes, and in his self-concept. It confers status. A general education which failed to find any place to consider something of such importance would be importantly defective. (p. 93)

DEWEY'S THEORY OF VOCATIONALISM

It is one thing to argue for a reconciliation of vocational and academic education – for vocationalism as an integral part of general education – and quite another to provide convincing justificatory arguments which might help to break down current prejudices and bridge the divide. Dewey's writings are helpful in this respect, since his starting-point was just these damaging dichotomies, divisions and prejudices which bedevilled educational debate, then as now. In fact, Dewey had a healthy dislike for all rigid divisions and argued passionately against the prevalence of 'either/or -isms' in educational theory. One of his major objectives was to break down the false dichotomy between the notions that 'education is development from within' or that it is 'formation from without' (Dewey, 1963, p. 17). Instead of this artificial opposition, educational activity is to be organized as 'intelligently directed development of the possibilities inherent in ordinary experience' (p. 89).

The gentry ideal of classical studies rested on Platonic conceptions of knowledge which were later supplemented by the writings of post-Cartesian philosophers such as Locke and Hume. According to this tradition, knowledge is essentially something which is acquired through rational reflection and, though it is always dangerous to apply general labels such as 'rationalist' and 'empiricist' to diverse schools of thought, even the empiricist strand of Enlightenment thought tended towards the view that knowledge and truth were to be pursued in a fairly passive spectatorial manner (see Hamlyn, 1987, pp. 206ff.). The pursuit of 'genuine' knowledge is, on this account, accorded a higher status (and so, by implication, were those, like Plato's philosopher-kings, who engaged in this activity) than the involvement in more practical endeavours. As Schofield suggests (1972), it was this tradition which gave rise to the belief that only 'disinterested knowledge has specific associations with the general culture' (p. 152), and this led to a rather one-sided view of what a general education should contain. Against this, Dewey favoured the Aristotelian tradition of education as a 'leading out', an activity designed to bring out the highest in human potential, and viewed the educational task 'not as a mere perpetuator of tradition, nor as a mere practical expedient, but as training in the art of inquiry' (Brumbaugh and Lawrence, 1963, p. 67).

The foundation of Dewey's epistemology is built upon the anti-Cartesian position originally developed by C. S. Peirce and later refined and modified by William James (Quinton, 1977). Labelled by Dewey himself as 'instrumentalism', this position differs in a number of important respects from the Platonic and Cartesian traditions. Unlike the passive spectator of Cartesianism, Dewey envisages an active pursuer and constructor of knowledge, working and interacting with others in a world of social beings and human products (Quinton, 1977, pp. 3–4). Knowledge and truth are neither given nor absolute, but constructed by humans out of their 'experience'. This concept of experience – which for Dewey is the 'name given to all that passes between the organism and its surroundings' (Geiger, 1958, p. 17) – holds a central position in Dewey's theory of knowledge. It is through experience that enquiry, or the pursuit of knowledge, is to be conducted, and, in Dewey's hands, this becomes a very practical activity, directed towards the solving of problems and the removal of obstacles in the way of general social progress.

Whitehead argued that the 'antithesis between a technical and a liberal education is fallacious' (1966, p. 74), and, in a similar way, Dewey attacked twentieth-century practice on the grounds that it had become 'highly specialized, one-sided and narrow'. It was an education

> dominated almost entirely by the medieval conception of learning . . . something which appeals for the most part to the intellectual aspect of our natures . . . not to our impulses and tendencies to make, to do, to create, to produce, whether in the form of utility or art. (Dewey, 1965, p. 26)

It should be stressed, however, that, in attacking the sterile features of traditional academic education, Dewey did not want to replace one extremism with another (unlike the contemporary 'industrial trainers'), but instead sought to break down the 'antithesis of vocational and cultural education' based on the false oppositions of 'labour and leisure, theory and practice, body and mind' (Dewey, 1966, p. 301).

This task was to be achieved in part by introducing into the curriculum the practical activities which Dewey called 'occupations'. An occupation is a 'mode of activity . . . which reproduces or runs parallel to some form of work carried on in social life' (Dewey, 1965, p. 132), and this notion of occupational activity – the 'continuous organisation of power along certain general lines' (p. 138) – figures prominently in the main recommendations for vocational education.

The idea of a vocation as something which 'signifies any form of continuous activity which renders service to others and engages personal powers on behalf of the accomplishment of results' (p. 139) is a broad one which, instead of standing in opposition to leisure and cultural pursuits, is made to embrace them. Such a conception includes

> the development of artistic capacity of any kind, of specific scientific ability, of effective citizenship, as well as professional and business occupations, to say nothing of mechanical labour or engagement in gainful pursuits. (Dewey, 1966, p. 307)

This wide-ranging vocational perspective is founded squarely on Dewey's pragmatic theory of knowledge which strenuously maintains the 'continuity of knowing with an activity which purposely modifies the environment' (p. 344).

The emphasis on the practical is carried over into proposals for a vocational curriculum. There is an insistence that the 'only adequate training *for* occupations is *through* occupations' (p. 310). It was mentioned in Chapter 1 that Dewey was a fierce opponent of the 'social efficiency' school of vocational education popularized by Snedden and Prosser at the beginning of the century, and argued forcefully against the idea of trade schools and the preparation of students for specific occupational roles. Instead, Dewey advocated a broad conception of vocationalism which was neither narrowly focused nor occupationally specific, but which allowed for a 'genuine discovery of personal aptitudes so that proper choice of a specialised pursuit in later life may be indicated' (p. 311). This connects well with the general preference for a pedagogy which exploits the learner's interests and experience and, ideally, has relevance to the solution of practical problems (Peters, 1977).

Dewey put forward two main arguments against a narrowly conceived vocational education, both of which have direct relevance to the contemporary debate about education, training and the post-16 curriculum. First, when 'educators conceive vocational guidance as something which leads to a definitive, irretrievable and complete choice, both education and the chosen vocation are likely to be rigid, hampering further growth' (Dewey, 1966, p. 311). More importantly, however, the needs of a constantly evolving industrial society can never be met by narrow skills training which neglects aspects of general education. Dewey was convinced that

> any scheme for vocational education which takes its point of departure from the industrial regime that now exists, is likely to assume and to perpetuate its divisions and weaknesses, and thus to become an instrument in accomplishing the feudal dogma of social predestination. (p. 318)

This warning is as relevant now in an era of relative economic recession, structural unemployment and post-Fordist industrial operations as it was when Dewey first wrote it about an earlier period of industrial development and organization.

EDUCATION AND WORK

Dewey's idea of what it is to have a vocation and his proposals for vocational education have much of value to offer those educators and trainers concerned with overcoming the vocational/academic divide and upgrading the status of VET. The central point about vocational preparation being on all fours with general education for life in society, though self-evidently basic, is never too trivial to mention and emphasize. By stressing the value of 'education which acknowledges the full intellectual and social meaning of a vocation' (p. 316), Dewey reminds us just how important it is to move beyond the damaging prejudices and dualisms which currently bedevil the education system at all levels.

One of the main implications of shifting our perspectives in the light of such considerations is that the notion of 'education for work' is taken seriously and incorporated into general education (through the National Curriculum and whatever post-school framework may emerge, be it a General Education Diploma or some other mechanism) as a key dimension and unifying element. The NCVQ approach to the problems and demands of VET has been to encourage the accreditation of *job* competences, and it is less than obvious that even this limited objective has led to the improvement of actual and usable vocational *skills*. What I am suggesting here is an emphasis, not on job skills, but on *work* skills and the development of knowledge and understanding about the nature and role of work within the wider framework of personal, social and educational development. Moreover, this is to be thought of, not as an optional element for students following a 'vocational' as opposed to an 'academic' route, but as a foundational component (a core or common learning skill or outcome, in contemporary terminology) of a 14 to 19 curriculum.

Such a core dimension builds on Corson's conception of 'studies in work across the curriculum' (1991, p. 173), but locates this within a context of general (or liberal) education in a way which is designed to be supportive of any specifically 'vocational' elements (of a BTEC, GED or GNVQ nature) of 14 to 19 education. Building on Dewey's ideas for practical enquiry and the values of liberal education outlined earlier, I suggest that a learning programme concerned with 'work' might include the following elements: the nature and value of work; work and employment; work and the community. It would be useful to comment on each of these in more detail before contrasting such an approach with more specifically vocational or CBET strategies.

The nature and value of work

In attempting to answer the question, 'What are the ingredients of the good life in pursuit of which we undertake to educate people?', Mary Warnock (1977) outlines a programme which contains three elements: 'Virtue, Work and Imagination' (p. 129).

What Warnock has to say about 'work' provides a useful starting-point for a description of this aspect of a 'work across the curriculum' dimension.

While agreeing with those educators who point to the dangers of narrowly focused vocationalism, Warnock maintains that

> work is, and must always be an important ingredient in the good life; that a life without work would always be less good than a life which contained it; and that to be totally unemployed is indeed a dreadful fate. One should help people, no doubt, to bear it, but should not accept it as a normal or ultimately tolerable condition. (p. 144)

This forthright account of the role and positive value of work in human life is based on and justified by a number of presuppositions. First, there is the notion that, even though a job that is boring, pointless and alienating can be regarded as no more than a necessary evil, it is still 'better to have it than not, and probably better to work hard at it than less hard' since 'money earned is better than money handed out as a right, divorced from any work done' (p. 144). Second, work can be regarded as a basic human need and motivation to act; in a Neitzschean sense, the 'will to power . . . is perhaps identical with the will to work', and it 'is certain that all work is effort to make or change things or reduce them to order, and that all these efforts are worth making' (p. 145).

The notion of money earned through work being superior to that received in charity could be regarded as a reassertion of the Protestant work ethic which was recently reincarnated in the form of the 'enterprise culture' which informed the vocational initiatives of the 1980s. It was a theme running through some of the TVEI and schools vocational schemes operated in this period (Shilling, 1989) and played a key role in the revival of citizenship education following the report of the Speaker's Commission in 1990 (Hyland, 1992e). In the National Curriculum Council document *Education for Citizenship* (which outlines proposals for citizenship as a cross-curricular theme), for instance, there are numerous references to the value of work in an enterprise context. In a section called 'Work and Leisure', for instance, teachers are asked to stress 'the importance to the society and the individual of wealth creation', and the 'Public Services' component is headed by an area of study designed to show 'how public services depend for their scope and effectiveness on the generation of wealth and are paid for by taxation – they are not free' (NCC, 1990, pp. 8–9). Beneath the apparent commonsensical and non-controversial nature of all this are unarticulated values about enterprise and individualism, and these are emphasized more by what is omitted than what is stated. There is nothing here about the fact, for instance, that the salaries of civil servants, politicians, the police and others are also paid out of taxation and 'not free', and definitely nothing at all about the social, economic and moral principles which underpin community services in modern welfare states.

What is missing from Warnock's justification of work is a clear articulation of the differences between work and labour or toil and, given that it is the latter which is realistically the common experience of most of the population, some attempt to place this within a context of broad values, principles and human motivations. Herbst (1973) uses a distinction brought out in the writings of Hannah Arendt to mark differences between work and labour which are of supreme importance for education. Although the concepts have a lot in common – both consume the time and energies of people, are directed to a purpose, can be done more or less effectively and conscientiously – work can be said to have some intrinsic value (the work is integrally related to its end-product), whereas labour has extrinsic or utilitarian value (it is done for purposes beyond itself, for money) and is, therefore, 'toil'; 'labour is hardship . . . the price which we pay for whatever advantages the rewards of labour will buy' (p. 59). Another way of expressing the difference is that 'work, unlike labour, must have a point which the workman [*sic*] can endorse, and a purpose with which he can associate himself' (p. 61).

This account seems to offer a far more accurate description than that of Warnock, who, though recognizing the menial and often futile nature of much so-called work, does tend to over-emphasize the creative work of artists and professionals. Against this, Wringe (1991) rightly points out that 'some kinds of work are not at all constitutive of the good life and are at best a necessary evil' (p. 37). Wringe has in mind here the sort of work which tends to be boring, repetitive, menial and futile (that is, 'labour' under Herbst's description), and suggests that, to a greater or lesser degree, most humans will have to face tasks of this kind. In fact, there is a good deal of evidence to suggest that school pupils are only too aware of these basic facts of life. The working-class 'lads' observed and interviewed in the research by Willis (1977) were almost fatalistically accepting of their future work in dead-end and menial jobs, and research in Australia by Walker (1991) produced similar findings. Shilling's work with youngsters involved in TVEI and schools vocational work-experience schemes was chillingly realistic in this respect. After experience of working in a large factory, the majority of students had developed negative attitudes and commented on the mechanical and tedious nature of most of the jobs. For these youngsters, any positive factors (easy work, good money) 'were not sufficient compensation for the labour process they would have been subject to'. Furthermore, 'far from making students more open to the possibilities of working in industry, this part of the course had alienated the majority from working in a large factory' (1989, pp. 124–5).

However, much of positive educational value can be gained from examining work in the light of such realistic experiences and expectations. If work of this kind is, for many people, a necessary evil, then to 'undertake one's share of this evil, and consequently to undertake such learning as will enable one to do so . . . may be a universal obligation as well . . . as being in itself an educative experience' (Wringe, 1991, p. 37). To be even more realistic, we need to move beyond the rather bourgeois notion (probably generated through the gentry ideal of education) that only professional or creative occupations can be intrinsically valuable, satisfying and self-affirming. Part of the 'morality of work' is to insist that 'work does not have to be sublime or spectacular . . . to be worthwhile. Many relatively mundane jobs can be challenging and varied and involve standards of logic, efficiency, integrity, judgment and so on' (p. 38).

This calls for considerations of work as 'craft . . . pursued for its own ends . . . as unconstrained occupational work' and thus 'similar to recreational work in having value for its own sake' (Corson, 1991, p. 171). However, in order to realize such ideals of occupational work (which are Deweyan ideals), and to move beyond negative notions of 'constrained labour', Corson suggests a framework for a learning pro-gramme which could reinforce 'the value that students see in their work and the significance of that work for themselves and for their society'; these include the following principles (p. 172):

(a)   there is no ulterior motive for work other than the product being made and the process of its creation;
(b)   the details of daily work are meaningful because they are not detached in the minds of workers from the product of the work;
(c)   workers are free to control their own working action;
(d)   craftsmen are thus able to learn from their work and to use and develop their capacities and skills in its prosecution;
(e)   there is no split of work and play and work and culture;
(f)   the work activity of craftsmen determines and infuses their entire mode of living.

These features of what Corson calls 'craftsmanship' are admittedly idealistic, but the suggestion is that nothing short of such radical reform can transform the nature of education for work. In the absence of such conditions, however, education still has a vital role to play in helping students to make sense of the less than ideal world in which toil may be a commonplace experience. Wringe has two key proposals to make in relation to the 'morality of toil and the division of labour' as opposed to the 'morality of work'. First, since 'toil, regular, serious toil cannot itself be a necessary part of the good life', the 'facts of human existence are such that preparedness to undertake it may be regarded as a necessary part of a life that is just' (Wringe, 1991, p. 40). Both vocational (technical) and moral education (concerning the values of work and distribution of goods in society) are, therefore, necessary components of an education for work curriculum, as are those elements of a general education (art, humanities, science, sport) which might give meaning to those aspects of life not taken up with work or labour.

A second consequence of the realism recommended by Wringe is that 'if toil is a necessary evil, training which enables it to be completed more efficiently and reduces the amount of time to be spent on it or enables it to be replaced by a more challenging or worthwhile form of work seems morally desirable' (p. 40). As with the other objectives outlined above, such an element will of necessity be just a part of a general education for work programme which incorporates knowledge, skills and values in the goal of promoting a critical understanding and full engagement with the nature of working contemporary society.

Work and employment

Warnock's argument that 'if children are to be educated in such a way that they can get jobs, it is reasonable that someone must try to work out roughly what kind of jobs there will be for them' (1977, p. 146) was written just before the onset of massively increased youth unemployment and, with hindsight, can perhaps be forgiven for a certain naivety. However, there is, as commentators on the 'new vocationalism' of the 1970s and 1980s point out, also a dangerous over-simplification in thinking that schools can either supply what industry wants or that education can in any way predict long-term job and industrial requirements. Although economic vicissitudes since the 1970s have generated a whole range of 'ritualistic' (Stronach, 1990) responses in the form of providing youngsters with job-specific and enterprise skills, there is scant evidence of any links between these activities and industrial requirements (Finn, 1990), and little justification for a belief in the efficacy of manpower planning (White, 1990).

The onset of structural unemployment generally from the 1970s onwards has caused some educators to argue that 'education about unemployment' (Furnham, 1984) is now a necessary component of any school or college curriculum. Certainly, any approach which heralded a movement away from what Lee *et al.* (1990) have called the 'immorality' of youth training which, under the guise of 'enterprise', sold 'unemployment relief as training' (p. 195), is to be welcomed. A more honest and realistic approach might seek to prepare students for the possibility of unemployment (Stirling, 1982), perhaps incorporating an examination of post-Fordist economics and operations and including ideas about flexible working, job-sharing and new attitudes to the place and value of work in the light of structural unemployment (Darcy, 1978).

However, even allowing for the 'quite serious difficulties about interpreting what the needs of industry are' (Finn, 1990, p. 48), there is still a crucial educational need for comprehensive careers advice and counselling. As Taylor (1991) has noted, although some sort of careers advice service is required from local authorities under the Employment Training Act 1973, this has always been patchy and unsystematic, and even this miminal provision is now threatened as the powers and resources of LEAs disappear as a result of central government policy. Drawing on the work of Watts (1984), Taylor recommends a careers education programme which includes 'employability skills' (job search, job acquisition and job retention), 'adaptability awareness' (to broaden the range of what is contemplated as possible) and 'survival skills' which would encompass an awareness of the psychological effects of unemployment and a knowledge of what support services are available in the community (1991, p. 199).

In addition, this aspect of education for work needs to emphasize that, in times of structural unemployment and fluctuating job markets, learning and education take on an increasing importance. On a general level, surveys of the labour force indicate that rates of unemployment are well above average for people without qualifications. In 1990, for example, unemployment among those without qualifications aged 20 to 24 and 25 to 30 was 20 per cent and 15 per cent respectively, twice the overall rates for these age groups. In addition, once unemployed, unqualified people are more likely than others to remain out of work for long periods (NCE, 1993, p. 243). However, though it is possible to show that 'learning pays' (Bennett *et al.*, 1992) at this level, qualifications are not necessarily the same things as skills and, on this foundation of general education, specific vocational training will need to take account of skill demands and shortages at a national and regional level (skills shortages are highlighted regularly in the Employment Department's Labour Market Report, see ED, 1993c).

Work and the community

In this section the place of work within the community and wider society will be examined in a critical manner which includes perspectives taken from alternative cultures and countries. The idea is to move beyond the standard descriptive approach recommended in *Education for Citizenship*, in which students would look at the 'opportunities and responsibilities of different types of work in industry, services and the professions' (NCC, 1990, p. 8), so as to enable students to analyse their experiences against the background of the social, economic and political developments and changes in society which have affected the lives of all citizens over the last few decades. The flip side of the 'enterprise culture', after all, is characterized by the centralization of state power, a growing gap between rich and poor, and the development of an underclass of underprivileged and disenfranchised people, and any rational programme of general education requires that this picture is also displayed to students.

In terms of recent changes in work and employment, there is an urgent need to examine the nature and causes of changing work patterns and the growth of unemployment and underemployment which has characterized modern industrial societies since the Second World War. There was a marked tendency for the 'new vocationalism' of the 1970s and 1980s to 'juvenalize and personalize' (Stronach, 1990, pp. 157ff.) the problem of unemployment as a means of suggesting that this was somehow caused by the deficiencies of young people. The preposterous nature of this wilfully misguided policy has been referred to in earlier chapters, and it will be important for an 'education for work' to engage with this problem in a realistic manner.

Instead of the personalization of the problem, students could be informed about the crises and difficulties which have beset all capitalist economies since the bubble of the post-war boom was pierced by the 'capitalist crisis of overaccumulation' (Armstrong *et al.*, 1984, p. 235) in the 1970s. This kind of study would draw on a number of disciplines (economics, history, politics), and might involve an examination of the role of work and basic economic principles in relation to different kinds of traditional and modern societies (materials produced for 'World Studies' in schools are valuable sources of material here, see Fisher and Hicks, 1985). In this respect, the history of post-war Britain provides fascinating material for study (with a wide range of accessible media and documentary material), and there is no shortage of explanations for our relative economic decline and de-industrialization in these years (Esland, 1990). In addition, some comparison of different patterns of economic and social development experienced in other countries (America, Japan and Third World countries for instance) would be of great utility and value.

In terms of this comparative dimension, it will be necessary to note that, although all modern industrialized nations have suffered as a result of the global recession over the last twenty years, some states have managed to cope with the difficulties rather better than others. As Shirley (1991) has argued, countries with 'extensive social policies' such as Denmark, Belgium, the Netherlands, Switzerland and Japan were more successful in keeping unemployment rates under control in the face of global recession than countries such as Australia, Canada, Britain and the United States, which were 'spectacularly unsuccessful' (p. 150) in this respect. A number of key factors are identified to account for these differences (pp. 152–3):

- A commitment to full employment both as a political priority and as the dominant ethic of economic policy
- State intervention geared to productive investment, both public and private, favoured over boosting consumer demand
- Active labour market policy measures including public works, vocational training and special employment in public services
- The creation of part-time jobs with full social rights in co-operation with trade unions favoured over a general reduction in working time
- A tax structure which reflected a trend away from pay-roll taxes and social contributions toward taxes on capital assets and consumption

- A labour movement committed to technological change and job flexibility under conditions of full employment
- A conscious decision by all parties not to use high unemployment as a means of securing other policy objectives

Any serious examination of such issues would draw on a whole range of different fields of study (more than satisfying the Peters' 'cognitive perspective' criterion of liberal education!), and would ideally involve the attempt to examine the broader themes in terms of their immediate impact on local and regional work communities. This sort of general 'education for work' provision would supplement and supply a theoretical and critical perspective on the more strictly 'vocational' elements of any 14 to 19 curriculum (in the form of work experience or schools–industry links, for example). In addition, it is crucial to locate all these vocational elements within a framework which examines critically the taken-for-granted assumptions about society and the economy, and explores a range of alternative positions and underpinning values.

Just as the 'new vocationalism' initiatives dishonestly suggested that education and unskilled school leavers were somehow to blame for Britain's economic crisis, so there is a similar disingenuous (and largely unquestioned) assumption that only a 'market forces' approach to industry and the economy can provide the solution to all the current ills which beset society (the application of this approach to educational provision is criticized in the next chapter). Similarly, a genuine 'education for work' programme needs to deal seriously with questions about the quality of working life and the social organization of work (Taylor, 1991), and challenge given assumptions about the inevitability of present arrangements. There is nothing immutable about the present nature of work and division of labour in society, and alternative possibilities can be constructed by drawing on the experience of different communities and different cultures.

MORALS, WORK AND SOCIAL JUSTICE

All this necessarily entails the exploration of values and basic moral assumptions about work, social organization and the general distribution of goods in society. To provide a foundation for the study of work and employment, which are central to the 'education for work' programme, it will be crucial to examine and reflect critically upon the values which inform and construct relations between people in all aspects of social organization. The revival of 'education for citizenship' in the early 1990s was referred to earlier, and the sort of instrumentalist/technicist approach to values which characterized this movement is typical of the incomplete and inadequate treatment of values in education in general and VET in particular. This technicist approach – translated into a concern chiefly with the rights of consumers – is a notable feature of the Citizen's Charter (Great Britain Parliament, (1991) issued by the government in 1991, which has spawned a whole range of similar specialist charters, including ones for schools and the further education sector (DFE, 1993c; FEU, 1993).

Calls for schools to concentrate greater attention on teaching pupils the difference between right and wrong occur regularly after outbreaks of social disorder or youth crime (the Speaker's Commission on Citizenship, for example, followed a series of riots in the inner cities, Hyland, 1992e), and moral education is thus called upon to provide a panacea for all our social ills. This places a monstrously misguided emphasis on morality as a mere technique for controlling social behaviour, and, in this respect, it is interesting how this 'technical' approach to values was popular in the 'personal and social skills' components of schools' vocational and youth training schemes (resurrected as a 'core skill' in the 1990s), and also in the 'moral competence' strategy (Wright, 1989) meant to provide a values dimension to NVQ programmes (an idea which, in spite of FEU support, seems to have been stillborn!).

However, all such technical and instrumental approaches to morality are fatally flawed and doomed to failure. The uncritical linking of prescribed behaviour with social norms can, at best, produce only a mechanical or conventional form of morality which, unsupported by 'justificatory reasons' (Straughan, 1982), would break down at the slightest challenge. Moral education cannot take the form of narrowly focused remedial programmes designed to respond to short-term needs (rather like many current VET schemes) in order to preserve the *status quo*. If such programmes are to be based on rationally justifiable grounds, they will need to call into question the morality of many contemporary social norms and practices (including issues surrounding work and employment) in order to provide young people with the wherewithal to adopt genuine value positions in relation to all aspects of social life.

Moral education is not simply a mechanical or descriptive operation designed to transmit values which happen to be socially or politically expedient (Trusted, 1987). Similarly, it is not possible to bring something called 'moral competence' into play so as to encourage young people to be reliable and conscientious at work. Employers' favourite values – honesty and reliability – are not, after all, just *occupational* skills or requirements, but moral *principles* which crucially govern all forms of human and social relationships. Similarly, the values underpinning good citizenship and the Protestant work ethic, though no doubt indispensable to the maintenance of order, stability and prosperity in modern industrial societies, are not especially 'capitalist' or 'civic' values, but old-fashioned *moral* values which need to be constantly renewed and critically inspected to guard against atrophy.

Lynch and Smalley (1991) are certainly correct in saying that citizenship education involves not just knowledge and understanding, but also the 'development of attitudes and values which underpin the notions of rights, duties and obligations' (p. 96). Yet there is barely a hint in the moral competence, personal skills or citizenship schemes that such rights, duties and obligations need to be examined critically, rationally justified and are, perhaps, open to change and revision in the light of empirical evidence and rational analysis. Criticism and autonomous reasoning are essential components of well-constructed programmes of moral education and development (Duska and Whelan, 1977), and this entails the fostering of questioning attitudes in students. In the sphere of education for work, this questioning must extend to a critical inspection of the values upon which the current arrangements of work, economic organization, the distribution of goods and services and general social relationships are based.

In terms of current VET provision there is a singular lack of criticism in relation to the basic values of 'individualism' and 'social market forces' which provide a foundation (though one which is rarely fully articulated and justified) for present social and economic arrangements in society. The dominant values associated with 'individualism' characterized the youth training of the 1970s, the 'new vocationalism' of the 1980s and continue to influence vocational initiatives in the 1990s (Lee *et al.*, 1990). The 'moral programme' of the enterprise culture was one of 'self-reliance and self-help, opening up economic and social policy to competition and market forces' (p. 3). Stronach (1990) chronicles in some detail the ritualization of such values in youth training programmes in which, through 'vocational profiling, the ritual moves the individual from experiential selfhood to social personhood . . . creating an archetype of the young citizen/worker in a series of idealized personal qualities (self-reliant, enterprising, thrifty, problem-solving, reliable, etc.)' (p. 176). Such 'individualistic' values were central to the citizenship revival in the early 1990s.

The unquestioned dominance of such perspectives and the moral assumptions associated with them will provide important and legitimate subject matter and areas for critical enquiry in the values component of any 'education for work' programme. Shirley (1991) explains that the

> doctrine of economic individualism is based on the belief that the history of western civilization is the history of free individuals engaged in intellectual thought. It is strongly rooted in the tradition of welfare economics . . . which maintains that all human behaviour is conditioned by the hedonistic aspirations of each individual wanting to maximize his/her productive capacities. (p. 154)

The popularity and attractiveness of these deceptively simple ideas are difficult to deny. Russell (1946, pp. 620–7) traces the growth of individualism in mainstream philosophy from the Greek Cynics and Stoics down through the medieval Christian tradition, until it finds its fullest expression in the writings of Descartes, which provided one of the chief sources of inspiration for the foundation of English liberalism in the seventeenth and eighteenth centuries. This Cartesian 'dualism' – the rigid division of mind and matter, subject and object – can be glimpsed behind all theories which stress the individual over the collective consciousness. Its influence is discernible in all fields of enquiry, even, as Eagleton (1983) argues, in such abstruse areas as literary theory, in which excessive individualism parallels 'possessive individualism in the social realm' and 'reflects the values of a political system which subordinates the sociality of human life to solitary individual enterprise' (p. 197).

Within the liberal tradition, individualistic notions went hand in hand with the growth of mercantilism, and in political theory the basic concepts date back at least as far as Hobbes and Locke and are encapsulated in the idea of 'possessive individualism' which asserts that 'the individual is essentially the proprietor of his own person, and capacities, for which he owes nothing to society' (Macpherson, 1964, p. 263). This theory and its implications provide one of the key philosophical foundations of the market economy and so-called 'free enterprise' system of modern capitalism. As Macpherson explains, possessive individualism holds that 'human society consists of a series of market relations' and that

> political society is a human contrivance for the protection of the individual's property in his person and goods, and (therefore) for the maintenance of orderly relations of exchange between individuals regarded as proprietors of themselves (p. 264)

It is these basic ideas which inform, either directly or indirectly, not just the neo-liberalism of the New Right (Whitty, 1990), but also the 'social market' (Ranson, 1993) model which over the last ten years or so has been applied to all manner of public-service provision from the health service to schools and further and higher education.

The appeal of such ideas often rests on intuitive feelings based on 'freedom' and what seems 'natural'. Hemming (1969), for instance, sees the development of individualism as a natural consequence of human evolution and the 'greater individuation of members of a species'. Accepting that the evolutionary trend is a 'good thing', he goes on to suggest that 'individuals have a responsibility to develop their individual capacities' and we 'should seek to help others to become themselves' (p. 26). Although some attempt is made to build bridges between 'self and society', Hemming remains committed to a system based on 'individual moral insight' (pp. 53–4, 62).

In a similar way, it is difficult to gainsay the values associated with individual autonomy which, in the writings of Kant, culminates in the moral injunction to treat people always as ends and never as means. Popularly expressed as 'respect for persons' (Körner, 1955, pp. 147ff.), this principle has influenced thought and practice in diverse fields of enquiry, and no one would want to deny that a society which defers to such a principle is, theoretically (and other things being equal), a most desirable one. A profound mistake is made, however, when the individualistic components of this system come to be divorced from the social ones. Possessive individualism is trivially correct in declaring that we are all the proprietors of our own persons (who else could be, after all?), but fundamentally misguided in thinking that the social context of personhood is irrelevant to such considerations.

This social context emerges as having special significance in relation to educational activity, and is also crucial to a consideration of systems of moral justification which, against individualism, may be used to undergird education for work programmes based on broad values of social justice. Although it is only in relatively recent times that individualistic values have been allowed full and free play in educational policy-making, their influence on theory and practice in this country has been around for some time. Such values, for instance, were influential in the development of a differentiated system of schooling based on competitive assessment and justified by a meritocratic ideology stressing individual achievement measured against prespecified norms (Broadfoot, 1979). The competitive ethos which underpins this market-forces approach is now applied with almost religious zeal to all aspects of educational policy and practice (Simon, 1992).

Cogent alternatives in the form of social-democratic and community-orientated approaches to provision have been proposed by a number of commentators, and these will be examined in greater depth in the next chapter. At this stage, it is worth stressing just how odd this individualistic ethos appears in the light of the broad socializing function of education which is the *sine qua non* of modern schooling systems. The 'hidden curriculum' of schooling, for instance, can be said to represent the 'enduring and powerful forces of a whole society socializing its members into compliance' (Meighan, 1981, p. 62). Moreover, demands that this hidden feature be made overt are regularly heard during times of moral crisis or social unrest (see, for instance, the recent outcry following the Bulger trial in which two 11-year-old boys were found guilty of killing a toddler; Bennathan, 1993, p. 17).

The causes of these strains and contradictions are to be found in the disingenuous attachment to a meritocratic ideology through which schooling has become, in Hargreaves' (1982) words 'deeply imbued with a culture of individualism' (p. 87). The main fault in this emphasis lies 'not in the humanistic sentiments and ideals which it enshrines', but in the 'repudiation of the nineteenth-century concerns with the social functions of education'. For Hargreaves the solution to the 'most central problems of our society' is to be found in the fostering of 'active community participation from its members' (pp. 93, 145). In a similar vein, Langford (1985) has attacked the obsession 'with the difference which being educated makes to an individual' (p. 3), and recommended instead a greater concern with the social dimensions of education and schooling. For Langford, 'to become educated is to become a member of society and so to have learnt what it is to be and to live as a member of that society' (p. 181). It is arguable whether the notion of active citizenship means anything at all without this social dimension of education.

Furthermore, we need such a social dimension in order to place such concepts as 'freedom' and 'personal development' in their proper perspectives. Such ideas are, in any case, hopelessly vague and tend to be meaningless until they are interpreted within certain social and moral frameworks. As Dearden (1972) has argued, by valuing freedom, personal development and autonomy in education, we do not thereby 'mark the eclipse of such other values as truth and morality' (p. 461). After all, 'great criminals are markedly autonomous men' (p. 461), but we would naturally wish to exclude the development of free criminals from our list of educational aims! In much the same way, the rather nebulous notion of 'individualism' only takes on meaning and import once it is located within a context of moral principles and social values (see Jonathan, 1993).

Any consideration of moral principles is, arguably, in itself sufficient to shift the area of focus from individual needs to social requirements, especially when the morality of work and employment is the chief concern. The mention of a specifically moral (rather than, say, a predominantly political or economic) framework inevitably raises questions about the nature of morality and moral judgement, and, although this is by no means a simple or straightforward question, there are fairly well-established ways of dealing with it. If we consider, for instance, why a woman's decision to have an abortion is thought to raise moral issues whereas, in the normal run of things, her decision to, say, eat a particular breakfast cereal does not, we move closer to the basis of morality. Undoubtedly the former state of affairs is far more complex than the latter, but the crucial question is *why* this should be so. The central difference seems to be that the abortion decision raises fundamental questions about human happiness, desires and interests in a way in which the decision to eat a particular sort of breakfast (normally) does not.

The traditional way of describing these features of morality has been to say that its nature and scope may be defined by the 'form' and 'content' of judgements (Hyland, 1986). Form covers the way in which moral judgements are characteristically expressed, and content refers to what morality is about; for instance, we can say that morality is generally about the sort of considerations brought to light in the example cited above, where basic human needs and interests are at issue. Hare (1981, pp. 22-4) suggests that the moral domain may be defined by reference to three features: prescriptivity, overridingness and universalizability.

Moral principles are prescriptive in the sense that, in holding them, we prescribe a course of action which we think ought to be followed by ourselves and others. Overridingness refers to the sense in which a moral decision overrides a merely prudential or selfish one. Universalizability, a concept first explored in Kant's moral philosophy, asserts that ethical principles have universal applicability, that is, if a course of action is morally right or wrong in a particular set of circumstances, then the same moral obligations are placed upon all people in relevantly similar circumstances.

Singer (1979, pp. 10–11) points to the fact that a diverse range of philosophers, as intellectually far apart as the existentialist Sartre and the Marxist Habermas, have all tended to agree that ethics must in some sense be universal. Moreover, although philosophers such as Hare place an excessive emphasis on the form of morality, the critical process ultimately tends to lead to the codification of content as well. In the end, moral decisions must be *about* something, and, although this area can only be mapped out in broad terms, there are grounds for regarding the general focus as 'human happiness or interests, needs, wants or desires' (Warnock, 1967, p. 55).

Any consideration of work, employment and the distribution of goods in society inevitably raises moral issues of this kind, and it is my contention that an 'education for work' programme needs to engage critically with such issues. The value assumptions underpinning the current arrangements for work, and the social structure which supports them, may be discussed and alternatives explored. In particular, it will be important to bring out the fact that beliefs about human nature which justify the individualistic and market-forces approaches are by no means the only logical conclusions from the basic premises described. Underpinning possessive individualism are beliefs that humans are basically hedonistic and self-interested, and the social, economic and political beliefs stemming from this position are meant to accommodate the so-called brute facts of human existence.

However, there are a number of serious weaknesses in this position. First, arguments about human nature prove very little by themselves, since this omnibus description can be manipulated to incorporate just about everything about humans which is not logically impossible! Second, even if hedonism or selfishness were deemed to be an accurate description of basic human behaviour, this would still not be all that decisive in terms of morality, since morals are not about what *is*, but about what *ought* to be (Snare, 1992). Moreover, the very premises of self-interest which are thought to yield individualistic conclusions are actually, when applied in contemporary theories of social morality, seen to be supportive of a more collective approach based on social justice and equity of interests.

Utilitarianism, one of the most widely endorsed and popular theories of ethics, for instance, is said by Singer (1979) to be approached by means of 'universalizing self-interested decision making' (p. 13). The basic idea is that morality is centrally concerned with the consequences which our decisions and actions have in relation to human needs, desires and interests. Actions and decisions are morally justified in so far as they further or maximize the promotion of interests or the satisfaction of wants. Accepting the fact that self-interest is a prime motivator of human behaviour, utilitarianism attempts to provide a way in which individuals may regulate their behaviour in the interests of the well-being of all (including themselves). Barrow (1975) summarizes the position succinctly:

> Although one of the arguments for utilitarianism is based on the suggestion that it is reasonable for people to strive for what they want, once utilitarianism has been accepted, it leads to the immediate attempt to regulate each individual's wants in a way that does justice to the overriding aim of equal concern for everybody's wants. (p. 113)

Hare (1981) suggests that there is a close connection between the basic utilitarian maxim, 'everybody to count for one, nobody for more than one' and Kant's categorical imperative, which enjoins us to 'act only on that maxim through which you can at the same time will that it shall become a universal law' (pp. 4–5). The key notion here is that, in so far as morality is concerned with the satisfaction of wants and the furtherance of interests, the only judgements and actions which have universal validity are those which place the interests of all on an equal footing.

Rawls (1971) offers a similar (though non-utilitarian) justification of social justice which is both powerfully persuasive and widely used in the justification of welfare rights and social legislation generally. Starting from the same basic 'facts' of human nature as those who would espouse individualism and competitive market approaches to society, Rawls accepts what has been described as the 'Humean model', which holds that the human condition is one of 'moderate scarcity . . . and limited altruism' (Snare, 1992, p. 170). This means (as individualists would agree) that there can never be enough economic or other desired goods around to satisfy everybody, and that there is too little altruism around to avoid conflicts arising from this scarcity. This leads to a 'vulnerability' the consequence of which is that 'in the absence of social rules and institutions no individual can be secure from attack' (p. 170). From this position the argument is pushed forward to the justification of some sort of 'social contract' which offers citizens mutual self-protection.

Starting with these basic conditions, Rawls asks us (as rational and self-interested citizens) to engage in the following thought experiment. Imagine that we are able to reconstruct society in any way that we choose (within the bounds of logic and practical feasibility), and that we are free to design social legislation, the distribution of goods and work, codes of behaviour and the general social and political structure in line with our wishes and preferences. The only limiting condition (and it is a supremely important one) is that we are situated behind a 'veil of ignorance' (1971, pp. 136ff.) so that we cannot know *in advance* the position in society in which we are going to find ourselves and thus cannot be sure of our future status and prospects. All this serves to sharpen the senses and concentrate the mind wonderfully! On reflection, we are likely (given the condition of rational self-interest) to realize that the most reasonable course of action is to design a society in which goods and services are fairly evenly distributed, in which the benefits and evils of work are broadly shared, in which justice and liberty under the law prevail, and which is characterized by quite a high level of respect for persons and the consideration of each other's interests.

Rawls described this favoured position in terms of 'justice as fairness' and expressed this by means of the technical formula of the 'difference principle', according to which 'social and economic inequalities are to be so adjusted that they are of the greatest benefit to the members of the least favoured social group' (pp. 75–8). Although different from Hare's utilitarian position, this contract theory has many parallels with it. In fact, Hare (1981) finally commits himself to a broadly similar line in admitting that 'the principles of economic justice which would be chosen by an impartially benevolent critical thinker would be moderately egalitarian' (p. 164).

Although theoretical at one level, such moral perspectives can be shown to have immediate practical relevance to any consideration of contemporary social conditions, since it is in the nature of the human condition that we can never know what the future holds for us in terms of health, employment prospects or life chances generally. Even the healthiest, most financially independent and socially successful people may at some time need to have recourse to the services and assistance of a society organized along mutually beneficent lines!

It is now widely accepted that 'thinking skills' (Whalley, 1987) should be an essential ingredient of general education (this is also argued in the National Commission report, NCE, 1993, pp. 85–7), and, applied to the key issues described above, I would suggest that a critical examination of the values underlying the nature of work and employment in contemporary society is an indispensable component of the 'education for work' programme outlined above. The unquestioned dominance of the individualist and market-forces models needs to be criticized and alternatives explored in the form of the moral perspectives described above. In this sense, not only are the general and vocational elements of the 14 to 19 curriculum more likely to be reconciled, there may also be a genuine opportunity to provide that 'balanced and broadly based curriculum' (Great Britain Statutes, 1988, ch. 1) asserted as an entitlement of *all* pupils in the Education Reform Act. Such a programme should also go some way towards meeting the current demands for vocational preparation being made by such agencies as the CBI and the National Commission on Education.

CONCLUSION: WORK, EDUCATION AND COMPETENCE

In terms of the range of vocational responses to economic and employment demands made on education in recent years, the introduction of NVQs can be regarded as supportive of the individualistic solutions to the alleged problems by claiming to supply the necessary job competences to people who are thought to be deficient in this respect. Enough has been said in earlier chapters to illustrate the monstrous folly and inadequacy of this policy. What can be added to these earlier criticisms is an illustration both of the inadequacy of the NCVQ enterprise in terms of the task of bridging the vocational/academic divide, and also of the tendency of CBET in general to stress the technicist and market-forces approaches to the issues which were criticized above.

The individualist thrust of NVQ assessment has been remarked upon by a number of commentators (Ashworth, 1992; Chown and Last, 1993) and has been mentioned on a number of occasions in earlier chapters. The quest for NVQ accreditation – often based on some sort of needs analysis, action planning and personal record of achievement – is a solitary one in which, under the guise of a spurious notion of autonomous learning, individuals are meant to take responsibility for their own achievements (and also failures!). There are many personal and educational benefits of student-centred and experiential learning, but the NCVQ approach does not appear to produce any of these. At the same time, the individualistic focus of NVQs directs attention away from the important interpersonal dimensions and social context of learning. Hodkinson (1992) is correct in noting that 'learning is not just about interactions between people, but also the interaction between people and their environment' (p. 33), and quite right in pointing to the shortcomings of the behaviouristic NCVQ model in this respect.

The idea of introducing the neo-liberal market-forces model into educational planning is based on the belief that 'markets promote autonomy by enabling all participants to make decisions for themselves; markets are myopic, offering what people want' (Ranson, 1993, p. 333). In particular, the 'social market' (Elliott, 1993,

p. 17) tends to view the educational enterprise as a business of offering consumers products with a certain utility value; in theory, the various 'suppliers' (schools, colleges) thus have to compete with each other for 'customers'. Not only is this conception of education and training monstrously distorted, but (as I explain in more detail in Chapter 10) it is also both dangerously mistaken and fatally flawed.

In terms of the present discussion, however, it is interesting how the notions of behaviourism, consumerism and prespecified outcomes can be seen to come together and complement each other in ensuring a perfect fit between NVQs and the social-market model of educational provision. Elliott's references to the 'social market' model of education and training have been mentioned in a number of contexts in earlier chapters. In relation to the present discussion, his description of recent trends in teacher education is both totally and uncannily applicable to the NCVQ enterprise. The basic principle of the social market, he argues,

> is that of behaviourism, with its implication that the significance of theoretical knowledge in training is a purely technical or instrumental one. Knowledge belongs to the realm of inputs rather than outputs. Its introduction can only be justified if it is a necessary condition for generating the desired behavioural outcomes of learning. (p. 17)

On this account, the outcomes of learning 'are construed as quantifiable products which can be pre-specified in tangible and concrete form . . . learning outcomes are conceived as behavioural, with an emphasis placed on the atomistic specification of discrete practical skills (competences)' (pp. 16–17).

The language of the market and 'possessive individualism' is translated and transmitted to customers in the NCVQ enterprise through talk of 'ownership'. Paralleling the obsession with private property in the larger market of economic individualism, the educational counterpart is, as Debling and Hallmark (1990) put it, that of the 'ownership of the facts, theories or principles needed for competent performance in an occupational role' (p. 10). The NROVA plays an important part in this process, since, for each VET consumer, it presents evidence of ownership in addition to symbolizing 'participation in the national system' (Jessup, 1991, p. 117).

This concept of 'ownership' has achieved a certain vogue in recent years in contexts in which learner autonomy and student-centredness are being discussed, though I suspect that those who use the term with the ideals of autonomy and experiential learning principally in mind are not fully aware of its wider proprietorial, individualistic and market-orientated connotations. There are a number of philosophical weaknesses in the notion of 'owning' the products of education such as knowledge and skills. In the first place, the 'scarcity value' of such products is quite unlike that of consumer goods. In the economic market individuals compete for commodities which are not available to everyone. However, my possession of a particular skill or body of knowledge does not prevent someone else from possessing that *same* skill or knowledge. Thus, there is a sense in which we can neither compete for educational goods (see Dearden, 1976, ch. 9) nor establish sole ownership over such goods.

That there is, undeniably, genuine competition for scarce resources in the contemporary social market of education arises from the fact that educational goods are deliberately constructed as 'commodities' (Chitty and Simon, 1993) and access to them (in the form of NVQ accreditation, GCSE or A-level grades, entry to higher education courses, etc.) is made into a scarcity by design (in order to restrict access to certain areas) or by economic necessity resulting in a limitation of resources and opportunities. But it is important to stress that there is no *intrinsic* reason for this scarcity of educational resources, nor any philosophical justification for this materialistic and legalistic conception of educational goods in terms of ownership and private property.

It is indeed ironic that the NCVQ enterprise is legitimated partly in terms of its policy of open access yet based on premises which hold that educational qualifications are essentially consumer goods 'purchased' by clients operating in an educational marketplace (of course this model now characterizes much of post-school education, as I mention later). Such contradiction, fuzziness and double-talk is a feature of much of NCVQ development, and is certainly characteristic of the folly of trying the upgrade VET and bridge the vocational/academic divide through programmes based on narrowly prescribed job competences. What I have suggested in this chapter is that these aims can be achieved only if, in the spirit of Deweyan vocationalism, a solid foundation is established in the form of an 'education for work' programme which would be a mandatory core element in a 14 to 19 curriculum for all students. Such a recommendation goes beyond the 'liberal vocationalism' described by Silver and Brennan (1988), which is concerned essentially with adding 'liberal' elements to 'vocational' courses, to the establishment of general education programmes (National Curriculum, GED, similar to the framework outlined and recommended at the end of Chapter 8) within which education for work is an indispensable component. Only in this way can we hope to overcome the damaging dualisms and prejudices and achieve Dewey's ideal of an 'education which acknowledges the full intellectual and social meaning of a vocation' (1966, p. 318).

Chapter 10

Competence, Education and the Learning Society

Along with the broad aims of the 'alliance' and National Commission referred to in earlier chapters, and the much-publicized NETTs, the slogan 'the learning society' has emerged as the currently most popular expression of our national aims for education and training. As with other fashionable notions such as access, learner-centredness, APL and CATS, the NCVQ recognized the importance of the 'learning society' bandwagon early on, and there are overt attempts to link NETTs and NVQs with the wider objectives encompassed by the slogan. Jessup (1991), for instance, waxes lyrical about the potential impact of NVQs and outcomes-led learning in this respect, and claims that a consequence is that 'continuing learning will become a natural part of life and employment. Companies, like colleges and training institutions, will become centres of learning' (p. 116). In much the same way, the proposals and recommendations in *Education and Training for the 21st Century* are designed to 'promote continuous learning from the age of 5 through education and throughout working life' (DES, 1992, vol. 1, p. 3).

The NETTs are, of course, centrally concerned with 'lifetime learning' and incorporate the key aim that 'by 1996 all employees should take part in training or development activities' (Debling, 1992, p. 5). In fact, the slogan has had a special attraction for those in the field of in-house training and development – especially since the 'Investors in People' initiative was launched by the Employment Department in order to 'help British business get the most out of its people' (ED, 1990, p. 2) through training and development – and the idea of the 'learning company' as one which invests in this way through schemes such as the Ford Employee Development and Assistance Programme (EDAP) now has wide currency. The chairman of the National Training Task Force which originally proposed the NETTs has proposed that 'one of the most effective investments a company can make in its future is to encourage and actively support the continuous self-development of its employees' (NTTF, 1992, p. 1), and, seeing the potential for higher funding and greater attention to adult education generally, organizations such as NIACE have positively encouraged the initiatives through conferences designed to publicize projects such as the Ford EDAP (NIACE, 1992).

As was mentioned in Chapter 2 when the idea of competence was examined as an educational slogan, a slogan can be powerfully persuasive without having any precise or fixed meaning. It has to be said that, for the most part, the 'learning society' falls into this category. All the force comes from the positive connotations associated with learning and development (which, like competence, is self-evidently a 'good thing' which no one could gainsay!), without offering anything like a clear account of what the learning and development in question will consist in.

The term has its roots in the adult education tradition of 'recurrent education' (Houghton and Richardson, 1974) and 'education permanente' (Schuller and Megarry, 1979) designed to challenge the stereotypical formal 'front loading' model of provision (see Molyneux *et al.*, 1988), and, indeed, it is so obviously attractive that it is surprising that its possibilities for fostering continuing education and training have not been exploited until now. However, the present ubiquity of the slogan more than makes up for its past neglect. The value of learning has apparently been rediscovered, and individuals and organizations of all kinds can, it is claimed, be revitalized by concentrating on their learning capacity. Expansion of the newly incorporated FE sector is explicitly linked with 'building a learning society' (Thomson, 1993, p. 7) and the 'learning university' (Duke, 1992) is proposed as the new model of higher education designed to be responsive to the social and economic changes required for life in the 1990s and beyond.

The common terminology, however, masks a world of difference between the sort of learning proposed by the adult education tradition – concerned with 'enlightenment' (Simon, 1990) and the fostering of 'critical practice . . . and direct engagement in definable concrete projects for social change' (Collins, 1991, p. 119) – and the aims of the NTTF and the CBI based on the 'economic utility' model of education mentioned in earlier chapters. Under the banner of the 'learning society', education, according to Ranson (1992), is 'being made a priority to serve the needs of the economy' (p. 28). However, the shifting of funds and priorities is piecemeal, limited and, linked to CBET and the NETTs, is likely to be as ineffective as past tinkerings with the system.

This much is recognized in the 1993 National Commission report which speaks of 'dutiful genuflexion rather than enthusiasm' (NCE, 1993, p. 321) about lifetime education and training, and makes positive recommendations for more intensive activity and investment from nursery to higher education. The key problem is that the mechanism favoured by central government as a means of bringing about the learning society is simply not up to the task. Market forces and economic individualism are no substitute for investment and strategic planning, and it is important to explore just why this is so before examining the role of the NCVQ and NETTs in the 'master plan' for education and training into the twenty-first century.

MARKET FORCES AND EDUCATIONAL PROVISION

Commentators such as Simon (1992), Whitty (1990) and Ball (1990) have produced comprehensive and detailed accounts of the way in which the New Right in British politics has succeeded in bringing about radical change in education policy-making and practice over the last decade or so. In terms of the broad ideological groupings identified by Williams (1961) – old humanists, public educators and industrial trainers – Ball (1990) argued that 'in the 1980s the public educators are in disarray . . . and the field of education policy making is overshadowed by the influence of the old humanists and industrial trainers' (p. 5). Since this comment, the 'industrial trainers' in conjunction with the 'neo liberals' (Whitty, 1990, p. 18) have tightened their grip considerably on all aspects of educational policy-making and legislation. Policy-formation now seems to be dominated by think tanks such as the Centre for Policy Studies (Judd and Crequer, 1993), and has degenerated into the 'impoverished' process described by Gipps (1993, pp. 36ff.).

Although there are strains and tensions in the general thrust of government policy since the period when the Reform Act was formulated (Lawton, 1989), the neo-liberal idea of allowing market forces to determine the shape of all aspects of educational provision has gradually emerged as a central unifying theme (Ranson, 1993). Strong and weak versions of the market-place approach to educational planning and provision are discernible in the literature, and I will be arguing that all such approaches are misguided and mistaken. In so far as the NCVQ enterprise is informed by these models, I suggest that this is yet another serious shortcoming of the strategy represented by this approach to education and training.

The strong thesis asserts that education is a business like any other and that 'markets and private sector management techniques can help provide answers to the perceived problems and deficiencies of the public sector, and that their imposition on schools will result in improvements in standards of provision' (Keep, 1992, p. 102). In order to achieve this, schools and colleges must be 'privatized' (though I will argue later that 'nationalization' is the more apposite term!) and must 'compete' for business by providing quality 'goods' to be purchased by 'customers' (students, parents, employers, etc.). The mechanisms for marketizing education along these lines have been developing apace since the Education Reform Act 1988. First of all, schools and colleges are 'freed' from local authority control (the former through the Reform Act and the latter through the Further & Higher Education Act 1992), and their funding controlled by central government through quangos (the Funding Agency for Schools and the Further Education Funding Council). Through 'efficiency' and the promotion of 'quality' products – manifested through the league tables now produced for FE colleges as well as schools (Dean, 1993) – the performance of educational institutions will be improved and consumer choice enhanced.

A weaker version of this thesis may be detected in attempts to introduce an 'enterprise culture' (Hyland, 1990, 1991b) into the control and management of education. Recognizing that, as a public service, education is not quite the same as private-sector industry, there is the implication that schools and colleges may operate *like* businesses by learning from their efficiency procedures and management systems (Keep, 1992). Income generation is a key aspect of this tendency, and many schools, for instance, have developed partnerships with local firms and initiated projects to boost their funds (Smith, 1990). In further education, the obsession with measures of 'quality' based on industrial standards such as BS5750 (Tysome, 1992b) has emerged as a prominent feature of the new culture.

EDUCATION AND THE MARKET: A CRITIQUE

Both the strong and weak versions of the thesis that education should be regulated by market forces can be shown to be untenable and, furthermore, self-defeating in terms of other generally approved aims such as promoting active citizenship, democratic decision-making, consumer choice and the establishment of a rational and coherent education and training system. There are a number of major flaws and shortcomings in the market-forces argument.

1. It is based on a mistaken or, at least, highly 'idealized' concept of how real markets operate. There are many types of markets and models of competition, and educational debates using the market model have conveniently avoided the messiness of 'having to refer to the quirks of actual markets' (Chambers, 1988, p. 47) and have also passed over the examples of outright market failure when attempting to deal in this way with the supply of public services such as education and training (Streeck, 1989; Evans, 1992).

In 'real-life' markets, pure and open competition of the sort envisaged for schools and colleges does not often exist. As Keep (1992) explains, 'unregulated competition . . . creates levels of complexity which make management impossible'; companies, often acting collectively, 'will therefore try to limit uncertainty' (p. 104) through such things as monopolies, cartels, franchising agreements and employer associations. In this respect, it is interesting that, in newly incorporated FE sector, employer's forums were established from the start (Evans, 1993), a Charter for Further Education (DFE, 1993c) was introduced to supplement the control of the FEFC and, in the absence of local authorities, colleges in some areas are grouping together to rationalize the provision of services (Tysome, 1992a). According to some commentators, it is only a matter of time before 'replacement LEAs' (Kenyon, 1993) need to be invented to facilitate strategic regional planning for the post-school sector.

This equivocation can, of course, be regarded as a natural and inevitable consequence of ambiguity on the part of central government over deregulation and the need for central control. No doubt partly arising from the neo-liberal and neo-conservative tensions in the New Right, educational legislation since 1988 has led to increasingly centralized control under the guise of giving more power to parents, schools, colleges or governors (Simon, 1992). However, the trick is now wearing a bit thin, and it is no longer possible to disguise a massive shift of power and control in education from the regions to the centre (Chitty and Simon, 1993) behind a 'power to the people' banner.

Against this background of centralized control, talk of market forces and competition in education can be placed in its proper perspective. Both the market and the competition are illusory or, at best, metaphorical and in no sense comparable to 'real' markets. As in the case of the introduction of performance-related pay into education and other public services, we are forced to conclude that, since all the available evidence shows no links exist between pay incentives and increased performance and enhanced quality (Caulkin, 1993), the determination to persist with patently inappropriate models of planning is generated by ulterior, non-educational motives.

2. The utter inadequacy of the market model when applied to education and other public services is brought out, on a common-sense level, by considering the so-called 'goods' that schools and colleges are said to produce. Although education may be 'commodified' and made into a 'positional good by definition in scare supply' (Ranson,

1993, p. 336), this is neither a rationally justifiable interpretation of public-service provision nor is it necessarily in the interests of consumers.

In order to function as commodities, the ends of education have to be viewed in an extrinsic and instrumental manner; in this commodity world, talk of intrinsically valuable knowledge and skills is replaced by the acquisition of capital (NVQs, A levels) which allows access to 'goods' which are in scarce supply (access to higher education, occupational roles and, increasingly, jobs of *any* kind). But it is pure sophistry to suggest that education can be regarded as a commodity in any sense other than this extended, extrinsic and technical-instrumental one (which, incidentally, fits uneasily with other branches of government policy concerned with improving standards!), and plain nonsense to think that, by introducing talk of commodities, we thereby open up education to market-place conditions.

The aim of industry and commerce is to make profits by selling goods and services; there *is no other aim*. Public services, such as health, education, the police and prison services, on the other hand, are called upon to perform a complex range of functions which are financed out of the public purse. Such services cannot make 'profits' in anything other than a wildly extended metaphorical sense (by introducing performance indicators and productivity gains, for example) for the simple (and wilfully overlooked or ignored) reason that they are not actually *selling* anything! As Keep (1992) argues:

> schools do not charge a price upon which they aim to make a profit, but instead have a public service obligation to provide a free service to all those who are legally entitled. There is also the expectation that schools are there to pursue social goals, such as the moral and religious development of the pupil and the fostering of the notions of citizenship, which are not normally expected of private sector organisations. (p. 114)

Although the case of post-16 education is slightly different, many of these simple and basic points still hold. Entitlements and goals vary in the case of further and higher education, but the service function remains, as does the chief funding mechanism in the form of taxpayers'/citizens' contributions.

Moreover, the evidence suggests that, whether in 'real' markets or the 'metaphorical' education market, since 'clout in the market derives from the power to subordinate others in competitive exchange', the paradoxical and unintended outcome is that 'consumer choice empowers the producers' (Ranson, 1993, p. 336). The process is explained succinctly by Ranson:

> Schools begin to differentiate themselves to fit specific niches in the educational market . . . The institutions begin to market what they believe to be their distinctive image, qualities and achievements. A hierarchy of distinction and public esteem emerges . . . It is likely in an education market, therefore, that the intention of increasing choice results not only in the product being altered but choice itself being reduced or eliminated. (p. 336)

These dangers are already being realized in the newly incorporated FE sector, in which fears are being expressed of a loss of community provision and colleges are being cautioned to resist the temptation to drift comfortably into a more conventional, prestigious academic provision and to accept a 'mission of answering to the education needs, from the basic to the advanced, of *everyone* over 16 in the community' so as to realize the 'national aspiration for universal education, vocational commitment and life-long learning' (Smithers and Robinson, 1993, pp. 2, 4). Hayes (1993) similarly urges colleges to note the difference between a 'business view and a public service view' and argues that they should be by all means 'businesslike' (p. 6) but avoid thinking of themselves as private-sector businesses.

As a public service, education is obviously 'more rigorously regulated than most private sector business markets' (Keep, 1992, p. 115) and it is state rather than self-regulated for the most part. Moreover, the various state mechanisms of control – OFSTED, the FEFC and HEFC – are subject to political and ideological directives in a way which is quite different from the private market. What is more, the centralized control exercised through the DFE is now sweepingly powerful and, in more and more cases, is used to further particular ideological ends (Judd and Crequer, 1993). In the face of such state control, the alleged autonomy of the so-called educational market and its consumers pales into insignificance.

3. Another particularly telling weakness of the market model of education concerns its equivocation about values, both moral values and those of a social-democratic kind. Although markets are founded on the assumption that the values associated with possessive individualism are shared by all rational, self-interested individuals, the market system could not function without the presence of other non-market values in society as a whole. As Poole (1990) explains, although markets are theoretically constructed solely on the basis that individuals will maximize their wants and preferences, the 'social relations constituted by the market presuppose a sphere of social life in which the individuals who participate in the market are themselves produced and reproduced' (p. 49). A market of self-interested individuals would not, without the existence of other values and motivations, reproduce itself. Poole argues that for reproduction of the system to happen

> it would require that purely self-interested individuals enter into relationships with each other in order to produce, nurture and care for other self-interested individuals just like themselves. To make sense of the apparent sacrifices of self-interest involved here we would at the very least have to assume the existence of goods of a quite different kind to those involved in ordinary market transactions. To comprehend the social processes necessary, we also need to suppose that there are human relationships – certainly those between parent and child, probably those between parents – which are conceptually distinct from the contractual and voluntary engagements for mutual benefit typical of the market. (pp. 49–50)

The operation of markets, therefore, is entirely dependent upon the inculcation of values of a non-market, disinterested kind (the 'family values' recently recommended as an antidote to youth crime!). In other words, it needs the values which education, as Ranson points out, is typically expected to transmit, namely, honesty, respect for persons and good citizenship. It is indeed ironic that schools are also being asked to conform with market principles which are often in conflict with such moral values!

In addition to all this, it needs to be said that the impact of the attempt to apply market principles to educational provision – particularly when this is combined with the increase in centralized control of the system – is profoundly and inherently undemocratic. As well as the loss of democratic control through the replacement of elected local education authorities by quangos appointed by central government (Hyland, 1992a; Bogdanor, 1991), the operation of the market reproduces the 'inequalities which consumers bring to the market place' and 'confirms and reinforces the pre-existing social class order of wealth and privilege' (Ranson, 1993, p. 337). The market 'entrenches the powerful beyond control', reinforces a 'traditional order of authority and power' and thereby leads to an 'attenuated democratic process' which succeeds in 'removing the social order from democratic scrutiny' (p. 339). It is quite breathtakingly disingenuous to manage such centralized and undemocratic control of education and the public services while maintaining a surface commitment to quality, rights and giving power to students, parents, citizens and the regions, and it is all achieved through the omnibus and all-purpose slogan of market forces!

COMPETENCE, MARKET FORCES AND THE LEARNING SOCIETY

The links between NVQs and the values associated with economic individualism and an educational market were referred to briefly in Chapter 9. However, there is much more to be said in this area, as indeed there is also in connection with the general centralizing thrust of recent educational policy and legislation. In order to ensure that the vicissitudes of the market do not interfere with the direction of government policy, regulation in the form of a National Curriculum and assessment system (bolstered by league tables and OFSTED inspections) was introduced to complement the process of removing schools and colleges from LEA control and placing them under the dispensation of quangos appointed by the Secretary of State for Education (Whitty, 1990; Simon, 1992). If this 'nationalization' of education at the school level is achieved through the National Curriculum, then NVQs and the central regulating power of the NCVQ is intended to achieve similar results at the post-school level. On this account, the spread of CBET throughout the system can be regarded as a means of ensuring that the education and training market functions in accordance with certain goals and objectives. NVQs and NETTs provide for the post-compulsory sector what key-stage testing does for schooling, and government policy in both these spheres of education is now transparent and overt (DFE, 1993a). The linking of FE and TEC funding to NVQ awards in combination with the general investment in public relations was supplemented at the end of 1993 by the expansion of the tax-relief scheme for training courses which lead to NVQs (Inland Revenue, 1993). In this respect, the FEU (1992b) scheme for a national system of credits for post-16 qualifications (though, no doubt, espoused for laudable educational ends) serves to legitimize the notion of education and training as a pre-packaged commodity which is (theoretically) on sale to all those with purchasing power.

NVQs are, in fact, ideally suited to the educational market-place; they are the commodities and goods which are purchased by self-interested consumers. As Theodossin (1990) has remarked:

> College marketing units ought to find it easier to sell products whose market-place value is clarified through the use of such devices as the NVQ kitemark, designated competency levels, and links and equivalency among the various awards. (p. 59)

Yes, indeed, and if such products are theoretically open to everyone, available in handy packages (units and modules) and have a simple and flexible assessment system, then so much the better for the market appeal and value of NVQs. Like action plans and training credits in the form of 'smart cards' (FEU, 1992a, p. 49), NVQs can be regarded as part and parcel of the new era of post-school education; privatized, marketized, commodified and, naturally, competence-based! It is, of course, true that the marketing of the system has not been as successful as the NCVQ and its supporters would have liked (Field, 1993a; Nash, 1993b), but this minor problem is nothing that cannot be solved by the injection of more public money into the advertising and marketing process (Targett, 1993)!

However, there is a yawning gulf between the rhetoric of the market and the reality of educational practice. Market forces and leagues table are about as unlikely to promote the learning society as NVQs are of upgrading the status of VET. The ends will not be achieved, because the means are fatally flawed. Treating learning as a commodity which can be bought and traded will not bring about the necessary cultural changes in attitude and motivation required to encourage people to view education and training as a worthwhile and lifelong process. Moreover, the technical-instrumental concept of learning which underpins this 'social market' model – linked with 'behavioural outcomes in the form of practical skills' (Elliott, 1993, p. 17) and appropriately serviced by the NCVQ model of CBET – is both educationally counter-productive and subversive of the aims of lifelong learning.

Indeed, as has been mentioned in earlier sections and stressed particularly in Chapter 4, there is a certain strangeness in the consideration of learning at all in connection with NVQs, since they are alleged not to be about learning, but only its outcomes. If this were true, how could the NETTs and the NCVQ development plan help to bring about a *learning* society? This question serves to remind us, once again, that the NETTs are after all only awards or certificates, not evidence of the develop-ment of knowledge and skills. More importantly, once it is recognized that the pur-ported independence of NVQs actually masks a behaviourism which narrows the focus of learning and leads to a loss of significant theoretical content, then the NCVQ role in all this becomes even more dubious. As was noted in earlier chapters, such a strategy leads to learning and behaviour which is 'programmed, repetitive and routine' (Argyris and Schon, 1974, p. 88) and which serves to de-skill VET (Callender, 1992; Smithers, 1993).

Ranson argues that the 'challenge for our time is to reconstitute the conditions for a learning society in which all are empowered to develop and contribute their capacities' (1993, p. 340) and he outlines the educational and socio-political conditions necessary for such a development. On the educational side, there is a need to 'progress from the post-war tradition of passivity . . . to a conception of the self as agent both in personal development and active participation in the public domain'. This entails a recovery of the Aristotelian conception of 'what it is to be and to develop as a person over the whole of a life and of a life as it can be led' and, 'since we can only develop as persons with and through others', this means that 'the conditions in which the self develops and flourishes are social and political'. Thus, 'self-learning needs to be confirmed, given meaning by others', since the 'self can only find its moral identity in and through others and membership of communities' (pp. 342–3).

Similar sentiments inform the NATFHE blueprint for the 'community college' (1992) appropriate to the new era of incorporated post-compulsory education and training. As an alternative to the emerging model 'based on inter-institutional competition, cutting costs and mounting courses on the cheap' (p. 1), the NATFHE vision is of a post-16 institution which is genuinely open and accessible to the whole community, and meets its needs. This includes all age groups, both sexes, all races, all abilities. It is based on a philosophy which asserts that all over the age of compulsory education have continuing legitimate educational needs relating to work, leisure and self-development. (p 8)

Such communitarian visions of the learning society run counter in every way to the market model of education and training and the NCVQ enterprise. In place of educational and economic individualism we need a social conception of development similar to the Langford model referred to in Chapter 9, and instead of an emphasis on pre-packaged products we require a Deweyan conception of active and experiential learning which places merit and value on the process of developing knowledge, understanding and skills (specific connections between the principles of lifelong learning and Dewey's social conception of education are made by Wain, 1987). Over and above all this, the learning society needs to be rooted and nourished by the civic virtues of active citizenship, as opposed to consumerist rights, for the 'values of caring or responsibility upon which can depend the confidence to learn derive any influence they may have from the authority of an underlying moral and social order' (Ranson, 1993, p. 344).

It is worth concluding with the 1993 National Commission's comments on the importance of encouraging lifelong learning:

Expanding educational achievement and opportunity is a community issue. For many people, continuing education is the means by which they may find a sense of personal worth by contributing within the community, rather than taking . . .

Continuing education provides important opportunities for increasing skills and knowledge and providing personal fulfilment. It also promotes social exchange and mutual understanding at a time when social cohesion is weakening. (NCE, 1993, pp. 334, 337)

In order to achieve all this we need the solid foundation of a general education entitlement for all which may be provided by a common 14 to 19 curriculum (along the lines sketched out in Chapter 8) coupled with a VET system in which an 'education for work' component of the kind described earlier is compulsory for all. The Commission was right to point out that our education system has 'concentrated for too long on the needs of the academically able at the expense of the rest' (p. 239); the enhancement of learning, education and training for *all* is the proper goal of the learning society. Not only have NVQs and the market model of education and training precious little to contribute to the promotion of this idea of lifelong learning, they are part of the problem which lifelong learning is intended to solve.

References

Ainley, P. (1988) *From School to YTS: Education and Training in England and Wales 1944–1987*. Milton Keynes: Open University Press.

Anderson, C. A. (1965) 'Literacy and Schooling on the Development Threshold', in Anderson, C. A. and Bowman, M. J. (eds), *Education and Economic Development*. Chicago, IL.: Aldine.

Argyris, C. and Schon, D. (1974) *Theory in Practice: Increasing Professional Effectiveness*. San Francisco: Jossey-Bass.

Armstrong, P., *et al.* (1984) *Capitalism Since World War II*. London: Fontana.

Ashworth, P. D. and Saxton, J. (1990) 'On Competence', *Journal of Further and Higher Education*, **14** (2), 3–25.

Ashworth, P. (1992) 'Being Competent and Having "Competencies"', *Journal of Further and Higher Education*, **16** (3), 8–17.

Austin, J. L. (1970) *Philosophical Papers*. Oxford: Oxford University Press.

Ayer, A. J. (1956) *The Problem of Knowledge*. Harmondsworth: Penguin Books.

Bailey, C. (1984) *Beyond the Present and the Particular*. London: Routledge & Kegan Paul.

Bailey, C. (1989) 'The Challenge of Economic Utility', in Cosin, B., *et al.* (eds), *School, Work and Equality*. London: Hodder & Stoughton.

Ball, Sir C. (1991) *Learning Pays: The Role of Post-compulsory Education and Training*. London: Royal Society of Arts.

Ball, S. J. (1990) *Politics and Policy Making in Education*. London: Routledge.

Barnett, R. (1990) *The Idea of Higher Education*. Buckingham: Open University Press.

Barrow, R. (1975) *Moral Philosophy for Education*. London: Allen & Unwin.

Barrow, R. (1987) 'Skill Talk', *Journal of Philosophy of Education*, **21** (2), pp. 187–95.

Bartram, D. (1990) 'An Appraisal of the Case for the Adaptive Assessment of Knowledge and Understanding in the Delivery of Competence-based Qualifications', in Black, H. and Wolf, A. (eds), *Knowledge and Competence: Current Issues in Training and Education*. Sheffield: Careers and Occupational Information Centre.

Bees, M. and Swords, M. (eds) (1990) *National Vocational Qualifications and Further Education*. London: NCVQ/Kogan Page.

Bennathan, M. (1993) 'Good Intentions Are Not Enough', *Times Educational Supplement*, 3 December.

Benner, P. (1982) 'From Novice to Expert', *American Journal of Nursing*, **82** (3), 402–7.

Bennett, R., *et al.* (1992) *Learning Should Pay*. London: London School of Economics/BP Education.

Berkovitch, I. (1977) *Coal on the Switchback: The Coal Industry Since Nationalisation*. London: Allen & Unwin.

Black, H. and Wolf, A. (eds) (1990) *Knowledge and Competence: Current Issues in Training and Education*. Sheffield: Careers and Occupational Information Centre.

Black, H. (1992) 'Sufficiency of Evidence', *Competence and Assessment*, **20**, 3–10.

Blackburne, L. (1994) 'Sir Ron Arrives with the Pruning Shears', *Times Educational Supplement*, 7 January.

Blackman, D. (1984) 'The Current Status of Behaviourism and Learning Theory in Psychology', in Fontana (1984).

Bloom, A. (1989) *The Closing of the American Mind*. Harmondsworth: Penguin Books.

Bloom, B., *et al.* (1956) *Taxonomy of Educational Objectives: Handbook 1 – Cognitive Domain*. London: Longmans.

Boffy, R. (1990) 'Occupational Competence and Work-based Learning: The Future for Further Education?', in Bees and Swords (1990).

Bogdanor, V. (1991) 'Where Will the Buck Stop?', *Times Educational Supplement*, 14 June.

Borg, R. W. (1981) *Applying Educational Research*. New York: Longman.

Bowles, S. and Ginitis, H. (1976) *Schooling in Capitalist America*. London: Routledge & Kegan Paul.

Bright, B. (ed.) (1989) *Theory and Practice in the Study of Adult Education: The Epistemological Debate*. London: Routledge.

Bristol Youth Award (1989) *Survey of Employers' Attitudes*. Bristol: Youth Award Scheme.

Broadfoot, P. (1979) *Assessment, Schools and Society*. London: Methuen.

Broadfoot, P. (ed.) (1984): *Selection, Certification and Control*. Lewes: Falmer Press.

Broudy, H. (1981) *Towards a Theory of Vocational Education*. Columbus, OH: National Center for Research in Vocational Education.

Brumbaugh, R. S. and Lawrence, N. M. (1963) *Philosophers on Education*. Boston: Houghton Mifflin Co.

Bruner, J. S. (1966) *The Process of Education*. Cambridge: Harvard University Press.

Bruner, J. S. (1974) *The Relevance of Education*. Harmondsworth: Penguin Books.

BTEC (1992) *BTEC Briefing: GNVQ Special Issue*. London: Business and Technology Education Council, Issue 10.

Bull, H. (1985) 'The Use of Behavioural Objectives', *Journal of Further and Higher Education*, **9** (1), 74–80.

Burgess, T. (ed.) (1986) *Education for Capability*. Windsor: NFER-Nelson for the Royal Society of Arts.

Burke, J. W. (1989a) 'The Implementation of NVQs', in Burke (1989b).

Burke, J. W. (ed.) (1989b) *Competency Based Education and Training*. Lewes: Falmer Press.

Burroughs, G. E. R. (1971) *Design and Analysis in Educational Research*. Birmingham: University of Birmingham School of Education.

Burwood, L. and Brady, C. (1984) 'Changing and Explaining Behaviour by Reward', *Journal of Philosophy of Education*, **18** (1), 109–14.

Callan, E. (1988) *Autonomy and Schooling*. Montreal: McGill-Queen's University Press.

Callender, C. (1992) *Will NVQs Work? Evidence from the Construction Industry*. Sussex: University of Sussex/Institute of Manpower Studies.

Cantor, L. M. and Roberts, I. F. (1983) *Further Education Today*. London: Routledge & Kegan Paul.

Carr, D. (1992) 'Four Dimensions of Educational Professionalism', *Westminster Studies in Education*, **15**, 19–31.

Carr, D. (1993) 'Questions of Competence', *British Journal of Educational Studies*, **41** (3), 253–71.

Caulkin, S. (1993) 'High Cost of Pay-by Results', *The Observer*, 12 December.

CBI (1989) *Towards a Skills Revolution*. London: Confederation of British Industry.

Challis, M., *et al.* (1993) 'Assessing Specified Competences in Medical Undergraduate Training', *Competence and Assessment*, **22**, 6–9.

Chambers, D. (1988) 'Learning from Markets', *Public Money and Management*, Winter, pp. 47–50.

Chi, M., *et al.* (1988) *The Nature of Expertise*. Hillsdale, NJ: Lawrence Erlbaum Associates.

Child, D. (1981) *Psychology and the Teacher*. London: Holt, Rinehart & Winston.

Chitty, C. and Simon, B. (eds) (1993) *Education Answers Back*. London: Lawrence & Wishart.

Chown, A. (1992) 'TDLB Standards in FE', *Journal of Further and Higher Education*, **16** (3), 52–9.

Chown, A. and Last, J. (1993) 'Can the NCVQ Model Be Used for Teacher Training?', *Journal of Further and Higher Education*, **17** (2), 15–26.

Clark, C. (1979) 'Education and Behaviour Modification', *Journal of Philosophy of Education*, **13**, 73–81.

Coates, P. (1990) *The Core Skills Initiative*. London: Further Education Unit.

Collins, M. (1991) *Adult Education as Vocation*. London: Routledge.

Corbett, A. (1993) 'The Peculiarity of the English', in Chitty and Simon (1993).

Corson, D. (ed.) (1991) *Education for Work*. Clevedon: Multilingual Matters Ltd.

COVTEC (1992) *An Introduction to NVQs*. Coventry: Coventry and Warwickshire Training and Enterprise Council.

Curtis, S. J. (1965) *An Introduction to the Philosophy of Education*. London: University Tutorial Press.

Curzon, L. B. (1985) *Teaching in Further Education*. London: Cassell.

Darcy, J. (1978) 'Education about Unemployment: A Reflective Element', *Oxford Review of Education*, **4**, 189–94.

Dean, C. (1991) 'Firms Unexcited by Revolution', *Times Educational Supplement*, 7 June.

Dean, C. (1993) 'Grandstand View of Vanishing Act', *Times Educational Supplement*, 19 November.

Dearden, R. F. (1968) *The Philosophy of Primary Education: An Introduction*. London: Routledge & Kegan Paul.

Dearden, R. F. (1972) 'Autonomy and Education', in Dearden, R. F., *et al.*, *Education and the Development of Reason*. London: Routledge & Kegan Paul.

Dearden, R. F. (1976) *Problems in Primary Education*. London: Routledge & Kegan Paul.

Dearden, R. F. (1984) 'Behaviour Modification: Towards an Ethical Appraisal', in *Theory and Practice in Education*. London: Routledge & Kegan Paul.

Dearden, R. F. (1990) 'Education and Training', in Esland (1990).

Dearing, Sir Ron (1993) *The National Curriculum and Its Assessment*. York: National Curriculum Council. Interim Report, July 1993.

Debling, G. (1989) 'The Employment Department/Training Agency Standards Programme and NVQs: Implications for Education', in Burke (1989b).

Debling, G. and Hallmark, A. (1990) 'Identification and Assessment of Underpinning Knowledge and Understanding in the Context of the U.K. Government's Standards Programme', in Black and Wolf (1990).

Debling, G. (1992) 'Competence and Assessment: Five Years On and What Next?', *Competence and Assessment*, **19**, 3–9.

Deere, M. (1993) *Guidance to Higher Education on GNVQ Level 3*. London: Standing Conference on University Entrance.

DES (1977) *Education in Schools: A Consultative Document*. London: HMSO.

DES (1985) *Better Schools: A Summary*. London: Department of Education and Science/Welsh Office.

DES (1987) *Managing Colleges Efficiently*. London: HMSO.

DES (1990) *Employment for the 1990s*. London: HMSO. Cmnd. 540.

DES (1991) *Education and Training for the 21st Century*. London: HMSO. Two volumes.

DES (1992) *The Reform of Initial Teacher Education*. London: Department of Education and Science.

Dewey, J. (1963) *Experience and Education*. London: Collier-Macmillan. Originally published in 1938.

Dewey, J. (1965) *The School and Society*. Chicago: University of Chicago Press. Originally published in 1899.

Dewey J. (1966) *Democracy and Education*. New York: Free Press. Originally published in 1916.

DFE (1992) *Initial Teacher Training (Secondary Phase) Circular 9/92*. London: Department for Education.

DFE (1993a) : *NVQs: Lead Bodies and the Education Service*. Letter to the Further Education Funding Council. London: Department for Education.

DFE (1993b) *The New Vocational A Levels: A Brief Guide*. London: Department for Education/ Welsh Office.

DFE (1993c) *The Charter for Further Education*. London: Department for Education.

DOE (1981) *A New Training Initiative: A Programme for Action*. London: HMSO. Cmnd. 8455.

DOE, DES (1984) *Training for Jobs*. London: HMSO. Cmnd. 9135.

DOE, DES (1985) *Education and Training for Young People*. London: HMSO.

DOE, DES (1986) *Working Together: Education and Training*. London: HMSO. Cmnd. 9823.

Dore, R. (1976) *The Diploma Disease*. London: Allen & Unwin.

Dreyfus, H. L. and Dreyfus, S. E. (1984) 'Putting Computers in Their Proper Place: Analysis Versus Intuition in the Classroom', in Sloan, D. (ed.), *The Computer in Education: A Critical Perspective*. New York: Teachers College Press.

Duke, C. (1992) *The Learning University*. Milton Keynes: Open University Press/Society for Research into Higher Education.

Dunne, R. and Harvard, G. (1992) 'Competences: Working with the New Criteria'. Paper read at the Universities Council for the Education of Teachers Conference, November 1992.

Duska, K. and Whelan, M. (1977) *Moral Development: A Guide to Piaget and Kohlberg*. Dublin: Gill & Macmillan.

Eagleton, T. (1983) *Literary Theory: An Introduction*. Oxford: Basil Blackwell.

Eastwood, G. R. (1964) 'Observations on Slogan Systems', *Canadian Education and Research Digest*, **4**, 208–18.

Ecclestone, K. (1993a) 'Accreditation in Adult Learning', *Adults Learning*, **4** (7), 178–80.

Ecclestone, K. (1993b) 'Why Do Teachers Have to Write Essays?', *Adults Learning*, **4** (10), 269–71.

ED (1990) *What Is an Investor in People?* Sheffield: Employment Department.

ED (1992a) *Examining Credits*. Sheffield: Employment Department.

ED (1992b) *National Standards for Training and Development*. Sheffield: Employment Department.

ED (1992c) *How to Accredit Work-based Learning*. Sheffield: Employment Department.

ED (1993a) *Systems and Procedures of Certification of Qualifications in the United Kingdom*. Sheffield: Employment Department Methods Strategy Unit. Research and Development Report No. 17.

ED (1993b) *Development of Transferable Skills in Learners*. Sheffield: Employment Department Methods Strategy Unit. Research and Development Report No. 18.

ED (1993c) *Labour Market Report*. Sheffield: Employment Department Skills and Enterprise Network, November 1993, published quarterly.

EDAP (1992) *A Unique Initiative In British Industry*. Basildon, Essex: Ford Employee Development and Assistance Programme.

Edwards, R. (1991) 'Winners and Losers: The Education and Training of Adults', in Raggatt and Unwin (1991).

Edwards, R. (1993) 'The Inevitable Future?: Post-Fordism in Work and Learning', in Edwards, R., *et al*. (eds), *Adult Learners, Education and Training*. London: Routledge/Open University Press.

Elam, S. (1971) *Peformance Based Teacher Education – What Is the State of the Art?* Washington, D.C.: American Association of Colleges of Teacher Education.

Elliott, J. (1989) 'Appraisal of Performance or Appraisal of Persons?', in Simon, H. and Elliott, J. (eds), *Rethinking Appraisal and Assessment*. Milton Keynes: Open University Press.

Elliott, J. (ed.) (1993) *Reconstructing Teacher Education*. London: Falmer Press.

Eraut, M. (1989) 'Initial Teacher Training and the NCVQ Model', in Burke, J. W. (ed.) (1989b).

Eraut, M. (1993) 'Implications for Standards Development', *Competence and Assessment*, **21**, 14–17.

Esland, G. (ed.) (1990) *Education, Training and Employment*. Wokingham: Addison-Wesley Publishing Co./Open University Press.

ESRC (1993) *Perceptions of NVQs in a Training Credits Pilot Scheme*. London: Economic and Social Research Council. Briefing Paper No. 7.

Evans, B. (1992) *The Politics of the Training Market*. London: Routledge.

Evans, R. (1993) 'Thoughts on the New FE Sector', *College Management Today*, **1** (3), 4–6.

Everton, T. and White, S. (1992) 'Partnership in Training: The University of Leicester's New Model of School-based Teacher Education', *Cambridge Journal of Education*, **22** (2), 143–55.

FEFC (1992) *Funding Learning*. Coventry: Further Education Funding Council.

FEU (1979) *A Basis for Choice*. London: Further Education Unit.

FEU (1984) *Towards a Competency-based System*. London: Further Education Unit.

FEU/PICKUP (1987) *Competency-based Vocational Education*. London: Further Education Unit.

FEU (1992a) *Flexible Colleges*. London: Further Education Unit.

FEU (1992b) *A Basis for Credit? London: Further Education Unit.*

FEU (1992c) Consultation on Qualifications Based on TDLB Standards. London: Further Education Unit.

FEU (1993) *A Charter for Further Education*. London: Further Education Unit.

Fennell, E. (1993) 'GNVQs: A Case of Critical Assessment?', *Competence and Assessment*, **22**, 11–13.

Field, J. (1991) 'Competency and the Pedagogy of Labour', *Studies in the Education of Adults*, **23** (1), 41–52.

Field, J. (1993a) 'Still Waiting for the Spring Offensive', *College Management Today*, **1** (5), 5–6.

Field, J. (1993b) 'Developments in Vocational Qualifications: Emerging Implications for Industrial Relations', *The Industrial Tutor*, **5** (7), 5–14.

Finegold, D. and Soskice, D. (1988) 'The Failure of Training in Britain: Analysis and Prescription', *Oxford Review of Economic Policy*, **4** (3), 21–53.

Finegold, D., *et al.* (1990) *A British Baccalaureat: Ending the Division Between Education and Training*. London: Institute for Public Policy Research. Report No. 1.

Finn, D. (1990) 'The Great Debate on Education, Youth Employment and the MSC', in Esland (1990).

Fisher, S. and Hicks, D. (1985) *World Studies 8–13: A Teacher's Handbook*. Edinburgh: Oliver & Boyd.

Fleming, D. (1991) 'The Concept of Meta-Competence', *Competence and Assessment*, **16**, 9–12.

Fletcher, S. (1991) *NVQs, Standards and Competence*. London: Kogan Page.

Flew, A. (1979) 'Sincerity, Criticism and Monitoring', *Journal of Philosophy of Education*, **13**, 141–7.

Flexner, A. (1915) *Is Social Work a Profession?* New York: Hildman Publishers.

Fontana, D. (ed.) (1984) *Behaviourism and Learning Theory in Education*. Edinburgh: Scottish Academic Press.

Furnham, A. (1984) 'Getting a Job: School Leavers' Perceptions of Employment Prospects', *British Journal of Educational Psychology*, **54**, 293–305.

Galloway, D. (1985) *Schools, Pupils and Special Educational Needs*. London: Croom Helm.

Gay, L. R. (1987) *Educational Research*. London: Merrill Publishing Co.

Geach, P. (1971) *Mental Acts*. London: Routledge & Kegan Paul.

Geiger, G. R. (1958) *John Dewey in Perspective*. New York: Oxford University Press.

Gibbs, G. (1988): *Learning by Doing*. London: Further Education Unit.

Gibson, R. (1986) *Critical Theory and Education*. London: Hodder & Stoughton.

Giddens, A. (1984) *The Constitution of Society*. Cambridge: Polity Press.

Gipps, C. (1993) 'Policy-making and the Use and Misuse of Evidence', in Chitty and Simon (1993).

Glasgow University (1992) *National Standards for Training and Development within Masters Programmes*. Glasgow: University of Glasgow Department of Education.

Great Britain Parliament (1991) *The Citizen's Charter: Raising the Standard*. London: HMSO. Cmnd. 1599.

Great Britain Parliament (1988) *Education Reform Act 1988*. London: HMSO.

Green, A. (1990) *Education and State Formation*. London: Macmillan.

Green, A. (1992) 'Education and Training: A European Perspective', *Forum*, **34** (2), 51–3.

Greenacre, L. (1990) 'Competence and Coherence: Opportunities for Education and Industry in the Emerging NVQ Framework', in Bees and Swords (1990).

Gribble, J. (1969) *Introduction to Philosophy of Education*. Boston, MA: Allyn & Bacon.

Griffiths, S. and Tysome, T. (1992) 'Jostle for Power in FE Sector', *Times Higher Education Supplement*, 30 October.

Griffiths, S. (1993) 'Proposals Widen Role for Schools', *Times Higher Education Supplement*, 10 September.

Gross, R. D. (1987) *Psychology*. London: Edward Arnold.

Guy, R. (1991) 'Serving the Needs of Industry', in Raggatt and Unwin (1991).

Haffenden, I. and Brown, A. (1989) 'Towards the Implementation of NVQs in Colleges of FE', in Burke (1989b).

Halliday, J. (1990) *Markets, Managers and Theory in Education*. Lewes: Falmer Press.

Hamlyn, D. W. (1987) *The Pelican History of Western Philosophy*. London: Penguin Books.

Hare, R. M. (1964) *The Language of Morals*. Oxford: Oxford University Press.

Hare, R. M. (1981) *Moral Thinking*. Oxford: Clarendon Press.

Hargreaves, D. (1982) *The Challenge for the Comprehensive School*. London: Routledge & Kegan Paul.

Hartnett, A. and Naish, M. (eds) (1986) *Theory and Practice of Education*. London: Heinemann Educational.

Haydon, G. (1973) 'Educational Relevance: A Slogan Examined', *Proceedings of the Philosophy of Education Society of Great Britain*, **7** (2), 223–38.

Hayes, C. (1989) 'Qualifications for an Uncertain Future', address given to the Association of Colleges for Further and Higher Education, 15/16 February 1989.

Hayes, C. (1993) 'Businesslike but Not a Business', *College Management Today*, **1** (1), 6–7.

HCTC (1991) *A Guide to NVQs*. London: Hotel & Catering Training Co.

HEC (1993) *NVQs: Implications for Higher Education*. Leeds: Leeds University/Higher Education for Capability.

Hemming, J. (1969) *Individual Morality*. London: Nelson.

Herbst, P. (1973) 'Work, Labour and University Education', in Peters, R. S. (ed.), *The Philosophy of Education*. Oxford: Oxford University Press.

Hertzberg, H. W. (1976) 'Competency Based Teacher Education: Does It Have a Past or a Future?', *Teachers College Record*, **78** (1), 1–21.

Hirst, P. H. and Peters, R. S. (1970) *The Logic of Education*. London: Routledge & Kegan Paul.

Hirst, P. H. (1974) *Knowledge and the Curriculum*. London: Routledge & Kegan Paul.

HMI (1989) *Post-16 Education and Training – Core Skills*. London: Department of Education and Science.

HMI (1991) *Training for Teaching in Further and Adult Education*. London: HMSO.

HMI (1992) *Hotel, Catering and Tourism Management*. London: Department of Education and Science.

Hodkinson, P. (1992) 'Alternative Models of Competence in Vocational Education and Training', *Journal of Further and Higher Education*, **16** (2), 30–9.

Houghton, V. and Richardson, K. (1974) *Recurrent Education*. London: Ward Lock Educational.

Houston, R. H. (1980) 'An Analysis of the Performance-based Teacher Education Movement', in Fardig, G. (ed.), *Prospects of Performance-based Vocational Teacher Education*. Orlando, FL: University of Central Florida College of Education.

Hoyle, E. (1983) 'The Professionalization of Teachers: A Paradox', in Gordon, P. (ed.), *Is Teaching a Profession?* London: London Institute of Education.

Hyland, T. (1978) *Open Plan Schools and Open Education.* Unpublished PhD thesis, University of Lancaster.

Hyland, T. (1979) 'Open Education – A Slogan Examined', *Educational Studies*, 5 (1), 35–41.

Hyland, T. (1986) 'Instruction, Rationality and Learning to Be Moral', *Journal of Moral Education*, 15 (2), 127–38.

Hyland, T. (1990) 'Education, Vocationalism and Competence', *Forum*, 33 (1), 18–2.

Hyland, T. (1991a) 'Vocational Studies That Won't Work', *Times Educational Supplement*, 20 September.

Hyland, T. (1991b) 'Taking Care of Business: Vocationalism, Competence and the Enterprise Culture', *Educational Studies*, 17 (1), 77–87.

Hyland, T. (1992a) 'Reconstruction and Reform in Further Education', *Educational Management and Administration*, 20 (2), 106–10.

Hyland, T. (1992b) 'Lecturing: Profession or Occupation?', *NATFHE Journal*, Autumn, pp. 10–11.

Hyland, T. (1992c) 'Expertise and Competence in Further and Adult Education', *British Journal of In-service Education*, 18 (1), 23–8.

Hyland, T. (1992d) 'Meta-competence, Metaphysics and Vocational Expertise', *Competence and Assessment*, 20, 22–5.

Hyland, T. (1992e) 'Moral Vocationalism', *Journal of Moral Education*, 21 (2), 139–50.

Hyland, T. (1992f) 'GNVQ Threat to GCSE', *Forum*, 34 (3), 73–6.

Hyland, T. (1993a) 'Professional Development and Competence-based Education', *Educational Studies*, 19 (1), 123–32.

Hyland, T. (1993b) 'Vocational Reconstruction and Dewey's Instrumentalism', *Oxford Review of Education*, 19 (1), 89–100.

Hyland, T. (1993c) 'Competence, Knowledge and Education', *Journal of Philosophy of Education*, 27 (1), 57–68.

Hyland, T. (1993d) 'Mismatches, Paradoxes and Square Circles: Making NVQs Fit Adult Learning', *Adults Learning*, 4 (10), 272–3.

Hyland, T. (1993e) 'GNVQs: Putting Learning Back into VET', *Educa*, No. 134, June, pp. 10–11.

Hyland, T. and Weller, P. (1994) *Implementing NVQs in Further Education Colleges.* Warwick University: Continuing Education Research Centre.

Inland Revenue (1993) *Tax Relief for Vocational Training.* London: Inland Revenue Press Office.

Irwin, A. (1993) 'Sciences Welcome NVQs in Degrees', *Times Higher Education Supplement*, 12 November.

Jackson, M. (1989) 'Access Ladder Aims to Add New Top Rung', *Times Educational Supplement*, 10 February.

Jackson, M. (1991) 'Vocational Council Snubbed', *Times Educational Supplement*, 13 December.

Jarvis, V. and Prais, S. (1989) 'Two Nations of Shopkeepers: Training for Retailing in France and Britain', *National Institute Economic Review*, 128, 58–75.

Jessup, G. (1989) Foreword, in Burke (1989b).

Jessup, G. (1990a) 'National Vocational Qualifications: Implications for Further Education', in Bees and Swords (1990).

Jessup, G. (1990b) 'The Evidence Required to Demonstrate Competence', in Black and Wolf (1990).

Jessup, G. (1991) *Outcomes: NVQs and the Emerging Model of Education and Training.* London: Falmer Press.

Johnson, T. J. (1972) *Professions and Power.* London: Macmillan.

Jonathan, R. (1993) 'Education, Philosophy of Education and the Fragmentation of Value', *Journal of Philosophy of Education*, 27 (2), 171–8.

Joseph, K. (1984) 'View from the Top', *Times Educational Supplement*, 13 January.
Judd, J. and Crequer, N. (1993) 'The Right Tightens Its Grip on Education', in Chitty and Simon (1993).

Keep, E. (1992) 'Schools in the Marketplace? – Some Problems with Private Sector Models', in Wallace, G. (ed.), *Local Management of Schools: Research and Experience*. Clevedon: Multilingual Matters.
Kelly, A. V. (1982) *The Curriculum: Theory and Practice*. London: Harper & Row.
Kelly, D., *et al.* (1990) *Making National Vocational Qualifications Work for Social Care*. London: National Institute for Social Work/Social Care Association.
Kelsey, B. and Cushing, S. (1992) 'Not So Great, Britain', *Times Educational Supplement*, 24 July.
Kenyon, B. (1993) 'The LEA Is Dead – Long Live the LEA!', *College Management Today*, **1** (3), 12–13.
Kerr, J. F. (ed.) (1968) *Changing the Curriculum*. London: University of London Press.
Kerry, T. and Tollitt-Evans, J. (1992) *Teaching in Further Education*. Oxford: Blackwell.
Knowles, M. (1970) *The Modern Practice of Adult Education: From Pedagogy to Andragogy*. New York: Cambridge Book Co.
Kolb, D. (1993) 'The Process of Experiential Learning', in Thorpe, M., *et al.* (eds), *Culture and Processes of Adult Learning*. London: Routledge/Open University Press.
Komisar, B. P. and McClellan, J. E. (1961) 'The Logic of Slogans', in Smith, B. O. and Ennis, R. H. (eds), *Language and Concepts in Education*. Chicago: Rand McNally & Co.
Körner, S. (1955) *Kant*. London: Penguin Books.

Labour Party (1991) *Today's Education and Training: Tomorrow's Skills*. London: The Labour Party.
Langford, G. (1978) *Teaching as a Profession*. Manchester: Manchester University Press.
Langford, G. (1985) *Education, Persons and Society: A Philosophical Enquiry*. Basingstoke: Macmillan.
Larson, M. S. (1977) *The Rise of Professionalism: A Sociological Analysis*. Berkeley: University of California Press.
Lawson, T. (1992) 'Core Skills 16–19', in Whiteside *et al.* (1992).
Lawton, D. (1989) *Education, Culture and the National Curriculum*. London: Hodder & Stoughton.
Lawton, D. (1993) 'Is There Coherence and Purpose in the National Curriculum?', in Chitty and Simon (1993).
Lee, D., *et al.* (1990) *Scheming for Youth: A Study of YTS in the Enterprise Culture*. Milton Keynes: Open University Press.
Lewis, T. (1991) 'Difficulties Attending to New Vocationalism in the USA', *Journal of Philosophy of Education*, **25** (1), 95–108.
Lynch, V. and Smalley, K. (eds) (1991) *Citizenship in Schools*. London: David Fulton.

Macdonald, B. and Walker, R. (1976) *Changing the Curriculum*. London: Open Books.
Macfarlane, E. (1993) *Education 16–19 in Transition*. London: Routledge.
MacIntyre, A. (1990) *Three Rival Versions of Moral Enquiry*. London: Duckworth.
Maclure, S. (1989) *Education Re-formed*. London: Hodder & Stoughton.
Maclure, S. (1991) *Missing Links: The Challenge to Further Education*. London: Policy Studies Institute.
Macpherson, C. B. (1964) *The Political Theory of Possessive Individualsim*. Oxford: Oxford University Press.
Mager, C. (1993) 'Progression from LEA to College Provision: The Role of Open College Networks, *Adults Learning*, **4** (5), 121–3.
Maguire, M. (1992) 'Training and Enterprise Councils', in Whiteside *et al.* (1992).
Mansfield, B. (1989) 'Competence and Standards', in Burke (1989b).

Mansfield, B. (1990) 'Knowledge, Evidence and Assessment', in Black and Wolf (1990).

Marshall, K. (1991) 'NVQs: An Assessment of the "Outcomes" Approach in Education and Training', *Journal of Further and Higher Education*, **15** (3), 56–64.

Martin, R. (1992) 'A Method for All Seasons', *Competence and Assessment*, Issue 19, pp. 9–10.

McAleavey, M. and McAleer, J. (1991) 'Competence-based Training', *British Journal of In-Service Education*, **17** (1), 19–23.

McCulloch, G., *et al.* (1985) *Technological Revolution? The Politics of School Science and Technology in England and Wales since 1945*. Lewes: Falmer Press.

McHugh, G., *et al.* (1993) *Why Take NVQs?* Lancaster: Lancaster University Centre for the Study of Education and Training.

McKelvey, C. and Peters, H. (1991) 'NVQs and Language', *Adults Learning*, **3** (3), 65–6.

McMaster, G. (1991) 'Japan's Secret of Success', *Times Educational Supplement*, 7 June.

Meighan, R. (1981) *A Sociology of Educating*. London: Holt, Rinehart & Winston.

Melia, T. (1993) 'When the Inspectors Start to Call', *Times Higher Educational Supplement*, 26 March.

Mendus, S. (1992) 'All the King's Horses and All the King's Men: Justifying Higher Education', *Journal of Philosophy of Education*, **26** (2), 173–82.

Mezirow, J. (1990) 'A Critical Theory of Adult Learning and Education', in Tight, M. (ed.), *Adult Learning and Education*. London: Routledge.

Millington, J. (1990) 'Engineering Training and Further Education: A Changing Relationship', in Bees and Swords (1990).

Minton, D. (1991) *Teaching Skills in Further and Adult Education*. London: City & Guilds/Macmillan.

Mitchell, L. (1989) 'The Definition of Standards and Their Assessment', in Burke (1989b).

Molyneux, F., *et al.* (eds) (1988) *Learning for Life*. London: Croom Helm.

Moon, B. (1990) 'Patterns of Reform: School Control in Western Europe', in Moon, B. (ed.), *New Curriculum – National Curriculum*. Milton Keynes: Open University Press.

Moore, R. (1989) 'Education, Employment and Recruitment', in Cosin, B., *et al.* (eds), *School, Work and Equality*. London: Hodder & Stoughton.

Moran, D. (1991) 'The Role of Knowledge in Competence-based Measurement', *Educa*, **115**, 8–9.

Mortimore, P. and Stone, C. (1990) 'Measuring Educational Quality', *British Journal of Educational Studies*, **39** (1), 69–82.

Moss, J. (1981) 'Limiting Competency-based Education', *Studies in Curriculum Research*, **19** (1), 14–18.

Mouly, G. J. (1970) *The Science of Educational Research*. London: Van Nostrand Reinhold Co.

MSC (1977) *Training for Skills*. Sheffield: Manpower Services Commission.

MSC (1988) *The PRD Evaluation of Caterbase: Early Delivery in Hotel & Catering YTS Schemes*. Sheffield: Manpower Services Commission Occupational Standards Branch.

Musgrave, P. W. (1966) 'Constant Factors in the Demand for Technical Education', *British Journal of Educational Studies*, **14** (2), 173–87.

Musgrave, P. W. (1970) 'The Definition of Technical Education 1860–1910', in Musgrave, P. W. (ed.), *Sociology, History and Education*. London: Methuen.

Nash, I. and Prestage, M. (1992) 'Promise to Train All Leavers Not Kept', *Times Educational Supplement*, 5 June.

Nash, I. (1993a) 'New Labels Herald Post-16 Overhaul', *Times Educational Supplement*, 16 July.

Nash, I. (1993b) 'An Award Shrouded in Ignorance', *Times Educational Supplement*, 5 November.

Nash, I. (1993c) 'The Independence Honeymoon Is Over', *Times Educational Supplement*, 3 December.

Nash, I. (1993d) 'UK Set for Training "Disaster"', *Times Educational Supplement*, 17 December.

Nash, I. (1994) 'Vocational Courses Get Welcome Boost', *Times Educational Supplement*, 7 January.

NATFHE (1992) *The Community College*. London: National Association of Teachers in Further and Higher Education.
NATFHE (1993) *Credit Limit*. London: National Association of Teachers in Further and Higher Education.
NCC (1990) *Education for Citizenship*. York: National Curriculum Council.
NCE (1992) *Towards a Well-qualified Workforce*. London: National Commission on Education.
NCE (1993) *Learning to Succeed: Report of the National Commission on Education*. London: Heinemann.
NCVQ (1988) *Initial Criteria and Guidelines for Staff Development*. London: National Council for Vocational Qualifications.
NCVQ (1989) *Assessment in NVQs: Use of Evidence from Prior Achievement (APL)*. London: National Council for Vocational Qualifications. Information Note 5.
NCVQ (1990a) *What's in It for Employers?* London: National Council for Vocational Qualifications.
NCVQ (1990b) *What It Means for Colleges*. London: National Council for Vocational Qualifications.
NCVQ (1991a) *Criteria for National Vocational Qualifications*. London: National Council for Vocational Qualifications.
NCVQ (1991b) *General National Vocational Qualifications*. London: National Council for Vocational Qualifications.
NCVQ (1992a) *Response to the Consultation on General National Vocational Qualifications*. London: National Council for Vocational Qualifications. Report No. 15.
NCVQ (1992b) *NVQ Update*. London: National Council for Vocational Qualifications. February 1992.
NCVQ (1992c) *NVQ Monitor*. London: National Council for Vocational Qualifications. September 1992.
NCVQ (1993a) *NVQ Monitor*. London: National Council for Vocational Qualifications. June 1993.
NCVQ (1993b) *NCVQ Information Note: General National Vocational Qualifications*. London: National Council for Vocational Qualifications.
NCVQ (1993c) *GNVQ Information Note*. London: National Council for Vocational Qualifications.
NCVQ (1993d) *GNVQs: Core Skills Units*. London: National Council for Vocational Qualifications.
NIACE (1991) *Adult Learners and the Colleges*. Leicester: National Institute of Adult Continuing Education.
NIACE (1992) *Adult Learners and the Further and Higher Education Act 1992*. Leicester: National Institute of Adult Continuing Education.
Nicholson, B. (1993) 'Cinderella's on the Ball', *Times Higher Educational Supplement*, 26 March.
Noah, H. J. and Eckstein, M. A. (1990) 'Business and Industry Involvement with Education in Britain, France and Germany', in Esland (1990).
Norris, N. (1991) 'The Trouble with Competence', *Cambridge Journal of Education*, **21** (3); 331–41.
NTTF (1992) *Releasing Potential: Company Initiatives to Develop People at Work*. London: National Training Task Force.
Nyberg, D. (ed.) (1975) *The Philosophy of Open Education*. London: Routledge & Kegan Paul.

O'Connor, D. J. (1968) *An Introduction to the Philosophy of Education*. London: Routledge & Kegan Paul.
O'Hanlon, C. (1993) 'The Importance of an Articulated Personal Theory of Professional Development', in Elliott (1993).
Osborn, S. J. (1993) *The Development of a Competence Based Vocational Education, Training and Qualification System for the British Coal Mining Industry*. Unpublished MA thesis. University of Warwick.

Otter, S. (1992) *Learning Outcomes in Higher Education*. Leicester: Unit for the Development of Adult Continuing Education.

Parry, G. and Wake, C. (1990) *Access and Alternative Futures for Higher Education*. London: Hodder & Stoughton.

Peters, R. S. (1966) *Ethics and Education*. London: Allen & Unwin.

Peters, R. S. (1977) 'John Dewey's Philosophy of Education', in Peters, R. S. (ed.), *John Dewey Reconsidered*. London: Routledge & Kegan Paul.

Peters, R. S. (1978) 'Ambiguities in Liberal Education and the Problem of Its Content', in Strike, K. A. and Egan, K. (eds), *Ethics and Educational Policy*. London: Routledge & Kegan Paul.

Phenix, P. H. (1964) *Realms of Meaning*. New York: McGraw-Hill.

Phillips Griffiths, A. (1965) 'A Deduction of Universities', in Archambault, R. D. (ed.), *Philosophical Analysis and Education*. London: Routledge & Kegan Paul.

Pickard, J. (1985) 'The Technical and Vocational Education Initiative', *Times Educational Supplement*, 3 May.

Poole, R. (1990) 'Morality, Masculinity and the Market', in Sayers, S. and Osborne, P. (eds), *Socialism, Feminism and Philosophy*. London: Routledge.

Powell, J. P. (1968) 'On Learning to Be Original, Witty, Flexible, Resourceful, etc.', *Proceedings of the Philosophy of Education Society of Great Britain*, II (1967–68), pp. 43–9.

Prais, S. (1991) 'Vocational Qualifications in Britain and Europe: Theory and Practice', *National Institute Economic Review*, May, pp. 86–92.

Pring, R. (1976) *Knowledge and Schooling*. London: Open Books.

Prosser, C. and Allen, C. R. (1925) *Vocational Education in a Democracy*. New York: The Century Co.

Prosser, C. and Quigley, T. (1950) *Vocational Education in Democracy*. Chicago: American Technical Society.

Pyke, N. (1993) 'Ill-starred Grade Changes', *Times Educational Supplement*, 19 November.

Quinton, A. (1977) 'Inquiry, Thought and Action: John Dewey's Theory of Knowledge', in Peters, R. S. (ed.), *John Dewey Reconsidered*. London: Routledge & Kegan Paul.

Radford, J. and Govier, E. (1980) *A Textbook of Psychology*. New York: Sheldon Press.

Raggatt, P. (1991) 'Quality Assurance and NVQs', in Raggatt and Unwin (1991).

Raggatt, P. and Unwin, L. (eds) (1991) *Change and Intervention: Vocational Education and Training*. London: Falmer Press.

Raggatt, P. (1994) 'Implementing NVQs in Colleges: Progress, Perceptions and Issues', *Journal of Further and Higher Education*, **18** (1), 59–74.

Ranson, S. (1992) 'Towards the Learning Society', *Educational Management and Administration*, **20** (2), 68–79.

Ranson, S. (1993) 'Markets or Democracy for Education', *British Journal of Educational Studies*, **41** (4), 333 51.

Rawls, J. (1971) *A Theory of Justice*. Oxford: Oxford University Press.

Reynolds, J. and Skilbeck, M. (1976) *Culture and the Classroom*. London: Open Books.

Richardson, J. T., *et al.* (eds) (1987) *Student Learning: Research in Education and Cognitive Psychology*. Milton Keynes: Open University Press/Society for Research into Higher Education.

Roland Martin, J. (1961) 'On the Reduction of "Knowing That" to "Knowing How"', in Smith, B. O. and Ennis, R. H. (eds), *Language and Concepts in Education*. Chicago, IL: Rand McNally.

Rowntree, D. (1977) *Assessing Students – How Shall We Know Them?* London: Harper & Row.

RSA (1992) *GNVQ Update*. Coventry: Royal Society of Arts.

Russell, B. (1946) *A History of Western Philosophy*. London: Allen & Unwin.

Ryle, G. (1973) *The Concept of Mind*. Harmondsworth: Penguin Books. Originally published in 1949.

Salford University (1993) *GNVQs as Progression Routes into Higher Education*. University of Salford.

Scheffler, I. (1960) *The Language of Education*. Springfield, IL.: Charles C. Thomas.

Scheffler, I. (1965) *Conditions of Knowledge*. Glenview, IL.: Scott, Foresman & Co.

Scheffler, I. (1973) *Reason and Teaching*. London: Routledge & Kegan Paul.

Schofield, H. (1972) *The Philosophy of Education: An Introduction*. London: Allen & Unwin.

Schon, D. (1987) *Educating the Reflective Practitioner: Towards a New Design for Teaching and Learning in the Professions*. San Francisco: Jossey-Bass.

Schuller, T. and Megarry, J. (eds) (1979) *Recurrent Education and Lifelong Learning*. London: Kogan Page.

Scott, D. (1989) 'In Defence of GCSE', *Forum*, **31** (2), 53–5.

Shackleton, J. (1990) 'NVQs: A Whole College Approach', in Bees and Swords (1990).

Shilling, C. (1989) *Schooling for Work in Capitalist Britain*. Lewes: Falmer Press.

Shirley, I. (1991) 'State Policy and Employment', in Corson (1991).

Silver, H. and Brennan, J. (1988) *A Liberal Vocationalism*. London: Methuen.

Simon, B. (ed.) (1990) *The Search for Enlightenment*. London: Lawrence & Wishart.

Simon, B. (1992) *What Future for Education?* London: Lawrence & Wishart.

Singer, P. (1979) *Practical Ethics*. Cambridge: Cambridge University Press.

Skinner, B. F. (1953) *Science and Human Behaviour*. New York: Macmillan.

Skinner, B. F. (1973) *Beyond Freedom and Dignity*. Harmondsworth: Penguin Books.

Smith, I. (1990) 'Commercial Ethos Puts Cash into the Classroom', *Times Educational Supplement*, 9 February.

Smith, R. (1987) 'Skills: The Middle Way', *Journal of Philosophy of Education*, **21** (2), 197–201.

Smith, R. A. (ed.) (1975) *Regaining Educational Leadership*. New York: John Wiley.

Smithers, A. (1993) *All Our Futures: Britain's Education Revolution*. London: Channel 4 Television Dispatches Report on Education.

Smithers, A. and Robinson, P. (1993) *Changing Colleges: Further Education in the Market Place*. London: Council for Industry and Higher Education.

Snare, F. (1992) *The Nature of Moral Thinking*. London: Routledge.

Spencer, D. (1993) 'Curriculum Brings Improvement But Distorts', *Times Educational Supplement*, 2 April.

Statham, J., *et al.* (1989) *The Education Fact File*. London: Hodder & Stoughton.

Steedman, H. and Wagner, K. (1989) 'Productivity, Machinery and Skills: Clothing Manufacture in Britain and Germany', *National Institute Economic Review*, **128**, 40–57.

Stephens, M. D. (1990) *Adult Education*. London: Cassell.

Stirling, A. (1982) 'Preparing School Leavers for Unemployment', *Bulletin of the British Psychological Society*, **35**, 421–2.

St John-Brooks C. (1992) 'Industry Rattled by New Training Plan', *Times Educational Supplement*, 30 October.

Straughan, R. (1982) *I Ought to But . . .* Windsor: NFER-Nelson.

Streeck, W. (1989) 'Skills and the Limits of Neo-liberalism', *Work, Employment and Society*, **3** (1) 89–104.

Stronach, I. (1990) 'Education, Vocationalism and Economic Recovery: The Case Against Witchcraft', in Esland (1990).

Sutton, A. (1992) 'The Reform of Vocational Education', in Whiteside *et al.* (1992).

Targett, S. (1993) 'Advertising Money Doubled', *Times Higher Education Supplement*, 12 November.

Taylor, P. H. and Richards, C. M. (1985) *An Introduction to Curriculum Studies*. Windsor: NFER-Nelson.

Taylor, W. (1991) 'School to Work', in Corson (1991).

Tennant, M. (1988) *Psychology and Adult Learning*. London: Routledge.

Tennant, M. (1991) 'Expertise as a Dimension of Adult Development', *New Education*, **13** (1), 49–55.

Theodossin, E. (1990) 'The College Marketing Implications of NVQs', in Bees and Swords (1990).

THES (1992) 'OU Abandons "Driving Test" in Latest Bid to Promote NVQs', *Times Higher Education Supplement*, 2 October.

THES (1993) 'NVQ May Force Institutions to Change Roles', *Times Higher Education Supplement*, 15 October.

Thompson, C. (1987) *The Responsive College Project*. Bristol: Further Education Staff College.

Thomson, A. (1993) 'A Lifetime of Learning', *College Management*, **1** (8), 7–8.

Trusted, J. (1987) *Moral Principles and Social Values*. London: Routledge & Kegan Paul.

Tuxworth, E. (1989) 'Competence Based Education and Training: Background and Origins', in Burke (1989b).

Tysome, T. (1992a) 'Sheffield United', *Times Higher Education Supplement*, 22 May.

Tysome, T. (1992b) 'FE Considers Three-pronged Quality Model', *Times Higher Education Supplement*, 28 Feburary

Tysome, T. (1993a) 'Shephard in Bid to Smooth Ruffled DFE', *Times Higher Education Supplement*, 12 February.

Tysome, T. (1993b) 'Vocational Take-over Bombshell', *Times Higher Education Supplement*, 8 October.

UDACE (1989a) *Understanding Competence*. Leicester: Unit for the Development of Adult Continuing Education.

UDACE (1989b) *Understanding Learning Outcomes*. Leicester: Unit for the Development of Adult Continuing Education.

Usher, R. (1992) 'Experience in Adult Education: A Post-Modern Critique', *Journal of Philosophy of Education*, **26** (2), 201–14.

Utley, A. (1993a) 'Final Leg of Funding March', *Times Higher Education Supplement*, 12 November.

Utley, A. (1993b) 'Schools Alerted to NCVQ Quality', *Times Higher Education Supplement*, 12 November.

Utley, A. (1994) 'Tests Spoilt for Choice', *Times Higher Education Supplement*, 7 January.

Wadd, K. (1988) 'Chicken or Egg?', *Times Educational Supplement*, 30 September.

Wain, K. (1987) *Philosophy of Lifelong Education*. London: Croom Helm.

Walker, J. (1991) 'Building on Youth Cultures in the Secondary Curriculum', in Corson (1991).

Wardle, D. (1976) *English Popular Education 1780–1975*. Cambridge: Cambridge University Press.

Warnock, G. J. (1967) *Contemporary Moral Philosophy*. London: Macmillan.

Warnock, M. (1977) *Schools of Thought*. London: Faber & Faber.

Watts, A. (1984) *Education, Unemployment and the Future of Work*. Milton Keynes: Open University Press.

Weinstock, A. (1976) 'I Blame the Teachers', *Times Educational Supplement*, 23 January.

Whalley, M. (1987) 'Unexamined Lives: The Case for Philosophy in Schools', *British Journal of Educational Studies*, **34** (3), 260–80.

Wheldall, K. and Merrett, F. (1984) 'The Behavioural Approach to Classroom Management', in Fontana (1984).

Whitbread, N. (1993) 'Beyond Irrelevance', *Forum*, **35** (1), 3.

White, J. P. (1973) *Towards a Compulsory Curriculum*. London: Routledge & Kegan Paul.

White, J. P. (1974) 'Intelligence and the Logic of the Nature–Nurture Issue', *Proceedings of the Philosophy of Education Society of Great Britain*, **8** (1), 30–51.

White, M. (1990) 'Educational Policy and Economic Goals', in Esland (1990).

Whitehead, A. N. (1966) *The Aims of Education*. London: Ernest Benn.

Whiteside, T., *et al.* (eds) (1992) *16–19 Changes in Education and Training*. London: David Fulton.

Whitty, G. (1985) *Sociology and School Knowledge*. London: Methuen.

Whitty, G. (1990) 'The New Right and the National Curriculum: State Control or Market Forces?', in Moon, B. (ed.), *New Curriculum – National Curriculum*. London: Hodder & Stoughton.

Wiener, M. (1981) *English Culture and the Decline of the Industrial Spirit 1850–1980*. Cambridge: Cambridge University Press.

Wigan Metro (1980) *Youth Opportunity Programme Trainees*. Wigan Metropolitan Borough: Youth Opportunities Unit.

Wilkinson, R. H. (1970) 'The Gentleman Ideal and the Maintenance of a Political Elite', in Musgrave, P. W. (ed.), *Sociology, History and Education*. London: Methuen.

Williams, R. (1961) *The Long Revolution*. Harmondsworth: Penguin Books.

Willis, P. (1977) *Learning to Labour*. London: Saxon House.

Wilson, J. (1972) *Philosophy and Educational Research*. Slough: National Foundation for Educational Research.

Wilson, J. (1977) *Philosophy and Practical Education*. London: Routledge & Kegan Paul.

Wirth, A. G. (1991) 'Issues in the Vocational–Liberal Studies Controversy (1900–1917)', in Corson (1991).

Winter, R. (1992) ' "Quality Management" or "The Educative Workplace": Alternative Versions of Competence-based Education', *Journal of Further and Higher Education*, **16** (3) 100–15.

Wojtas, O. (1993) 'Scotland Employs Best Test Pilots', *Times Higher Education Supplement*, 8 January.

Wolf, A. (1989) 'Can Competence and Knowledge Mix?', in Burke (1989b).

Wolf, A. (1990) 'Unwrapping Knowledge and Understanding from Standards of Competence', in Black and Wolf (1990).

Woodhall, M. (1990) 'Human Capital Concepts', in Esland (1990).

Woods, R. and Power, C. (1987) 'Aspects of the Competence–Performance Distinction: Educational, Psychological and Measurement Issues', *Journal of Curriculum Studies*, **19**, 409–24.

Woolhouse, J. (1993) 'The Case for Reform', *NATFHE Journal*, Spring 1993.

Wright, D. (1989) *Moral Competence*. London: Further Education Unit.

Wringe, C. (1991) 'Education, Schooling and the World of Work', in Corson (1991).

Young, S. (1993) Review of *Learning to Succeed*. *Times Educational Supplement*, 19 November.

Youthaid (1992) *A Broken Promise: The Failure of Youth Training Policy*. London: Youthaid.

Name Index

Subject Index